Unshakeable Faith

By Monroe and Jeri May

WestBow Press books may be ordered through booksellers or by contacting:

WestBow Press
A Division of Thomas Nelson
1663 Liberty Drive
Bloomington, IN 47403
www.westbowpress.com
1-(866) 928-1240

ISBN: 978-1-4497-7877-4 (e)
ISBN: 978-1-4497-7878-1 (sc)
ISBN: 978-1-4497-7879-8 (hc)

Library of Congress Control Number: 2012923222

Printed in the United States of America

WestBow Press rev. date:12/21/2012

Introduction

So why write a book about my daughter's illness and death? Why would you want to read such a depressing topic? I suppose I want you to be drawn to McKenzie's story not because of the end of the story, but because of the heart of her story. McKenzie was a fighter, she had to be. But not only was McKenzie a fighter, everyone in our family is a fighter. We've had to fight our way through her illness and death and fight to stay together even today. In Luke 22:31, Jesus tells Peter that Satan has asked to "sift you as wheat". When you sift wheat, you separate it. You separate the good from the bad, the weak from the strong. I have felt that Satan has asked to sift my family as wheat. Satan's desire is to tear my family apart. He desires to tear apart my marriage. He desires me to question my faith in Jesus Christ. I refuse to let Satan succeed. We are strong because Christ lives in us and we will survive; even live eternally because of that.

At the heart of McKenzie's story is salvation. Growing up in a Christian home, I don't remember a time when I didn't have Jesus in my life. I remember thinking what a boring testimony I had- accepted Jesus early in life, grew up, married a Christian man, and had children whom we were raising in a Christian home. When McKenzie was diagnosed, the issue of salvation and testimony became paramount. I knew that my God was and is a merciful God. He would not let her die and deny her entry into heaven because she was a child. But I questioned the age of accountability. I wrestled with assurance of her eternal fate and my belief in a God who would allow a child to suffer so greatly. I believe to this day that God never intended for cancer and disease like McKenzie's to be part of our world. Illness and pain are a result of fallen man's sin. So I don't believe that God gave McKenzie cancer, but I do believe He allowed it. And I believe He allowed it for many purposes. I hope you'll see some of those purposes as her story unfolds in these pages.

Another aspect of her story is comfort. We received comfort from so many different directions as McKenzie's illness progressed. People we hadn't seen in years showed up to be the hands and feet of Christ to us. We were comforted by the words that people wrote on the website in the form of guestbook entries. You'll see some of those here. We've even been comforted by writing this book. And as we've been comforted, we'd like to comfort someone else. We know there are other parents out there going through the hell of childhood cancer. When McKenzie was diagnosed, we knew of one other couple who had traveled that road and they became a walking guidebook for us. We saw other books that talked about the medical aspects of the disease and even one that walked you through the red tape of medical insurance as it related to childhood cancer, but none that addressed the details of what it was like to spend those horrible nights in the hospital with your sick baby. You'll find that here. It's possible to survive the nightmare intact. We have and we hope to offer you comfort if you are wearing those shoes right now.

Above all, I want to offer you faith. I was talking via email to a friend a few months ago and she asked how we were doing. I filled her in on current details of our healing and she said to me, "Jeri, I can't wait to hear more about your unshakeable faith." That is where the title of this book came from and that is my hope for the legacy of McKenzie's story. You can have unshakeable faith in God alone. He alone can carry you in the palm of His hand through whatever tragedy you find yourself. He carried me. He carried us. As I said before, I refuse to allow Satan to shake my faith. I refuse to let him win. You, too, can have an unshakeable faith in Jesus Christ. My faith is built on the solid rock of His Word and His Love alone. I will not be moved. You, too, can stand firm if you place your trust in the Author and Perfector of my faith.

Come on our journey with us for a little while. See what the Lord did in our lives and know that He can do much in your life, too.

Author's Note: Monroe and I have written our stories separately and then combined them. I think you'll be able to tell the different tone in our voices, but I've labeled the passages to help you know the difference. We have also included entries from our caringbridge.org website- both our own entries and many from our guestbook. These help chronicle our journey as only actual warriors can in journal form.

Foreword

By Caroline May (McKenzie's Older Sister, Age 14)

The sky turns into a pink mess as the balloons float high above the church's roof. This is it; this is my last goodbye, and I know that she is watching from heaven, telling me not to cry as she enjoys the pink mess turned masterpiece.

On December 8, 2009, my four-year-old sister died from a long fight with a cancer called neuroblastoma. This is a rare kind of cancer that begins in the nerve tissue. The doctors measure the stage of the tumor on a scale of I to IV with I being the least dangerous and IV being fatal. McKenzie's tumor was a stage IV. Following her first diagnosis and eight-month treatment, she was miraculously healed for some time. However, when the second diagnosis was made, the cancer spread too quickly to stop.

I'd like to say that I was shy about it and didn't burden many other people with my sadness, but that wouldn't be true. I'm pretty much an open book; if I don't like something, I let it show in my face. The only time that I remember trying to contain my thoughts was when I was having a really bad day and all I could do was refrain from crying, but I'm not writing this to make you feel sorry for me. I'm writing this to share how I was lifted up out of my sadness through my friends and family.

I believe in friends. I believe in family. I believe in love. I believe in dedication. Most of all, I believe in hope. In my case, these values go together in more ways than one.

My friends were my family and my family members were my friends. Not everyone I knew was like this, though. Many of the kids around me at school knew my situation but didn't care. Life would go on for them no matter what happened to me. That's where I found my want for love, because I knew that I wanted to care about others even if they didn't care about me. Dedication is an obvious value in my situation. I could not give up. This, however, does not show dedication alone; it also shows hope.

Hope is my life. I have to hope. Without hope, I can no longer move forward. I have to keep going so that I can find out what is on the other side of my despair. It's like the saying, "The grass is always greener on the other side of the fence." Of course, this is normally in a different context. Instead of this motto implying that you should be happy with what you have, I look at it as motivation to get to the other side.

In this world, so many people with situations like mine exist in desperate need of hope. Though they may not know it, their minds crave the idea of having something to look forward to, something to jump the fence for. All it takes is a little encouragement. Imagine the chain of caring that we could set off with just a little bit of hope.

All about McKenzie

It all started in 2004. We had 3 beautiful children. Courtney was 10 years old, Caroline was 7 years old, and Monroe Jr. was 3 years old. We lived in an ideal neighborhood where everyone was close. The girls attended a small school where I volunteered whenever possible. Monroe Jr. attended a preschool nearby. Monroe had a wonderful job with a medical device company and I was involved with Bible Study Fellowship, PTA, and the swim team. We were living a blessed life.

We had talked about having another child. I was so busy with running our lives that I didn't think I really had time for another little love. Monroe worried, as always, about the financial implications of another child. Having another would mean paying for another college education and another wedding. I think he worried, too, about the demands of another baby on my time. We weren't actively trying to avoid getting pregnant, but we certainly weren't trying to get pregnant either. McKenzie was a surprise to both of us no matter how you look at it. With our first three children, I had prayed for and received them as gifts from God. I had asked God to give us healthy children and He had graciously answered our prayers with our two girls, Courtney and Caroline. I had prayed earnestly about having a boy before we even began trying to have Little Monroe. With McKenzie, she was simply all God's idea. He had the plan to put her into our lives from the very beginning. We never asked for her and had no idea of how she would change our worlds from her very conception. But God had a plan. He still does.

Monroe

My wife Jeri and I met each other in the spring of 1984 while attending Winston Churchill High School in San Antonio, Texas. We dated for a while and then lost touch, only to reconnect around Christmas of 1989. We dated and became engaged and eventually married in January 1991.

When we'd been married almost 3 years, we had our first healthy daughter, Courtney. In December 1996, we had our second healthy daughter, Caroline. In February 2001, we had a healthy son, Monroe Jr. We were sure we were done. However, God had plans for us to have one more. In February 2005, Jeri delivered our fourth child, McKenzie Jo May.

The birth of our fourth child changed our world almost as much as having our first child. It seemed like from the time we found out the Jeri was pregnant with McKenzie; everything in our world began to change regularly. All of a sudden, our house and our cars were too small, our bills too large. This little girl rocked our world and would change our family forever.

Jeri

When I began to think I might be pregnant, I was not unhappy about it. Never mind that this was not our plan. I knew from McKenzie's conception that God had ordained this path for our lives. My prayer at that point was for "one more little Christian." Courtney had accepted Christ and been baptized in May 1999. Caroline had also been baptized at age five and we were doing everything we could to train up little Monroe in the way he should go.

I recall a humorous story about finding out whether or not I was pregnant. I took a pregnancy test one day when Monroe was out of town. I was not yet ready to tell him my suspicions. The test came out positive. It was surreal. I just could not believe it yet. That same day I had one of the children at the pediatrician for some childhood issue. I was still building a relationship with our doctor, Jeanne Lovett. She became a major player in the story of McKenzie. This day was just the beginning. I casually asked Dr. Lovett if she had privileges at North Central Baptist Hospital. I already had thought out the implications that, if I was pregnant, I wanted to deliver my baby there. It's funny how my woman's brain worked this all out in the matter of a few hours. She looked at me with a funny expression and asked to see me in the hallway when the examination was complete. Once in the hallway, she asked the reason for my question. I told her I had taken a pregnancy test and that it had been positive, but that I wasn't even sure if I was really pregnant. With honesty that I have since come to completely treasure, she said to me bluntly, "Jeri, there are no false positives on pregnancy tests- only false negatives." From then on, I knew she was right. This was not a false positive, but rather a gift from God.

Monroe's reaction of complete shock is one I remember. I don't think he was prepared at all for what God had just begun to do in our lives. He moved on with quick responses and determination as he always does. Within a couple of months, he had his appointment for a vasectomy, because "this was not going to happen again." I was a little concerned about somebody "messing with my man," but I knew, too, that he was right. This was only the beginning of the changes that God was ushering into our lives.

One story of my pregnancy was not as humorous as my belief in "false positives." It was the story of where we would live. Acts 17:26 says that God determines where we should live. He showed Himself in a mighty way in determining where we would live during this time. Once we started realizing that we really didn't fit into our cozy little Hidden Forest home with our new addition, we began weighing our options. We looked at remodeling and adding a bedroom onto our home, remodeling the kitchen (I love to cook and really wanted a "new" kitchen), and adding some more office space for Monroe who keeps an office at the house. We had several bids, but one of the gentlemen trying to sell us his company's services made an interesting statement. He said, "It really sounds to me like what you want is an altogether new house, not a remodeled one."

So we began looking to move within our neighborhood. We loved Hidden Forest and did not want to leave it. We contacted the real estate agent from whom we had bought the house because he was- and still is- a "Hidden Forest expert." We began looking for a five-bedroom house with office space, a formal dining room, and a formal living room to house our grand piano. We wanted at least three bathrooms because a friend had remarked one day that four children sharing a bathroom made us "just one viral infection away from disaster." That was a prophetic statement; just wait. We found a wonderful home within the neighborhood that fit all of our specifications. It also had a swimming pool, not something I felt I needed, but was a little excited about. Our current home went on the market and we placed a contingency contract on that home. Being in the neighborhood, I would often drive by on the way home. One day I drove by to find two carloads of people looking at "our new house." I had a gut feeling that they would buy it out from under us and I was right. It was November and our current home was not moving. I cried for about two weeks straight- it was silly to cry over a lost home deal, but I was a little hormonal. Finally, between Monroe and my mother, they were able to talk some sense into me. I needed to get up and stop moping about this. There were no other homes on the market in our neighborhood, so we began looking for new homes. We had always been advised against this, but when we found a floor plan that was designed, it seemed, exactly for us and fit our budget (well, a little more than Monroe wanted to spend...), we decided to build. This is where several circumstances seemed to converge to begin a snowball effect from which we would not recover for over seven months.

First, McKenzie Jo May was born on February 8, 2005. We actually chose her birthday. We induced at thirty-eight weeks into my pregnancy. We talked my obstetrician into inducing a couple of weeks early because we were going on a trip to Hawaii. I know, it's ridiculous! But, neither one of us had ever been to Hawaii and we were going on a free trip! Monroe had been blessed in 2004 with a wonderful year with his company. In fact, he was "Sales Rep of the Year" and we were invited to go to Kauai on a rewards trip. We did not want to miss it! My other children had tendencies of wanting to be carried up to forty-two weeks of pregnancy which would have taken us right up to the date of the trip! So, my obstetrician agreed after much measuring and checking and belief that McKenzie was developed enough to be born. She thought I was crazy and still does! However, throughout McKenzie's illness, that same wonderful obstetrician has been one of my personal strongest advocates. Shortly after McKenzie was born, she adopted triplets and then found out she was pregnant a brief time later. She now knows what it is like to be the busy mother of four children and has been so wonderful to call and check on me periodically. Anyway, McKenzie was born without health concerns to either of us and Dr. Lovett did have privileges at North Central Baptist Hospital. Little did we know how much time we would spend there with her almost three years later.

McKenzie has always been everyone's baby. When Caroline was born, I used to say she was Courtney's baby to hold as much as she wanted. When Monroe was born, I said Caroline could take care of him and love on him. When McKenzie was born, she was everybody's baby. Everyone even got to help choose her name. My original plan was to name her Masden. That was Monroe's grandmother's maiden name. The name had been used previously in the family for middle names and only for boys. I thought it would make a darling little girl's name. However, Courtney was appalled. She insisted that I could not do that to this child! So, I bought a baby names book and we took a family poll. I remember one day in particular we took a day trip while I was pregnant. I brought out the book in the car and began reading all of the girls names beginning with "M". I wanted a name to begin with "M" because we had "Courtney and Caroline" and I wanted "Monroe and Mmmmmm". You get the picture. Any name that anyone liked, I placed a tally mark beside. Then, I took the top five names and Monroe and I chose

"McKenzie". It went well with "Jo". We had chosen "Jo" as the middle name as that is my mother's middle name.

So, McKenzie Jo May came into our lives. When she was two weeks old, we had Caroline into Dr. Lovett's office because Caroline wasn't feeling well. In fact, she was feeling awful. She tested positive for influenza. I had received my flu shot in the fall so I was protected, but McKenzie would be highly susceptible. Dr. Lovett recommended removing the baby from our house. McKenzie and I went to live at Meemaw and Grandpa's house, my parents. It turned out to be a good thing since little Monroe was diagnosed quickly after with influenza, too. Monroe and his mom (who had her flu shot, but was affected anyway) cared for the two "sickies" for two weeks in between caring for themselves. Courtney was the only one who did not actually get sick. McKenzie and I stayed protected at our safe house until danger passed.

By the time the danger passed, it was time to pack up and go to Hawaii. I don't remember a lot about that trip as much of it was spent caring for a newborn, but I remember the beauty of the island, the wonderful food, the good friends made, and the baby in the bag. I had taken a sling for McKenzie to travel in. She was so good when out in public. She slept in the sling always when we were out of the room. People joked with us that there really wasn't a baby in there because she was so good and quiet. As soon as we would return to the hotel room, she would be awake for hours on end. We even tried to rig a way to hang the sling on the back of a chair in hopes that she would sleep there, but to no avail. Monroe took her some mornings to the beach so I could get a little sleep. He says, to this day, that he has seen some of the most beautiful sunrises because of

McKenzie. Nonetheless, it was a good trip and one that marks McKenzie's entry to our family.

We sold our Hidden Forest house in April and moved in with my parents the first week of June. We lived there for four months while our new house was being built. The time for the kids with Meemaw and Grandpa was priceless. Even Monroe's and my relationship with them survived!

The weekend that we moved into the new house, McKenzie was dedicated to the Lord at our church at the time, Trinity Baptist Church. We had attended Trinity since before Courtney was born. We had so many wonderful friends there and we would soon see the power of Christ through many of these same people.

So, McKenzie came into our lives. In so many ways she changed and shaped our lives. God was using her to turn us into the people we needed to be without our knowledge. We changed houses, the kids changed schools, and Monroe took a management position with his company in order to more stably provide for all of us. We knew life had changed, but we had no idea of the challenges ahead.

Diagnosis

We settled into the new house. We met new neighbors. The kids settled into their new schools. I was called into leadership with Bible Study Fellowship. McKenzie went to Mother's Day Out at Coker Methodist Church just as Caroline and Monroe, Jr. had done before her. She started a little younger, just 18 months. She was never the "easy" baby we had hoped to find in our fourth child. You know, some mothers describe their youngest children as easy and say that they just go with the flow. That was never McKenzie. In fact, I described her as the strongest willed of the four children. Little did we know that God had designed her so that her strong will would serve her as a will to live. Don't get me wrong. She was and still is a joy. She was and is a beautiful child. As she grew, her hair came in thick, dark, and curly. Her older brother and sisters all had blondish hair. Two of them have blue eyes. I was thrilled that I finally had a baby who actually resembled me with my dark curly hair and dark eyes. McKenzie, like all of our children, was a big child. I never liked to use the word "big" to describe any of them because I felt like it had such a negative connotation. However, that is truly what she was. She, again like her siblings, was very tall for her age. She eventually lost the May child tummy that we thought was just part of her chunkiness. I preferred to describe her as tall. Tall she was, but it was her girth that caused us to be buying her size 6 and 7 clothes when she was just two years old. Size 5 clothes would have been about the right length, but would not accommodate her large belly. Now we know why. My new neighbor has a little boy close to Monroe Jr.'s age who was small by comparison. She and I used to joke about how if only McKenzie was a boy, she could pass down clothes to him as she grew out of them.

She had many ear infections throughout her second year. Dr. Lovett got to know her well during this time and I am so thankful now that she did. We had tubes put in her ears in October 2007. I look back now and think about how maybe her immune system was not in full force because it was fighting a terrible predator elsewhere in her little body. We also blamed her lack of good night time sleep on her ears. Going back to day one, she was never a good sleeper. She would cry many times during the night. Had we any idea of why she slept so restlessly, we might have caught her disease earlier. But then God would not be glorified so mightily by the works of His hands.

McKenzie in October 2007 as Tinkerbell

We bought a lake house in May 2007. We enjoyed that place so much! We bought a boat that my dad and Monroe chose together. The house was an old fixer upper. My mom and dad spent a weekend painting it with me. It was a large house (for a lake house), 2200 square feet with lots of rambling rooms. It was a great getaway. The kids got a Ping-Pong table for Christmas just for the lake house. It gave them a place to play. We spent hours shopping garage sales to furnish that big old house and took donations of furniture whenever friends or family members were clearing things out. We eventually had the exterior painted, too, and I think it turned out to be a pretty cool place. It was a block off the water, but had a beautiful lake view and was close to a city park where we could launch the boat. The kids could roam the area exploring the parks and playing on the playground equipment or swinging on our tire "horse" swing. We had a small fire pit where countless evenings were spent making fire and s'mores. Monroe's aunt and uncle and cousins had a place on the same lake and we enjoyed countless hours of "cousin" time with the kids playing and the adults telling stories and laughing. It was so much fun. In fact, one of the first nights we were all staying in the house, the cousins came over and the kids were all running around crazy. McKenzie happened to run into a corner of a wall with her forehead. Oh, how she cried. She got a huge goose egg immediately and we were worried about a concussion. I think in that situation, I wondered just for a split second what it would be like to lose her. Don't we all wonder that as parents? We think about those things in the quiet recesses of our minds, but usually just stuff those feelings away. Maybe we say a quick little prayer that God protect us from losing a child. Maybe we just refuse to think about it overmuch. Either way, I believe God prepared me just a little that night.

Our family made a trip to Disneyland in November of 2007. I had never been and Monroe wanted to take us as a family to experience the fun of Disney. It was so much fun! We stayed at a suite hotel property. We took turns sleeping with McKenzie on the pull out sofa bed. Monroe claims now that he should have known something was wrong with her the way she never really got into a deep sleep. She cried through the night and tossed and turned. He presumed as I did that it had to do with sleeping in a new place and possibly with being frightened of some of the characters at the park. Our first morning at Disneyland, we walked into a breakfast seating with characters visiting the guests. It wasn't planned. We were just hungry for breakfast and thought it would be a great kickoff to our trip. McKenzie took one look at Winnie the Pooh and began screaming! Monroe ended up taking her out of the restaurant so that the rest of us could enjoy the experience. He still jokes to this day about the expensive character breakfast he paid for, but didn't get to take part in. But he also says how much he enjoyed the time spent alone with McKenzie elsewhere in the park. He bought her some pink Mickey ears with her name embroidered and took her on the Dumbo ride. He says now it was time well spent even if he didn't get to eat until lunch! We had several experiences like that while at Disneyland. She would act unusually or have stomach problems that we didn't understand. But, that was just parenthood. We did what we had to do. Don't all parents? We never dreamed that maybe she was hurting.

Disneyland 2007 Family Trip

You know, prior to McKenzie's diagnosis, it seemed to me that we led a "charmed" life. I don't really believe in being "charmed." I believe only in the sovereign will of God, but I hope you get my meaning. Everything seemed to have gone smoothly in my life. I was born and raised in a middle class Christian family by loving parents. I married a wonderful Christian man and we had four beautiful children. We had never had tragedy strike in our lives. We had experienced the cancer illness and subsequent death of Monroe's father at what I believed to be much too young of an age, fifty-nine. We had experienced the usual young couple "stupid" money mistakes which could have easily led to our bankruptcy if not for having family and friends mentor us past it. We had experienced the usual childhood illnesses, broken bones, and problems that any young family does. But, I think I honestly thought that nothing bad would ever happen to us. That is why, on that Disneyland trip, I had our little family pose in front of a sign that reads, "and they lived happily ever after..." and used it as our Christmas card picture in 2007. I think I really believed that we would live happily ever after. Little did I know that a storm was about to blow in that would shape our "ever after" forever after.

We spent Christmas 2007 the same way we always had-Christmas Eve with Monroe's family, Christmas morning at home, and then Christmas Day with my family. We decided, however, to spend New Year's Eve at the lake house. I don't think the cousins were even up there (it was an hour's drive from home). I remember watching New York midnight on television and then going to bed. McKenzie had gone to sleep much earlier much easier than ever. She even slept late the next morning. We drove home to San Antonio later that day and McKenzie took a great nap. Then on January 2nd, she slept late again. I was relieved and thought maybe her sleep pattern was improving. She put herself down for a nap about 10 or 10:30am that morning. I just went upstairs to check on her and found her asleep in her bed. I thought that was weird, but that was nothing compared to her sleeping until about 4pm that afternoon. And it was at that time that Monroe went upstairs and actually woke her up. He brought her down and she seemed very sleepy. She could barely hold her eyes open. She looked drunk. We agreed that she could not have gotten into anything unusual anytime recently that might have chemically altered her. Monroe then tried standing her up and she crumpled to the floor. She was unable to bear her own weight. We tried several times and then Monroe took her to the sofa and just held her while I called the pediatrician. Since it was so late in the day, the nurse and I agreed that we would bring her in first thing Thursday morning. She didn't appear to be in any pain, so there didn't seem to be any reason to take her into the emergency room. It could wait till morning. I don't remember having any anxiety that evening or even the next morning as we headed for the doctor's office. Looking back at the signs, how could I not have known how sick our baby girl was?

Thursday morning, Monroe and I loaded McKenzie up and took her to Dr. Lovett's office together. I think Monroe must have believed something was seriously wrong while I naively believed she had a virus or something easily fixed. We met for quite a while with the doctor. As I said before, she knew McKenzie pretty well and was definitely surprised by her current lethargic state. She kept asking if McKenzie could have possibly gotten into any type of poisonous chemicals, anything from under the kitchen sink or anything at the lake house she could have been allergic to or stung by. Monroe and I racked our brains and could come up with nothing. We showed her how McKenzie was unable or unwilling to stand. That was the final thing that made Dr. Lovett send us to North Central Baptist Hospital. She called ahead and had the staff ready to admit her. We didn't do much to her that first day it seems like. I seem to recall only weighing her and inserting the I.V. line. I remember her just lying there sleeping and sleeping. Monroe spent the first of many nights in the hospital with her that night. He was ever the protective father, so loving to his baby girl. I think the first test we ran was an EEG to check her brain waves. I think that was done on either Thursday or Friday. It must have been Thursday because I know on Friday we did an MRI to look for a brain tumor. Again, Monroe was faithful to stay by her side throughout that test. The next was a spinal tap in the ICU to look for anything bacterial that could be causing these changes. Repeatedly following these tests, nothing was found.

Sometime during all these tests, Dr. Lovett talked to us about bringing in another doctor to help figure out McKenzie's case. She claimed he was "the smartest man in San Antonio". His name was Dr. Mahendra Patel. He was extremely busy, she said, and could only come at odd hours to review the test results as they were being done. I recall walking by the nurses' station several times to see a group of doctors circled around a computer screen studying results and discussing options. Almost always, Dr. Lovett and Dr. Patel were among this group. I didn't actually meet Dr. Patel until Sunday morning, but I was impressed with him because Dr. Lovett was impressed with him. I didn't know at that time that his field was Hematology/ Oncology. I don't think I knew what Hematology was, but I did know what Oncology was and it's probably best I didn't know his specialty. I was impressed with his dedication and willingness to look at our little girl. I had no idea how important he would become to our lives.

Monroe

This part of our journey began on January 3rd 2008 at North Central Baptist Hospital in San Antonio, Texas with our then 2 year 11 month old daughter McKenzie Jo May. Once there, McKenzie underwent several procedures until an abdominal CT scan revealed a large mass in her abdomen. She went under the care of Dr. Mahendra Patel and for the next 23 months our family endured a life changing series of events.

Below is a detailed account of McKenzie's battle and those who were close to her and our family. It is a story of love between parents and a child and a community and our family. It is also a story of facing life's challenges head on and on the shoulders of God.

Jeri

I look back at the person I was then and I look at the person I am now and I am truly amazed. I see a different person. I thought I trusted God then. I know I trust God now. My faith had not been truly tested. I used to think I had a boring testimony. Now, I feel like I have so much more to tell others. I remember walking cheerily into the children's ward at North Central. I was so naïve to think that everything really was going to be okay with her. I still believe that none of this happened without the approval of God Almighty. I believe that everything that happens to me as a believer and follower of Jesus Christ filters first through God's hand. I don't believe God caused this tragedy, but I do believe He allowed it. Why? Well, I'm getting ahead of myself, but truly I believe He allowed it for His glory.

Monroe stayed with her every night while in North Central Baptist. He said nights were horrible. This would only be the beginning of his dislike and disdain for the night staff of nurses in any hospital. He complained that neither she nor he got any rest because there was a constant parade of staff coming in to check on her. I would soon find out that he was totally not exaggerating.

On Saturday, January 5th, Monroe and I "celebrated" our 17th wedding anniversary in McKenzie's hospital room. I remember sitting in the room with all 3 grandparents opening cards and talking about how hopefully, this would all be over soon. Little did we know that, even on our 19th wedding anniversary, we would be still feeling that this was far from over.

The doctor came and told us that morning that McKenzie appeared to be suffering from a severe case of Narcolepsy, a severe sleep disorder. They were sending her blood samples off to Stanford where, we were told, they were doing a great trial on Narcolepsy. We would get this all figured out. But, just in case, just to rule anything else out, they would do an abdominal C/T that Saturday afternoon. I remember Monroe going home, exhausted, to get some much needed rest while I walked down with McKenzie for the C/T. She was still sleeping most of the time and didn't really fight them on this one. I remember vague complaining from her wanting them to leave her alone, but nothing like the feistiness that we would come to know in future procedures. I remember the technician asking me why they were doing this test. I told him confidently that it was simply a precaution. I still don't know if the doctors suspected something in her abdomen or if they really were just ruling out all other possibilities. Maybe I'll have to ask Dr. Lovett or Dr. Patel when I see them again. In any case, the findings were about to rock our world.

Monroe spent Saturday night again with her. I remember him saying this would be the last night he could physically stand to stay. Sunday night would be my turn. So, I enjoyed my sleep, as I always do. Sunday morning, I decided to get up and take the kids to church. We were all getting ready to go when Monroe called and told me to get there quickly- the doctors had something important to tell us. I didn't know whether he knew the diagnosis already, I didn't take the time to ask him. But he definitely knew something bad was coming. He told me to leave the children at home, call my parents and have them meet us there. His mother was already there. I scrambled to get there fast. That drive, in retrospect, was the longest drive of my life. It wasn't all that far from our house to the hospital, but I'm sure I stopped at every red light between those two points and prayed all the way. I think I knew it was bad, very bad. I couldn't get there fast enough. Time dragged on. I finally arrived and went down the hall to McKenzie's room. She was there resting comfortably as usual and Monroe and his mother were there with tears in their eyes. My parents arrived soon after and Dr. Patel came in to explain things. I remember the details of the treatment he sketched on the whiteboard. I remember the word "cancer" and learning to spell "neuroblastoma". I remember the tears in my husband's eyes and the look of resentment I saw against "cancer" rearing its' ugly head in our family again. I remember Monroe asking what would happen if we didn't treat the disease. Dr. Patel's answer was that McKenzie would live four to six weeks at most. This was stage IV neuroblastoma. She would not survive. I remember Monroe, his mom, and I talking together in the hall. I asked Jane if she had it all to do over again with her husband, knowing that he would die anyway, would she treat him again? She said yes, she definitely would. Monroe was skeptical, not wanting to watch his daughter endure the horrors of chemotherapy, radiation, and surgery that he'd watched his father endure 11 years earlier. I held onto verses in the Bible I'd read urging us to choose life. Deuteronomy 30:19 (NLT) says, "Today I have given you the choice between life and death...Oh, that you would choose life, so that you and your descendants might live!" NIV If we chose not to treat, we were choosing certain death for McKenzie who could not choose for herself. We were her advocates and I was certain we had to choose to fight this new demon in our world. Monroe remained unconvinced, but agreed to move forward with at least the first round of treatment. This was the first time in our marriage where, I felt, we were diametrically on different sides of an issue. I can see his reasoning now, but then I had a hard time seeing the suffering that would go, hand in hand, with the treatment that was prescribed. We would have this same choice again and we would choose differently the next time. I still question the sanity of the second choice, but I do not ever question the sanity of the first choice. We chose life for McKenzie on January 6, 2008. It was like a life that we had never known and I pray we never know again. It was the life of a cancer patient fighting the demon pursuing them. It was a physical battle and a spiritual battle. There are scars and casualties existing today that can never be changed. We won some fights and lost many others. Lives were changed. In fact, very few lives that came in contact with McKenzie Jo May were not changed.

Monroe

As a parent of four children, I always had a fear that something serious would one day happen to one of them. In January 2008, my wife, Jeri, and I were living a happy life with our four children in San Antonio, Texas, not knowing that soon something would happen to change our lives forever. Courtney was fourteen and in 8th grade. Caroline was eleven in 5th grade, Monroe Jr. was six in 1st grade and McKenzie Jo was one month shy of her third birthday. We had just celebrated Christmas with family and we were looking forward to a new year.

Little did we know that life would change for our family on January 6th with the diagnosis of stage IV cancer in our youngest child, McKenzie. We would be faced with many decisions and many unpleasant situations as a family. Below is our family's story much as it was chronicled on our website www.caringbridge.org/visit/mckenziemay1_.

We were deeply concerned about our little girl. We hoped for the best however, we feared the worst. As her father, I spent the first three nights with McKenzie in the hospital. The nights were long for me but she mostly slept. The days were filled with scans, blood draws, an MRI, a spinal tap, and finally an abdominal CT that would ultimately indentify the problem.

On Sunday morning, January 6th, the day after Jeri's and my 17th wedding anniversary, we received the diagnosis. In much the same fashion I had witnessed with my father, eleven years earlier when he was diagnosed with pancreatic cancer, the doctors came in and asked me to call our family to the hospital. I had an immediate flashback to sitting with my father in a similar hospital room and listening as his doctor described his condition. The extent of the disease and the course of treatments he would face were explained.

I knew from the seriousness of Dr. Lovett's face that the news was not good. I called Jeri and she headed to the hospital as quickly as possible. As I awaited her arrival, my mother, Jane, showed up and I finally could not wait any longer and asked Dr. Lovett to please come in and share the diagnosis.

There we sat: McKenzie, my mother and me. Three generations of family together to face yet another cancer diagnosis. This time it would be stage IV, neuroblastoma, a very rare form of childhood cancer. It was a large mass that covered most of McKenzie's abdomen. It began on her adrenal gland and attached to ALL major organs: heart, lungs, stomach, spleen, and kidneys. My worst fear for my youngest child was confirmed.

When Jeri arrived, we had the doctor come in again to share the diagnosis. Even when I heard it a second time, I still had difficulty accepting what was happening to McKenzie. Jeri's parents, Jerry and Thelma, were called and arrived shortly. During this time, Dr. Lovett had called Dr. Mahendra Patel to consult. His specialty was Pediatric Hematology/Oncology and he was to us introduced as the "smartest man in town". Our lives would be tied closely to this physician for the next two year.

Dr. Patel came into the room and began telling us about options, odds and treatments. The treatments would be long and very rough. McKenzie would be treated with chemotherapy, a bone marrow transplant, and finally surgery. In order to gain the best results, we would begin the next morning with bone aspirations of both hips, a biopsy, and a port placement. Odds of her surviving for 12 months were at best 50/50, odds of survival longer then two years where less than 25%.

After Dr. Patel spoke with Jeri and me, we finally had a chance to talk to each other in the hall and discuss what we would do. After prayers and tears, Jeri convinced me that we would FIGHT! WE went back into the room and began what would be a very long process. We stood united with our daughter and with each other.

We also agreed that we would be honest with our other children and share with them the truth. Courtney, Caroline and Monroe had been left at home while Jeri and I were at the hospital. I would need to leave and go and explain the situation the best I could. I left to drive home and have a family discussion while Jeri remained at the hospital.

McKenzie was weak and under three years of age. Her explanation would come with time as she asked questions. For now, all we explained to our daughter was that she was in the hospital and was sick. We told her that she had a "boo boo" in her tummy.

So on that Sunday afternoon, I went home and gathered the kids together to break the news. We sat in our den and I began to explain the situation to Courtney, Caroline and Monroe. Without a doubt, this was one of the hardest things I had ever had to do. I prayed for strength and just the right words to explain the situation.

One of the challenges was that there was a 7 year age gap. Although I did not want to frighten any of them, I wanted them to understand how serious the situation was for McKenzie and for our family. I do not remember exactly what I said, however, I do remember after I finished my explanation, Monroe age 6 asked, “Is she going to die?” My other two girls began to cry and I answered that “Yes, that was a possibility.” We all hugged and cried for several minutes, and then Monroe said “OK, can I go to a friend’s house?”

Courtney and Caroline each headed to their rooms. They needed time to process what they had just been told. None of us had faced this situation before so we each had to find our own way through the process. There was no “right” or “wrong”, only the reality of the situation. At times we all needed space and at times we did not want to be left alone. Jeri and I would try to make sure that the children always had someone near by.

Looking back, it is very interesting to me how different each of us would handle McKenzie’s illness throughout the next two years. There would be many times where each of us would fall apart. Through it all, rarely would Jeri and I fall apart at the same time. This was a blessing from God; He gave us strength to be there for all of them.

That afternoon, the two older girls decided they wanted to go to the hospital to visit McKenzie. I took them to see their little sister. Courtney and Caroline painted her nails, did puzzles, and tried to cheer her up. They showed a sweetness that would continue throughout her illness.

Also, on that afternoon we began what was the first of many difficult medical challenges. McKenzie was not eating or drinking and the physicians wanted to start an IV on her. Jeri and I watched as the nurses tried seventeen times to start an IV. McKenzie screamed and squirmed and cried as Jeri and I sat and held our baby. Finally, we told them to quit and they agreed. This was a valuable lesson and I swore that from that point forward we would act as McKenzie’s voice in the hospital. I would not allow her to be needlessly poked and stuck.

This was also the beginning of many difficult and painful procedures. It is very hard to sit and watch your baby in pain, even when you know that the medical community has the best of intentions. When your child cries, screams and begs for things to stop, and you allow them to continue, you create many questions in your mind. Is this for the best? Why are we continuing? And will this help? These are a few that continued to rattle around in my head.

On that Sunday night, I made a phone call to two friends I knew understood what we were facing, Rick and Lori McGrath. They were the only two people I knew that possibly could understand. Several years earlier, they had lost a daughter to brain cancer. In fact she had passed away on the same floor where McKenzie was currently staying. Rick and Lori dropped everything and came to the hospital to visit. They brought food, magazines and a wealth of knowledge that no parent should have. They understood what we would be facing.

I had first met Rick and Lori when they moved to San Antonio for Rick's job and they began attending Trinity Baptist Church with us. Rick was in Medical Sales and so was I so we struck up a friendship. I had visited Rick and Lori throughout their daughter, Marin's illness and had even visited the day she passed away. I hated to call but did not know who else to turn to. They graciously began to walk Jeri and I through what would be a long, long battle.

That night, I spent the night with McKenzie. Jeri stayed at home with the other three children and helped them prepare to return to school on Monday morning. It would not be easy. Sunday was also the last day of Christmas break. So, in addition to the new diagnosis, we had to get the other three children ready to return to school.

That night at the hospital was especially long for me. McKenzie slept and I prayed and listened to music. I remember playing the George Strait song, "I Saw God Today", Garth Brooks' "The Dance" and Steven Curtis Chapman's "Cinderella" over and over again. I sat and watched McKenzie sleep. This would be the first of countless sleepless nights watching her and praying for her. The nights are the longest and worst parts of spending time in a hospital with your child.

Also, on that night very late, I began writing to my daughter as she lay in bed sleeping. I would find that writing would be an outlet for concerns moving forward.

January 6, 2008- Dad's Notes

Dear McKenzie,

It is one month before your 3rd birthday and you are turning our lives upside down once again. It is just before six in the morning and I am sitting with you at North Central Baptist. We have spent the last three nights and this will be the fourth day at the hospital. You have had an EEG, Spinal Tap, MRI, Abdominal CT, blood tests, and urine tests. Currently, we have Dr. Lovett, your pediatrician, a neurology-pediatric specialist, Dr. Patel (Hematology/Oncology Specialist), and several other doctors working with us to try to figure out what is wrong with you.

You started sleeping more and more last Saturday, and by Wed. we could barely wake you up, and when you were awake you were not able to walk or stand on your own. So needless to say you are scaring your mother and me to death. You have so many people praying for you I am sure that God hears our prayers. My Mormon friends in Salt Lake are praying for you, our Baptist friends are praying for you, our Episcopal, Lutheran, Catholic, and CBC friends are all praying. We are just hoping someone can figure out what is wrong.

I have spent the nights with you and Mommy is spending the days with you. Because in addition to worrying about you, Courtney, Caroline and Monroe are at home and need to be taken care of as well. I can tell you that we have blessings coming out of this already. Our family and friends are all helping out to make sure that everyone is taken care of. Dee Dee, Mee Maw, and Grandpa are helping with the other kids. Aunt Kate and Aunt Gaye call non-stop all day long to check on you, and we have many different friends coming by to see you during the day. All we need now are some answers!!!!

You are sleeping again, and we had a few good minutes this morning. You sat in my lap, ate some animal crackers, and drank some juice. You were fairly alert, however, you were not willing to stand or walk. It is really tough to watch you this way because we are all so used to you jumping up and running around. You have never been a baby that did not move.

I am trying hard to focus on all the fun we have had over the last year. In May of 2007, we bought a lake place at LBJ and we got a boat. You love going to the lake and love being on the boat. You like playing in the water and you love the new tire swing you got for Christmas. In November of 2007, we took a trip to Disneyland in California and you loved it all. But your favorite part was all of the Disney Princesses. We even bought you a Snow White outfit that you wore on the plane coming home. As we were walking through the DFW airport, some of the flight attendants thought you were so cute that they paged you over the intercom, "Snow White to gate C22, Snow White to gate C22." It was really cute.

So through all of this, I am trying to focus on the happy times, but I've got to tell you it is a challenge. Please get better and please get better quickly. We all love you and can't stand to watch you like this.

January 7, 2008-Dad's Notes

3:00 a.m. Well, McKenzie yesterday we got our answer and it was not at all what we had hoped for. The Doctors came in around 9 in the morning and told us that you had a large 12cm tumor growing in your abdomen. They call it Neuroblastoma and informed us that this was a very rare type of cancer that only 100-200 children in the United State contract each year. Well you seemed to hit the jack pot, but not the kind we had hoped. So this morning I am sitting with you once again in the hospital waiting with you for the next step. In about three and a half hours you will undergo surgery to have a chest port, a bone biopsy, and a piece of your tumor to be removed. From there we will hopefully go home on Monday night and you will then go on Tuesday to check in at the Methodist Children's Hospital to begin treatment for this disease. Wow, this is so much for such a little girl. My hope for you is that you will grow up and someday look back on this and have some idea of what you lived through. I know you are a fighter, and I know you can make it through this if you try. Fight, Fight, Fight, don't let that green eyed monster beat you!!!!

10:30- We did not make it home; we were sent straight to Methodist Hospital and it looks like we will be here for a while. Possibly we could stay here for up to 3 weeks. We will hope for the best. Tuesday will bring more tests and more trails for you. Stay strong and stay precious.

Treatment

Jeri

The treatment plan was laid out. I had agreed to it although, as I stated before, I had so little understanding of what I had agreed to. Monroe reluctantly agreed. The afternoon of that first day is still very clear. My parents stayed with McKenzie while Monroe and I began to talk through the realities of all we had agreed upon. We made phone calls informing friends and family of her diagnosis.

One of my first phone calls was to Jennifer Gonzales, the Teaching Leader in my Bible Study Fellowship class where I was a Discussion Leader. I facilitated the discussion of 15 women studying the book of Matthew that year. Arrangements would have to be made for someone else to facilitate the group. I would need to step out of leadership for as long as it took to complete McKenzie's treatment. But, the greater reason I made that phone call was the support that the large circle of leaders offered. From the beginning of "choosing life" for McKenzie, I was on a mission to see her cured. "Cure" became my battle cry. Knowing it was a long shot, I was sure that God would answer with healing McKenzie and allowing her to live a long and happy life. So I asked for the leaders in my circle of believers in Christ to pray along side me. I knew that whatever was happening in McKenzie's treatment, every Tuesday morning there were many women praying for me, for McKenzie, and for my entire family. I came to believe that, like Peter in the gospels, Satan had asked to sift me as wheat. I believe that God did not send McKenzie's cancer. I believe cancer comes straight from Satan. Sin and disease entered the world at the time of Adam and Eve's fall in the book of Genesis. Cancer is just one of Satan's more ingenious masterpieces. He is crafty, I'll give him that. However, I also believe that greater is He that is within me than he that is within the world. Satan went to God and asked Him to afflict us with this awful disease. Satan wished to destroy my marriage, he wished to destroy my family, and he wished to destroy my faith in Jesus Christ. But, God had other plans. God allowed, definitely not caused, this awful illness to permeate the otherwise tightly woven fabric of our lives in order to glorify Himself. So many lives would be changed and, I believe, faith strengthened because of the witness of this little girl who loved Jesus so much. The lives of the women in the leadership circle of the day women's BSF class in San Antonio, Texas were changed. I know because I am one of them.

We began the job, even without knowing it, of becoming McKenzie's advocate. I never really thought about the fact that one needs a mediator between themselves and the hospital staff. I always naively assumed that the doctors and nurses just automatically had your best interest in mind and always made wise choices. This is not so. Doctors and nurses are not evil people. But they are only people like you and me. They don't have any more supernatural wisdom than you and I.

By January 6th, McKenzie needed a new I.V. So that day, they attempted to put in a new one. I am not proud of this next part. Looking back now, I would have done this so differently. Hindsight is 20/20. Monroe was not there until later in the afternoon or this would never have happened. My mother and I tried to help the staff by alternately holding McKenzie. But, the sad fact is that we allowed them to stick her 17 different times without success. Just thinking about it now makes me feel like the worst mother of all times. I just didn't know that I could say, "NO!" or "STOP!" We were still at North Central Baptist in a regular children's wing. The staff didn't have the expertise to adequately find a vein and get what they needed with her so squirmy. They called many different staff members from other departments who had more experience, but all failed. I don't remember how or why they finally stopped trying. Maybe they finally just admitted defeat. I know I should have stopped them after two or three tries. I know that now. But I didn't know it then. They finally agreed to let her do without an I.V. for the night and have one done while she was under anesthesia the next day. If you learn nothing else from this book, learn that you are an advocate for your loved one in the hospital. You have rights and so does your loved one. You can say "no". It's your choice.

Having spent so many nights in the hospital and with no end in sight, Monroe went home to rest a little. The job that waited for him at home was explaining this new diagnosis to our other three children. Courtney was 14 years old, a straight A student and active musician and athlete in the 8th grade. Caroline was 11 years old, also a straight A student and a budding musician in the 5th grade. Little Monroe, as we call him, was 6 years old and just active. In 1st grade, Monroe just loved to run and play often citing recess and P.E. as his favorite subjects in school. I think it is easiest for the younger children to accept difficult things in their lives, especially spiritual matters like life and death. And maybe because he is a boy he simply takes the information given to him and doesn't emotionalize it like we women do even from an early age. My very tired husband, both physically and emotionally, sat the children down when he got home and gently told them that their sister had cancer. I wasn't there so I don't know all the details except for what Monroe shared with me later. But, I picture a very tender scene. The way I picture it Caroline and Courtney began crying quietly. I do know that Monroe told me that little Monroe asked two questions: 1) is she going to die? And 2) Can I still have my birthday party next month? Such simple questions from one so young... To the first question Monroe answered, "Maybe." To the second question the answer was "of course!" I know there were many other questions from the girls and he also gave them an abbreviated version of the upcoming treatment plan. Their lives were also changed from that moment on. They grasped the seriousness of the situation. Their loves deepened for each other and for their parents (take that, Satan). Already, God's love was triumphing rather than Satan taking the victory. Now, don't think it was all peace on earth at our household. Our children still fought ferociously with each other. They still do. They still fought ferociously with McKenzie. They loved her deeply and tried at first to handle her with kid gloves. But with McKenzie, the gloves came off. She became a fighter like you've never seen. She fought ferociously with them. God used McKenzie's illness to shape my other three children into people He needs them to be. Like rock against rock, bits and pieces of each of them were chipped away and sparks flew often. Some of their childhood innocence was stripped away. We know why God made McKenzie come to us with so much spunk. She needed every ounce of fight to complete her journey. We don't know yet, though, why God is shaping these other three into such strong personalities. Time will tell. I know His purposes will be fulfilled in each of their lives. A great deal of His shaping began that day for them.

Monroe has a large family. While his immediate family consists of only him and his sister, he has many aunts and uncles and cousins. His father, as I mentioned, passed away in 1997. His father has two brothers. One of his uncles is Jim and the other is David. I have much to say about Jim, all good, as he really stepped up as the patriarch of the family following his brother's death. He is intricate to our story. However, David's life is greatly intertwined in ours as well. When Monroe and I married, it took a long time to feel accepted with his extended branch of cousins and such. But one person with whom I always felt loved was David. He was the rambunctious little brother that you've seen in many families. He is loved by all. He was married early in adult life and had two children- a boy and a girl. Then he divorced and dated and then remarried. At the time of Monroe's and my engagement, he was married to one of the most delightful women I've ever met. Her name is Nancy. In fact, I found Nancy so engaging that I once joked that if David ever divorced her that I would keep her and forget about him. She was also married previously and has two equally delightful daughters. Her darling daughters were junior bridesmaids in my wedding. They were in elementary school at the time. I was unable to find dresses that I liked for them. Nancy was so kind that she even sewed them dresses to mirror my bridesmaids. They were pretty detailed and I was impressed. The girls were tiny enough to be flower girls, but were at that preteen age when that would have been condescending. So, we made them junior bridesmaids and they were incredible. Fast forward seventeen years. David and Nancy were separated by January 2008. My heart was broken because I loved them both very much. It was a touchy subject in the family. Sides were chosen, but I was not about to choose sides. I cared too much about both of them to let either one of them out of my life. So on the day of McKenzie's diagnosis, I think I called Nancy. Someone did and she and the girls came to the hospital to see us. Healing began for every one of some of the hurt of the divorce. That is part of the good result of McKenzie's illness. Lives were reconciled; wounds were touched by the Healer. Nancy doesn't do anything in a small way. She came to the hospital with her daughters and the husband of her oldest daughter. (We would later attend the wedding of her younger daughter during McKenzie's remission.) They brought the first of many very lavish gifts that little girl would receive. I loved having them there. I was so glad they came. I had missed them so much. It was healing for me. While they were there, another cousin and his family arrived. It was a little tense for a minute, but quickly, I think, everyone realized that they had to put aside their differences for this little girl who was so sick. There could be no petty disagreements while we fought for her life. This happened many times during the two years we fought cancer with our baby. I used to be a big grudge holder. However, God showed me that life is too short. I still get mad. But, He brought about a new peace in me and in many. Many of us learned that you can't let differences keep you occupied. You must keep your eyes on more important things like healing.

The next morning, Monday, January 7, 2008 McKenzie had her first operation. She had a double port surgically placed on her left side below her armpit. That port would serve as the administration site of all medications. It would prevent having to find a vein for an I.V. every time she needed medication or blood. Also during the anesthesia, Dr. Patel did the first of several bone marrow aspirations. He withdrew bone marrow from her left hip to see the extent of the cancer's effect. We found out later that, yes, the cancer was found completely through the bones and bone marrow. The surgery was done at North Central Baptist and the plan was to move her quickly to Methodist Children's Hospital where we would begin chemotherapy shortly. Monroe stayed still with her through all of this until he would almost fall over from exhaustion and I would send him home to catch a little shut eye. She recovered from surgery in her same room and then later that day was dismissed from North Central Baptist for the last time. I wished that we could do treatment at that hospital because it was so much closer to our house, but they were not equipped for the intensity of treatment she would need. So my mother and I packed her up in my Yukon XL and drove her, still groggy and sleepy, to Methodist Children's Hospital for the first of many, many visits. We were told that we should expect a month long stay for this first visit.

We were met on the fourth floor, the Hematology/ Oncology- or Hem/Onc wing, as it is called, by Carlos. Carlos was McKenzie's first nurse there. He was my guardian angel through this scary maze of cancer that first night. He so kindly took all of her pertinent information and showed me the ropes on the floor. My little McK was beginning to rouse from surgery and he endeared himself to her right away. It would be Carlos that she asked for every time we stayed there. He was her favorite coloring partner and the most efficient at talking McKenzie into allowing him to change her needles (which needed to be changed every five to seven days). He facilitated moving us into a larger more comfortable and more private room where we wouldn't have to share with another patient during that first stay.

Of course, once the staff got to know McKenzie and her feisty temperament (and her feisty father), they would move heaven and earth to get us into a larger, private room. I know of at least twice during different stays that we moved at 1am or 5am to a better room because once the morning began the room would be occupied or that was just the earliest it was available and clean. We only shared a room once that I know of. It was with another of Dr. Patel's patients, a little girl named Rachel. I felt sorry for them for having to room with us. We were a pretty demanding lot and I'm sure they felt invaded when we were brought in. But, there was no other room in the inn and it was necessary. That stay was one when McKenzie and I were moved in the middle of the night to a private room when one came available. I just wonder who made the more urgent pleas- me or Rachel's poor father!

Carlos was just the first of many wonderful nurses we encountered on the fourth floor. I think, though, that I will save some of those precious jewels to share as our story unfolds. I will say that Nancy was another staff member who came to me early and helped me understand the intricacies of chemotherapy. She brought a notebook and placed in it all the several page thick descriptions of the many drugs we would encounter on just the first round of treatment. Now, I am not a naturally organized person. Monroe is, but not me. So when

Nancy, the nurse, brought this notebook in, I just thanked her and set it aside for him. What I really appreciated was the time she spent talking through all the drugs and their possible side effects. It read like one of those tiresome commercials you see where they are suggesting a certain drug for you and then while the pretty picture is playing you hear five minutes of "do not take this drug if you are pregnant, nursing, or breathe on a regular basis" and "discontinue use if you experience headaches, hair loss, or seeing red spots on your white sheets." It seemed to me that the side effects could be more devastating than the cancer, but that is kind of an oxymoron. Nothing is more devastating to me now than cancer. And this would become Monroe's mantra- is this treatment really worth all this pain we are inflicting on her? But, all I could see at that point (and to some degree still do see) was the cure. I prayed and hoped that God would really CURE her. Nancy was patient to explain it all and remained an advocate for us throughout our journey.

Monroe insisted on spending the first night with McKenzie in the "new" hospital. He was and is still such a good dad. He said this was worse than the first one. He complained that the staff came in and out all night long. This would become an issue with him throughout her treatment and beyond. I mentioned it recently in a discussion I had with Dr. Patel and he said a wise thing, "If you want rest, don't come to the hospital. If you want rest, go home." And he's right. But, my thought at that time was that you come to the hospital to get well. And you can't get well if you don't get some sleep. And I know I'm a grouchy parent when I don't get any sleep! But sleep was something we seldom got when in the hospital overnight. What I figured out eventually was that the night staff was responsible for collecting data. They were to gather the blood samples, the weight measurements, the urine input/output data, and the respiratory information that the lab technicians and the doctors would expect to be waiting for them when they arrived at 7am. But this never sat well with Monroe and I certainly understood.

Monroe

Note to McKenzie January 7, 2008- 10:30pm- We did not make it home, we were sent straight to Methodist Hospital and it looks like we will be here for a while. Possibly we could stay here for up to three weeks. We will hope for the best. Tuesday will bring more tests and more trials for you. Stay strong and stay precious.

The plan was to have surgery at North Central Baptist and do a tissue biopsy, bone biopsy and port-a-cath placement in order to deliver medication and fluids when needed. We then hoped to check out of the hospital and take her home for twenty-four hours. We did not make it. Instead, we checked out of the NC Baptist and went straight to Methodist Children's Hospital to begin our first round of chemotherapy. We had no choice but to move ahead aggressively.

Jeri

My first night was Tuesday, January 8th. I didn't know what exactly to expect. I took my nightgown and kind of thought I might sleep through their comings and goings. I am a heavy sleeper generally. Monroe used to say that all I required for sleep was my eyes being closed. Upright, horizontal, it didn't matter as long as I could close my eyes.

But, that first night I heard every noise. I heard every nurse that came and went. Now I should explain that every patient room has a bathroom in it, but that restroom is for patient use only. From the beginning, every output from McKenzie's body was measured. She was completely potty trained at this time, but because of her lethargic state was wearing pull-ups round the clock. Each one was weighed when we changed her for bodily fluid output. As she became less lethargic and began asking to go to the restroom, each time she urinated it was measured and recorded. This told the doctor if she was retaining fluid or needed a diuretic. The parents of the patients were to use the restroom in the "family room" across the hall. This became more natural to me over time, but was certainly uncomfortable this first night. I was accustomed to sleeping in a nightgown and mistakenly assumed I would be sleeping this night. Monroe had warned me, but I didn't get it. That was the last night I took a nightgown in which to "sleep" in the hospital. I quickly adjusted my expectations and assimilated into a wardrobe of sweat pants and soft long sleeve t-shirts overnight. The room was always cold and when I inevitably jumped up to help McKenzie or talk her into letting the nurse complete a procedure with her, I was comfortable and so was the nurse with my new nighttime wardrobe. McKenzie and I (or Monroe or Meemaw) were often woken from a sound sleep by the sudden noise of the hospital room door being swept abruptly open by the members of the night staff who were sure they were "just doing their job." I came to believe that many of them were so upside down in their sleep habits and therefore so crabby about being awake at night that they wanted to make us crabby, too. You know the old saying, "Misery loves company."

We complained many times about the night staff, but really, it never changed.

There was one definite exception to my general dislike of the night staff (and okay, a couple of others). Her name was Kerian. I could not for the life of me figure out how to say her name at first. She finally told me that it was like "carryin'" a baby. She was the first night nurse McKenzie had while I stayed over and I will be forever grateful for her kind indoctrination of me to hospital nights. She wore a light around her head like a miner and only turned it on when necessary. That woke up McKenzie far less than the members of the staff who breezed in turning on every light in the room so they could perform their task. Kerian was even known to take McKenzie's blood sample without waking her! That is one talented nurse! There were a couple of others who could do this, too, but they were few and far between. It always seemed like we would get one good night nurse for every four or five nights of challenging ones. I'm still not sure if it was them or us that were the problem! I always felt bad when I would stay and have a good one and then Monroe the next night would complain so badly about the overnight he'd had and then I would figure out it had been the same nurse.

Monroe and I were on a rotating 24-hour schedule while in the hospital. He would stay with her for about 24 hours and I would be at home with the other children. Then I would go up and relieve him for 24 hours while he went home, slept a little if the children's schedules would allow, have dinner with them, do homework with them, attend their evening activities with them, sleep at home in our bed, then come up to the hospital to relieve me and do it all over again. It's no wonder having a sick child is such a stress on marriages. You rarely see one another.

When you do see each other, it is in a hospital room under less than ideal circumstances. McKenzie would often be sleeping and we would need to talk quietly or in the hall. Sometimes the nurses were kind enough to sit with her while we slipped out and had a few minutes together in the elevator foyer. That was always less than private as Methodist Children's is a very busy place. We would bring the other children to visit McKenzie as often as possible. Whoever was available of the children (not in school or at a weekend activity) would come and visit during what I came to call our "shift change". Then they would leave with the tired parent and head out. Those short visits were so good for McKenzie. She loved and missed her family so much during hospital visits. It was good for the "sibs", too, as Dr. Patel calls them. They got to see that their sister was alive and fighting. They also got to see the seriousness of what we were dealing with. They might walk in to find her puking up her guts. They might walk in to find her sleeping under heavy drug influence. They might walk in to find her smiling and happy to see them, desperate for a new playmate for a few minutes. Those were the happiest times for me. To see Courtney, Caroline, or Monroe Jr. curled up in bed with her coloring, painting, or blowing bubbles did me a world of good. They all worked so hard to love on her. Monroe and I both worked so hard to make sure the "sibs" were never alone. They are why we designed the "24-hour on, 24-hour off schedule" at the hospital. We never wanted them away from home if they didn't have to be. We tried very hard to maintain a "normal" schedule in this new totally "abnormal normal" we'd been forced into. As it turned out, little Monroe spent most of those two years with friends. He was simply happier there. He was spoiled and that wasn't completely a bad thing. He was spared much of McKenzie's wrath and much of the despair that settled around our home from the stress of dealing with a terminally ill child. Let me just interject here that today Monroe is my "big project." He may not like now being the center of my attention, but he needed much discipline when our journey with McKenzie ended. He needed the shaping that he missed over those two years. Don't get me wrong; the incredible friends who cared for him did a great job. I could not have survived without them and Monroe might not have survived either- either of the Monroe's! But there is nothing that can replace the discipline of a parent. I owe those friends a huge debt of gratitude. Stephanie and Eve, you were my right hands. I love you so much for all you did for me and my little boy. Courtney and Caroline spent time with friends, but were also with us for the majority of our fight. They saw a lot more. They, too, were helped by a host of friends. They were and remain today very active girls. They want to be involved in church, music, and sports. They want to do it all and still maintain an "A" in all academics. Because of the help of so many friends including Lisa and T.C. Carter, Marsha and Bob Nelson, Melanie and Ken Drummond, Christie and Ray Hoese, they got where they needed to go day after day. These people went out of their way to ensure our daughters were always picked up so Monroe and I could rest or care for McKenzie and not have to get her out when we were at home.

I was blessed to stay at home and not have to work outside the home throughout McKenzie's illness. Of course, I was able to do that because my dear husband was blessed with a wonderful job. He was a regional manager with a medical device company when McKenzie was diagnosed. This meant he hired, trained, and occasionally fired the sales reps. for the company in his part of country. He covered at least five states at any given time and traveled quite a bit. When McKenzie was diagnosed, he made the decision to limit his travel whenever she was in the hospital. That was most of the time, at least at first. He was blessed with a company that was and is very family oriented. They told him to do whatever it took. Monroe would not travel if she were in the hospital because there would be no one to be at home with the kids while I was in the hospital with McKenzie. I know his boss covered his travel at least a couple times and I believe other regional managers helped, too. They had our back. They still do. They have been the most supportive company I've ever heard of. The people at the home office in Salt Lake City, Utah sent gift cards. They gave blood. They sent encouraging emails and notes. They sent gifts to McKenzie. I consider them all family.

Because Monroe and I grew up in San Antonio and have lived here most of our forty years, we know a lot of people. We've been active in our churches, communities, and Bible studies. Monroe has kept in touch with most of his high school friends and, as I mentioned, he has a large family. So, you can imagine how the phone calls began to pour in as the word of our daughter's illness began to spread. We recognized that it was an outpouring of love and that we would not be able to field all the calls. Someone recommended that we create a website to handle the inquiries. So we did. Monroe's sister, Kate, created McKenzie's caringbridge.org site as we were driving over from the Baptist hospital to the Methodist. If you've never had anyone seriously ill near to you and experienced this wonderful resource, you're almost missing out. For us, it became a lifeline to the world. It became a journal of our thoughts and feelings so that we could have an outlet for those locked inside. It became a mission field where we shared our love for Jesus Christ and the way He cared for us on this journey. We were able to receive notes from people and they really poured in from all parts of the world. Because Bible Study Fellowship is an international organization, we had people praying for her from all over the world. It was so encouraging. We linked a carecalendar to the website as well and people could sign up to bring us dinner. I was overwhelmed from day one with loving friends and family vying to bring us food. It was more than I could handle while still juggling the circus that was our family life and McKenzie's life. It was wonderful to have such a resource as caringbridge.org and carecalendar.org. The love of our family and friends was evident as those websites filled up quickly. We recently had the entries from our caringbridge site printed and they filled up two very large volumes!

Monroe

Between Sunday afternoon and Monday afternoon, Jeri and I received well over a hundred phone calls and emails. As word spread, the numbers grew, neither of us had the strength to keep up with the callbacks and return emails. Our friends the McGrath's suggested we begin a web site. My sister, Kate Wilson, helped to get us started, and we discovered Caring Bridge.

On January 8^{th,} we began our journey with caringbridge.org in an attempt to keep our family and friends posted as to what was happening with McKenzie. Our journal entries became the basis of this book. This site became the outreach for Jeri and me and kept people we knew informed as to what was going on. It was a true blessing to our family and saved us many many phone calls. It gave us the ability to update our world anytime day or night.

Wednesday, January 9, 2008 5:21 AM, CST

Good Morning everyone. Jeri here. We've had a restful night. At least as restful as you can have in a hospital where they check on you every fifteen minutes! We had our first blood transfusion and continue with fluids. We begin chemo at 9am and it should be a 6 hour or more process. I am praying that this treatment will CURE this precious girl. I am feeling the prayers of every one of you. God hears and answers. He is worthy of all my praise. Y'all please post me a message in the guestbook. And if you want to bring a meal, click on the link to the care calendar. Talk to you soon.

Wednesday, January 9, 2008 6:20 AM, CST

Wow. McKenzie has woken up in a great mood. She is laughing and joking with me and the nurses. Her world will be rocked later today with the chemo, but for now I am seeing my precious princess!

Wednesday, January 9, 2008 1:50 PM, CST

Hello Everyone. I wanted to tell you all how much we appreciate the overwhelming response to the website as well as all of the kind words, thoughts and emails.

The Dr. has told us that, now that we have begun Chemo, we can no longer have any stuffed animals or toys in her room. ***So I would like to ask, for the moment, please do not bring***

***any toys or gifts for McKenzie**. It is difficult for her to see them and then NOT be able to play with them.*

Chemo. today is going well and she is sleeping through most of the medication process.

Thank you all for your continued support, your good thoughts, and your prayers.

Monroe

As we began to journal more and more, we received many notes of encouragement through the guestbook portion of the Caringbridge web site. Many people responded with kind thoughts and encouraging words. It often lifted our spirits during the roller coaster of events that would occur on a daily and weekly basis. We were extremely thankful for all of the thoughts and prayers.

Tuesday, January 8, 2008 10:22 PM, CST-Journal

May Family, you are all in our thoughts and prayers during this difficult time. Know that there are so many people that care about you and love your family. Take care! Love the S. Family

Julie S.

Janice has lit a candle for your family at St. Patrick's in New York.

Let me know anything I can do.

John H.

Wednesday, January 9, 2008 11:02 AM, CST

I love you McKenzie.

Dee Dee

Jane May

San Antonio, TX

Wednesday, January 9, 2008 10:55 AM, CST

Monroe and Family,

My thoughts and prayers are with little McKenzie and your family during this time, I have a three year old boy and I can't imagine how tough this must be for you. I know I am far away but if there is anything I can do just let me know.

Hang in there, stay strong.

Shannon T.

Shannon T.
Seattle, WA

Wednesday, January 9, 2008 10:39 AM, CST

Hi sweet baby girl, may God bless you, comfort you, protect you, and watch over your precious little body soul and spirit as you go thru this. May He bless your mommy, daddy, brother and sisters too. We love you, we are praying for you and we want you to feel better.

Love, Joan

joan the g.'s
San Antonio, TX

Wednesday, January 9, 2008 10:20 AM, CST

I sure appreciate you letting us into your world through this website. We have been thinking of you and your family non-stop and this allows us to be close to you guys without imposing during the sensitive times.

We're with you,

Amy N.

Wednesday, January 9, 2008 10:20 AM, CST

Jeri, I am so glad that you are using CaringBridge. This site is invaluable in keeping up with all the details of life right now. God used it greatly during Jon's illness. Now, just know that I am praying today for McKenzie's reaction to chemo. I pray that she trusts the people around her and that God will protect her physically, mentally and spiritually today. May he use this drug to cure her body. He is the Great Physician. Love you all, Faith

Monroe

Many of these notes helped to remind us that God was still in control and thus strengthened our faith that we would get through this with Him alone.

Jeri

So, as Wednesday, January 9th dawned, I was at the hospital and our first chemotherapy session was due to begin around 9am. I wasn't sure what to expect, but I was anticipating something BIG! I had been given the lists of side effects that might accompany the long list of medication she was to receive. We were told that hair loss was inevitable and I really thought that by 5pm her hair would be gone. We were told that nausea was inevitable and I really thought that by 9:05am she would lose her breakfast. She had been given doses of drugs to help her fluid balance, steroids to help her maintain her weight, and anti-nausea drugs to keep her from vomiting. I was surprised when a beautiful nurse arrived that morning who was obviously several months pregnant to administer the chemotherapy. She took many precautions to protect herself such as a sterile gown and special gloves, but I was concerned nonetheless. She assured me her little one would be fine and the last time I saw Melissa, she assured me that he was. We became friends. I loved hearing about her children and those of the other nurses as well. So many of the nurses on the 4th floor I count as friends because of their angelic, tireless care of their young charges. I was especially grateful for Melissa and the way she so kindly guided me and McKenzie through our first chemotherapy session. The day ended pretty quietly as it had begun. The immediate results of the poisonous drugs to McKenzie's little body were not evident until at least later that night when it was her daddy's turn to stand sentry. By the next morning, she could no longer hold anything down. And so began a cycle of chemo. We would beef up her appetite with steroids and she would often become wildly energetic, angry, and so hungry she might eat my arm if I didn't get her something NOW. She would get the chemo drugs for five days at a time with a continuous infusion of fluids to balance her nausea. And then we would wait to see results.

Thursday, January 10, 2008 6:03 AM, CST

Good morning everyone, just a quick update. Last night was rough and did not go quite as well as we would have hoped. But McKenzie continues to be feisty and a fighter. We all have to watch her legs, because she kicks like a mule. It is really kind of funny; I may quit warning everyone, because when she gets a good shot in it makes her laugh.

We have added a couple of links to some websites which might be useful if you want to know more about Neuroblastoma.

Thank you again for all of your kind words and thoughts.

Wednesday, January 9, 2008 9:57 PM, CST

Hi Everyone! Wow! I am amazed at the outpouring of love, prayers, and support. You all are holding us up with your prayers. I cannot thank you enough for every note I have read. I cannot thank you enough for all the prayers. The kids are enjoying the food at home. As Monroe said, today went much better than expected. We had no nausea or vomiting so far. Dr. Patel has struck a wonderful balance in the drugs. I know it may not last, but we'll take it when we can get it. Tomorrow will be fluids only with at least one procedure thrown in. Please keep up with notes. I love to look at them. You can pray specifically for the decision we have to make about whether or not to cut McKenzie's beautiful curls before they fall out. She has never had a haircut. I'm worried that it may traumatize her. Monroe offers to shave his, but I think that may traumatize all of us! We don't know what's under there! Posting new pictures soon. With love, Jeri

Wednesday, January 9, 2008 9:10 AM, CST-guest book

Dear May Family,

Ever since Kate let us know on Friday what was going on; our hearts and prayers have been focused on all of you. McKenzie is a blessed little angel and we know she is getting the best care and that your family is getting wonderful support from those around you. There are no words to fully let you know how Chris and I feel; but, I know the Lord is busy hearing and answering all of the prayers being said for all of you. Please let us know of anything else we may do.

Beth T.

Wednesday, January 9, 2008 9:45 AM, CST-guest book

Psalm 22:24

For he has not despised or disdained the suffering of the afflicted one, he has not hidden his face from him but has listened to his cry for help.

Psalm 9:9
The LORD is a refuge for the oppressed, a stronghold in times of trouble.

Monroe
LETTER TO MCKENZIE, FROM DAD-Personal Journal:
January 10, 2008

Well "Son of a Nutcracker", as we say, things have not gone well. All of the original diagnoses were correct: Stage IV Neuroblastoma, in the bones. Since we arrived at Methodist Hospital, the staff has been great. They are very sweet to you and try hard to make you comfortable. Yesterday was your first round of Chemo and it lasted almost seven hours. You did very well through it all and then, during the night, the vomiting began. You are a brave, strong little girl and I love you. It is so difficult to sit and watch everything you have to go through, but from time to time you have a bright moment and it really makes it all worthwhile. Today you will have: a Chest X-ray and a MIBG test.

We launched your web site about thirty six hours ago and you have already had over one thousand hits on the web. You are being prayed for in all fifty states as well as by many different denominations. You have become the interest of many, many different folks. And whether you know it or not, you are bringing people together in ways I cannot understand.

One day at a time, one week at a time.

McKenzie in the hospital shortly after diagnosis

Jeri

Now remember that McKenzie had been next to catatonic because her little body was literally dying before our eyes. She slept on and off for much of the trip to Methodist and most of the first few days we were there. But with the steroids and the chemo, she began to wake up. We began to wake the sleeping giant. Her personality began to emerge. When the nurses would check on her, she would protest. Dr. Patel, that wise soul, quickly figured out how to deal with the Princess (as she began to be called about this time). The first day of chemo, Dr. Patel came in the afternoon to check on her. She was actually awake for the first time since he had joined our battalion. He walked in and greeted her with a smile. She told him in no uncertain terms to get out and stay out. I don't know any other two year olds who would react any differently to being strapped in a bed, stuck with needles, and pumped twenty four hours a day with poisonous drugs even though they are “for her own good”. I’m not sure how I expected Dr. Patel to react. I knew he had been practicing a while and had surely encountered countless fussy kids in his specialty field, but this was my little girl and I was a little embarrassed by her lack of grace. I love his reaction to this day! He put up his hand as if to shield his face and told her, “Don’t look at me, Genius! Just don’t look at me!” This would become his battle cry with McKenzie. I’m sure he said it to her every time he saw her up until their parting. She actually reacted with a laugh! She reacted that way every time she saw him and he offered their customary greeting. She still didn’t readily allow him to examine her, but she began to look forward to his visits and later couldn’t be in his presence without hugging him. Dr. Patel later told me that he had never used reverse psychology like this with a patient, but that it simply came to him at that moment to try it with McKenzie. It worked mightily. I know Who sent Dr. Patel that message and it was “genius” of God to offer us all a tool we would use with McKenzie for the next two years. We all became the perfecters of “reverse psychology”. Even up until her last days, if I wanted McKenzie to do something (and I use this on Monroe, Jr., too!) I simply said, “You don’t really want to do so and so, do you?” To which she would reply, “Yes, of course I do!” It worked most of the time. She caught on quickly. She was smart as a whip. But, if it was a new issue, she really had to think about it. I credit Dr. Patel with this brilliant move and he says it simply came to him. It was nothing he’d tried before. I believe I know Who whispered in his ear.

Knowing that McKenzie would lose her hair was one of the hardest things for me. I believe it was all my vanity. My first two daughters are beautiful blondes. McKenzie was a brunette with gorgeous ringlets. I always said I had to have four children to get one to look like me. She had my curly brown hair and my big brown eyes. Her hair hung to her shoulders when dry, but when wet it was much longer. She was almost three years old and we'd never cut her hair. I was worried about how she would react when her hair was gone. I was also worried about how I would react. Dr. Patel assured me that the other children in his practice who lost their hair really didn't react. I wasn't so sure this would be the case with McKenzie and I really didn't want all that curly brown hair to come out in huge clumps. So, I decided that McKenzie needed her first haircut. A good friend of mine was a hairdresser and even agreed to come to the hospital. It was a service for which I will be forever grateful. We gave McKenzie a darling little "bob" cut and I think she really liked the attention. She continued to be more and more awake. It was like watching a miracle before our eyes as her body responded to the chemo drugs. Of course, she became feistier and feistier, but it was good to see her fight return. Later, when we had been released from the hospital and her hair was falling out in earnest, Monroe decided to "vacuum" it off her back. We have some really cute video of him using the vacuum on her back and she is just laughing and running around the house. Little Monroe even got in on the action wanting his dad to vacuum him, too! You know the old saying, when life gives you lemons, make lemonade. We did this many times during her illness or at least tried. Once McKenzie's hair was completely gone, she was even cuter. I always tried to keep a hat on her when we were out and about, but she never liked to wear her hats. Sometimes it was necessary to protect her from the sun and sometimes I wanted it to go with her outfit, but most of the time I just didn't want her to have to deal with the stares of strangers. I was so sure that she would live a good long life and didn't want her to feel the emotional scars of being different. Looking back now, I know God made her different for a purpose. She had little clumps of hair still hanging in her head and she didn't care. She just wanted to go out of the house like she previously did. Her curls grew back in when she was in remission and even at recurrence her hair loss bothered me greatly. I get a pit in my stomach just thinking about it now. But she was always beautiful to me. She still is.

From the time of McKenzie's first hospitalization, she received gifts. She received so many gifts! Even when we were still at North Central Baptist, people began bringing her things. She was too sleepy then to even think of playing with anything. And remember, this was two weeks after Christmas, so she had a full house of new things waiting for her at home. But, I came to understand that it made people feel better to bring her things. Everyone wanted to do something for her and for us so they brought or sent gifts. My friend, Stephanie brought a great monogrammed bag stuffed with toys and I still have that bag. We eventually just called it "the McKenzie bag" and almost always toted it with us on every doctor appointment and hospital stay. The final time I cleaned it out made me sick to my stomach because I associated it with McKenzie and working toward the cure. The children's minister from our previous church brought some great things. We received books and puzzles and coloring books and pages and stickers and dolls and stuffed animals and I can't even tell you what else for her to play with. We received quilts and prayer shawls and new dresses. We received picture frames and some beautiful crosses. We had absolutely every item made by Disney with every Disney princess on it. Most of this came throughout the first six months of her illness. We kept what she loved and gave away what she didn't. Many of her friends benefited from these giveaways. McKenzie might receive three of the same coloring books and she certainly didn't need all three so I gave the other two away if I could without her even seeing them. We had so many stuffed animals and toys at the hospital that when she began chemo, the nurses made us clean house and take everything out. There were fears that the stuffed animals carried germs and would infect her. So we made a clean sweep only to have the room fill up again within days. We had asked on her website for no more stuffed animals, so people brought other things! McKenzie fell in love with everything "Disney princess" and "Fancy Nancy". My friends would scour the stores for books and costumes she didn't own and bring them to the hospital and I would use them as incentives for completing procedures or cooperation. To this day, I have a difficult time seeing little girls in princess dresses without picturing my baby girl all dressed up and it always brings a tear to my eye. She had favorite coloring pages and I know one of my friends searched every Target and Wal-Mart in San Antonio for these reusable marker sheets before ordering them online. She was given so much and loved it all so much. She became so full of life following treatment. She played so hard with all of her things. She was easy to spoil and I don't regret giving her anything.

Monroe

When your child is having Chemo, everything that comes out of your child's body is toxic and the risk of infection is very high. The hospital had many rules and Jeri and I had to adapt very quickly to what was allowed and not allowed in the hospital room. We could only change her diapers while using latex gloves, we could not have any stuffed animals in the room and McKenzie was allowed very few visitors. It was a total change of our mindset in what we did and how we helped our baby.

Jeri

So, we began chemo. She was treated for a month while staying in Methodist Children's Hospital. We had many rocky days during this stay. She had been so out of it for so long and hadn't had a bowel movement. We finally ended up giving her an enema. I had a hard time with this for some reason. My mom and one of the very brave nurses, Angie, handled this while I prayed in the hall listening to my baby scream. McKenzie lost weight due to constant nausea. We watched for fever, which would signal an infection. Her compromised immune system would be a source of concern for the rest of her life.

Thursday, January 10, 2008 2:05 PM, CST

Well, we are having a pretty good day. McKenzie's big sister, Courtney, was able to come and visit. That was very good for McKenzie. Courtney and I washed her hair. The nausea has stopped for the time being. She is eating and drinking very little today, but she did tolerate some goldfish and Gatorade.

We are going down for an MBIG (another abdominal scan) soon. We have made the decision to trim her hair tomorrow night. She has never had a haircut, so please pray that she is relaxed about it (I don't want it to be another "procedure" she has to endure). I started talking to her about it today. She is resting now. Talk to y'all soon. Jeri

Friday, January 11, 2008 2:43 AM, CST

Good Morning Everyone! It's 2:45am and McKenzie and I are watching Barbie Nutcracker. We are NOT sleepy. I hate to post personal messages because I would like to send one to each of you, but I am unable to email out right now. Melissa, where did you get those fabulous slippers? We are hooked and need another pair because we have soiled the ones you brought. Let me know where and we will send someone for some. Love, Jeri

Friday, January 11, 2008 3:14 AM, CST

3:15am We are still NOT sleepy!

Friday, January 11, 2008 5:31 AM, CST

Now we are watching Cinderella, they say some of the steroids may be giving her all of this energy. I've given up hope of sleep for today! We begin Day 2 of Chemo at 9am. A two hour treatment today is scheduled, another MIBG, and a visit from big brother "Mo". Yeah!

Friday, January 11, 2008 10:22 AM, CST

McKenzie is starting chemo treatment day 2 this morning. She will be undergoing this for the next several hours. We will update later this afternoon after the daily round of tests. Thank you all again for the kind words and prayers.

Friday, January 11, 2008 5:38 PM, CST

Hello everyone, just a quick update. McKenzie is finally sleeping this afternoon and is peaceful. That is a true answer to prayer.

I know that the weekend is upon us and that many of you may be planning a trip to the hospital. Please understand that McKenzie will be continuing her chemo on Saturday and Sunday this weekend. Therefore, we will probably not be able to let you come into the hospital room where she is staying. If you come by we will do our best to come out and say hello, however, it may be for only a brief minute.

Our other children all have weekend activities that will require either Jeri or myself to be away from the hospital. So, if we come out in the hall to talk, McKenzie will be alone in the room. We are trying to avoid leaving her alone.

*Also, **PLEASE DO NOT BRING ANY TOYS OR BALLONS FOR MCKENZIE, SHE CANNOT HAVE ANYTHING ELSE IN THE ROOM.***

Thank you all for the support we continue to receive. Your tributes and prayers are truly seeing us through this time. Enjoy your families this weekend and treasure every moment with your children. God bless you all.

Monroe

LETTER TO MCKENZIE, FROM DAD-Personal Journal:

January 12, 2008

We are on day three of chemo- first round. Today was pretty good. You had your first haircut and look really cute. I was concerned because you kept getting sick and it was difficult to keep it out of your hair. So today, Cherie came and gave you a trim. Last night you spent the night with your Meemaw. She was nice enough to stay with you so Mommy and I could spend a night home together. It is really difficult because when we are at the Hospital we want to be home, when we are away from you we want to be at the hospital. You are so important to us that I love you and want desperately to be around you. Last night you had to have an enema because it had been almost two weeks since you took a poop. I was very upset because I did not want to see them do anything else to you. However, it seemed to make you feel better and you were in a very good mood today. Your new website continues to amaze us all. You have almost 2500 hits and this only day three. It is helpful because we are able to keep people updated without having to use the phone. Your web address is www.caringbridge.org/visit/mckenziemay1. People have left messages from all over the United States and we are able to give updates about your condition as well as post pictures and links to other web sites. This continues to be quite a journey you are taking us on. Remember I Love You.

Saturday, January 12, 2008 9:26 AM, CST

Hello again everyone. I have relieved my mom now and it is a good morning so far. McKenzie ate some breakfast this morning after having refused all food/beverage yesterday. You can pray that she will take orally her laxative this morning so that we don't have to have another enema. Talk to y'all later.

Saturday, January 12, 2008 4:59 PM, CST

We have had a good day. McKenzie got her first haircut ever today (Thank you, Cherie!) and has much of her usual spunk. She even got mad at me at one time because I wouldn't fold her up like a taco in the electric bed. She threw everything at me including her slippers, pillows, and her baby doll. Now her sisters are visiting. Caroline brought one of her American Girl Dolls freshly returned from the Doll Hospital. The doll is wearing a hospital gown and has a balloon just like McKenzie. I am posting some new pictures from the day.

Sunday, January 13, 2008 3:20 AM, CST

Well Good Morning Everyone, our Little McKenzie is still wide awake. We have watched Beauty and the Beast *four complete times tonight and she is still going strong. Earlier this evening McKenzie had a visit from her cousin Rusty. This made her very happy. She gave him a big hug and even let him have one of her balloons. It was very cute.*

Well only twelve more hours until the Cowboy game, I hope I will be awake at kick off. Happy Sunday morning to all.

Sunday, January 13, 2008 6:15 PM, CST

McKenzie has had a very busy day. She really didn't sleep all day until about 4pm. She is sleeping very restlessly and often waking up screaming. Once again, the steroids are pumping her up. I'm not posting any pictures today because she won't let me bathe her really or get her new haircut cleaned up. She is just highly irritated right now. She threw a major fit earlier including trying to bite me and Monroe said she threw him a right hook earlier that would put a boxer to shame. I guess it is good that we still have our little fighter. I'm trying to use the mentality of a newborn baby and rest when she is resting, so I'll make this brief. Have a good night everyone. I truly feel your prayers.

Sunday, January 13, 2008 8:48 PM, CST

I just want to thank everyone once again for all of the kind prayers, cards, emails, meals, stuffed animals, toys, books and balloons. We are truly blessed to be surrounded by so many friends and family members who want to help us get through this battle with cancer. We are truly humbled by the outpouring of kindness that has been showered down upon us. Thank you also to everyone who has donated blood in McKenzie's name and also to my aunt, Sally M., who is working to get a blood drive together at her Elementary School on February 4th. These acts of kindness are what are getting us through this battle one day at a time. Thank you all very much.

Monday, January 14, 2008 7:13 AM, CST

Well, you know the old song "The Lion Sleeps Tonight"? That was our theme song last night. Her nurse, Meredith, and I decided about 10:30 that her hair needed washing and that she was just going to have to scream through it. So we did it. It must have made her feel better because about 1am she finally drifted off. She is still asleep at 7:15. They made me wake her about thirty minutes ago to get her weight, but I just picked her up and stood on the scale with her (and then they subtracted her weight from mine or wouldn't that mess up their calculations!). But, she is back to sleep. She finally figured how to get onto her tummy which I think helps. Well, y'all have a great day! Today is day five of chemo, the last day for this round. Not sure what's next. I think just wait and see...

Monroe

LETTER TO MCKENZIE, FROM DAD-Personal Journal:

January 14, 2008-Methodist Children's Hospital

It is my turn again to sit with you and what a pleasure it is for me to have this time with you. Today was the last round of your first chemo treatment. You did well and Dr. Patel has been able to control the nausea very well. We are beginning to notice a few more hairs on your pillow, so I know that the hair is going to go soon. The last two days have been horrible on you and all of us. You have been receiving "steroids" to help fight disease and possible stop some of the inflammation. You have been a baby on steroids. No sleep for almost thirty six hours. That happened to be my night to stay with you. We watched movies all night long and I tried to keep you happy. Besides not wanting to sleep you have had mood swings and have become very angry. Wow, I am glad that last night you finally slept for a while with Mommy. Today you are alert and fairly happy and seem more like yourself.

Monday, January 14, 2008 4:02 PM, CST

Okay, chemo day 5 is behind us! It's been a good day except for a little weekly procedure that she hated- re-accessing her port. A little nap, a little playing- she colored some pictures this morning and we read some books about Cinderella and Snow White. She remains such a girly girl. Trish- the Cinderella balloon is a favorite. Daddy is there- it's his night. You can pray for Monroe and me to remain healthy. We both feel a little run down physically. I am loving hearing from some cousins with whom I have been out of touch for a while! Y'all keep those notes coming.

Monday, January 14, 2008 5:24 PM, CST

Hello Everyone, we just had a visit from McKenzie's doctor, Dr. Patel, and we received some very encouraging news. We may possibly be able to take McKenzie home on Wed. Her counts are all moving in the right directions and he feels like she has responded well to the chemo treatments. This is very welcome news and we are very excited. We feel like McKenzie has almost made it through the first round and we know she would love to be able to go home and be with her family in her own room. Thank you all for your continued prayers.

Tuesday, January 15, 2008 7:01 AM, CST

Good morning all, it was a pretty good night last night. McKenzie, however, has turned into a bit of a night owl. We stayed up watching movies until around 1:00 o'clock and then she finally drifted off to sleep. Her sleep is somewhat restless at times, but then again it has been going on most of her life. We have already had the morning round of blood tests, blood pressure, temperature reading and weight. She is holding her own at this time and we are very proud of her.. The Cowboys may have gone out in the first round, but I know McKenzie is going to make it to the Super bowl, and she already gets my vote for MVP(Most Valuable Patient). Thank you again for all that you are doing to take care of the May Family. Your thoughts and prayers are felt daily, hourly, and by the minute.

Also, please everyone at Merit, go out and sell something. We need to have a good first quarter.

Tuesday, January 15, 2008 4:53 PM, CST

Hello Everyone. McKenzie is having a good afternoon. She is eating a little, but still not interested in drinking more than 2 sips of water all day. The nurses say that is okay because she is still getting fluids. But, we can't go home with those! We have another little bump in the road with McKenzie's big sister, Caroline. She is having some x-rays done right now at North Central Baptist of a sore tailbone. Please pray that we again get a clear diagnosis, but that this is easily treatable and nothing as serious as McKenzie's illness. Meemaw will take a turn with McK tonight. Pray for Meemaw's stamina as McK is just drifting off for an afternoon nap at 5pm! We'll keep you posted.

Jeri

But we made it somehow through this first round of treatment and prepared for the next step: taking her home. It scared the heck out of me. The hospital was a sterile environment. I was scared that home would bring exposure to infection and that we would end up quickly back at the Methodist. Monroe began to say that he believed she would thrive better at home. I began to pray he was right. He was. Dr. Patel predicted we would return to hospital within two weeks. I began to pray he was wrong. He was. We took our baby home despite my fears. It was much like bringing home your first newborn for the first time. You are not sure you know what to do and you are scared you will do it wrong. I was scared I would break her just as I was scared when I brought Courtney home for the first time.

Wednesday, January 16, 2008 9:10 AM, CST

We are headed home! Dr. Patel came in this morning and said she was doing well enough to get out of here for the time being. We will have an appointment in his office on Friday to see how she is doing. Everyone is excited to go home except McKenzie. She says she wants to stay. I think we will take her with us anyway.

We will post an update later today.

Wednesday, January 16, 2008 11:54 AM, CST

We are home! I feel like a mother of a newborn baby in that I don't want to break her! She did come with some instructions which we will follow to a "t". McKenzie ran through the house looking at all of her toys and was so excited to see her pets. It is great to have her here. They say we will be going back soon as her fever will spike soon in the future. We are working to keep the house as sterile as possible. NO Germs!!! Talk to y'all soon. With Love, Jeri

Jeri

She came home and was so happy to be there! We began convincing her to wear a sterile mask whenever out of her hospital room or out of the house. We didn't go anywhere for months except for Dr. Patel's office. We were very careful whom we invited to the house. No one was allowed inside except family and closest friends. And those were even banned if they had even the slightest sniffle or heaven forbid, a sore throat! These were necessary precautions to safeguard our baby. They worked because we beat the odds and avoided hospitalization between our first and second rounds of chemo!

Monroe

After thirteen days in the hospital, we finally went home for the first time. It was exciting and scary taking our sick little girl back home. Courtney, Caroline and Monroe were back in school and trying to carry on a "normal" existence. Jeri and I would finally have a few days to try to figure out what would happen next and how we handle the "new normal".

In a matter of two weeks time, our world had been turned upside down. Our youngest child was diagnosed with stage IV cancer, she had spent almost two solid weeks in the hospital, and she had been forced to endure what would be the first of many rounds of chemo. Each round lasted a week.

There is really no way to describe the sense of hopelessness that filled our family at this time. The list of things outside of our control was very, very long. Jeri and I would struggle to keep our relationship going and essentially work at just making it from day to day. Every morning we would look at what needed to be done and how we would make it through.

Oh, yeah, and I had to keep working, I needed to get back on the road for my job. Jeri would have to run the house by herself, take care of McKenzie, not sleep, and get everyone else everywhere they needed to go. The road ahead would be bumpy, and we knew that we would not be able to get by alone. We prayed and turned to God for guidance and strength. It was all that we knew to do. We had to hang onto the faith that God would see that things would get better.

Jeri

Between the first and second rounds of chemo fell McKenzie's third birthday. Her birthday is February 8th and her big brother's birthday is just two days earlier so we had previously done family parties together for them and this year would be no exception. This year, we were just a little more grateful for her life and those of all of our family members! Monroe had celebrated his 7th birthday with his good friend, Drew, a week earlier at Laserquest. Drew's mother, my good friend, Stephanie volunteered to plan a party for the boys together since Drew's birthday falls about ten days before Monroe's. The two boys have tried to celebrate their birthdays together ever since! So out of chaos came a new tradition. I was so grateful to Stephanie for handling this. That would be the first of many times she stepped in and simply handled things! McKenzie received a beautiful yellow dress from Meemaw and Grandpa that was an exact replica of Belle's dress from "Beauty and the Beast" for her birthday. She wore it to the family party (no germs allowed!) and she looked so beautiful despite her little clumps of hair that remained and her chapped lips from the medication. She wore some winter gloves with her dress because Belle wore gloves and she was sure they matched! And she received more presents! She got her very own full size handmade dollhouse from her grandmother, Dee Dee. She had this HUGE Disney princess cake from HEB and she chose the same cake the next year for her fourth birthday. Monroe had a monster truck cake (again, thanks to Stephanie!). We had a blast at that party. I was so glad that we still had her and her brother and sisters, too!

Monroe

One of the new challenges with McKenzie was our every-other-day trip to the doctor's office for blood work. At the beginning of each appointment, the nurse took her weight, blood pressure and temperature- all of which would be a challenge. McKenzie did not feel well, did not want to go to the doctor, and did not want to cooperate. Even though she had gotten to know Dr. Patel while in the hospital, she was still getting to know his office staff. She made sure that everyone knew she was angry.

Jeri and I also struggled with how to discipline a three year old with stage IV cancer. What was appropriate, what was acceptable? It was a constant challenge to keep boundaries for McKenzie, and at the same time be sympathetic to how she was feeling. It was a constant "mine field"; we never knew when she would explode!

Jeri

We marched on through four more rounds of chemotherapy. We had five days of chemo with two to three weeks in between. The first round we did outside the hospital was extremely difficult. Being on chemo is always difficult. But, having a three year old on chemo with round the clock fluids being infused from home is a major challenge. It's even more difficult when you have a spirited little girl on steroids. We would generally show up at Dr. Patel's office on Day One of that round with a big bag of toys knowing we would be there six to eight hours. We would also be armored with lots of money for snacks that she would order throughout the day. It didn't matter what food we brought or what food the staff at the office had on hand,

McKenzie always wanted "**something else.**" She would start out watching a movie. We would infuse her with fluids and anti nausea drugs for about two hours and then begin with the chemotherapy drugs. The anti nausea drugs, if a good balance had been struck, would make her sleepy and she would rest for a little while. This didn't happen often, though, and even if it did it would always follow a MAJOR fit. I was always embarrassed by her fits in public and at this time in her life, Dr. Patel's office was as public as we got. The staff was so kind. They tried to distract her, watch movies with her, color with her, visit with her or me, all while trying to juggle an office full of sick kids. They are an awesome group of people. We would receive a long dose of chemo on the first day and then begin the long trip home around 5 or 6pm. We lived a twenty to thirty minute drive from the medical center without traffic, but in rush hour traffic it became a forty five to sixty minute drive. Usually on that trip, McKenzie would become nauseous and the car would need detailing AGAIN! We had tons, actually we still do, of those little sleeves they dispense in the hospital or big pink plastic buckets for her to get sick in. It didn't matter how prepared we were, she usually missed! Poor baby, she really tried.

Dr. Patel's office and nursing staff are such an awesome group of people! From Tonya who met us at the window every visit to Sylvia who checked us out every visit, I grew to appreciate them more than I can tell you. Sylvia would usually answer the telephone, too, during office hours when I would call. She is a master at managing requests both for the doctor's time and attention and mediating/arranging hospital procedures. Sylvia, at first meeting, struck me as tough, a hard shell, someone I wouldn't care for. However, I was wrong. She may wear a slightly tough shell, but inside she is one of the most caring individuals I've ever encountered. She had a row of little figurines at her desk. McKenzie asked one day while we were in the office if she could play with them. Sylvia quickly said "NO". McKenzie began to fuss. Sylvia explained to me that one of the children Dr. Patel had treated and lost had given her the figurines. It made sense to me. It endeared her to me. The compromise we made was that McKenzie could play with "Domino", the stuffed Dalmatian puppy Sylvia also kept on her desk. So every time we went to the office, whether it was for five minutes or five hours, McKenzie babysat "Domino". Also, I made sure to bring Sylvia something whenever we traveled. I hope she treasures them like she treasured her gifts from her other patients. She is such a dear lady. The nurses quickly grew to understand McKenzie, as I believe they worked to understand every patient they treated. Carole was in charge of administering McKenzie's drugs. She is truly a special lady. She and I share our Christian faith and she lives her out in such a tangible way. She is the hands and feet of Christ to many. She has a beautiful singing voice and blessed me in that way, too. She was so adept at timing McKenzie's fluids, anti nausea drugs, and chemo drugs. When we were on chemo, McKenzie's port would remain accessed even when we went home in the evenings. We would be responsible for changing bags of I.V. fluid and pushing the anti nausea drugs. McKenzie would carry all of these things along with the portable drug pump in a little backpack that Carole would have prepared for us. Several times we had to make return trips to the office for Carole to fix one thing or another. She was always so patient. Well, almost every time. On our first round of chemo while staying at home, on day four, McKenzie was painting at the kitchen table. Monroe and little Monroe were going out in the backyard to do something and McKenzie wanted to go, too. I was busy in the kitchen and told her just a minute and I would help her get her mask and hat on before she went out. She got angry and impatient and got up to go out on her own. I tried to slip on her hat on her way out the door and this just further infuriated her. She took the backpack with her pump and fluids and threw them to the kitchen tile floor. The pump started beeping, screaming at me! I pulled it out and tried everything I knew to silence it. New batteries, resetting the program, nothing worked. I quickly called the office and spoke to Carole. She said we better come in. So I drove my angry, steroid hopping three year old (actually it was the day before her third birthday) the forty five minutes to the medical center and we traipsed into Carole's office. McKenzie seemed repentant while Carole fussed at her. It turns out she had actually broken the pump. Last time I mentioned it to Carole; she said she never had gotten it working again. I felt awful and offered to pay to replace it, but of course, she wouldn't let me. She said she'd never had a child so angry as to actually break one of her pumps. Well, we all knew McKenzie was special!

Home life while McKenzie was on chemo was greatly altered. The other three children went on with their "normal life" whenever possible. They attended school, played sports, played music, and played with friends. While they did that, Monroe and I changed our schedules to focus on McKenzie and her needs while we fought the cancer monster. Therefore, the lives of the other children were altered because we were not able to focus on them. We were not free to drive them because we were either at the doctor's office or dealing with a very fussy little girl. McKenzie ruled the roost at home. She would take up residence on what we now call the "chemo couch." On the "chemo couch", she watched T.V., movies, vomited, received medication, slept, ate and ate and ate, received countless gifts, and requested toys or outfits to fit her mood. While she slept, everyone else was quiet. When she was awake and wired from the steroids, everyone else was kept awake. Trying to make a steroid induced girl to rest or stay quiet is like trying to put toothpaste back in the tube. It's a lesson in futility. We built our world around her. And there's a country song that goes, "You're gonna miss this, you're gonna want this back. You may not know it now, but you're gonna miss this." (You're Gonna Miss This by Trace Adkins) And I do. I would alter our lives again if it meant we could keep her happy and healthy. I have some wonderful pictures of my sweet baby girl during those chemo days. If she wasn't throwing up, she was usually ready to ham it up for the camera. If she felt up to dressing up in one of her many costumes, she wanted me to snap a photo of her. She always wanted someone to dance with her. She always wanted someone to watch T.V. with her, but we grew tired of the same shows. And we watched them anyway. I've seen Beauty and the Beast more times than I can tell you. We watched countless episodes of Little Bill, saw E.T. at least a hundred times, and when the Hannah Montana movie came out we wore it out, too. We were always on the lookout for some new show or movie to show her in hopes that we could make a change from the show we'd been watching over and over for weeks.

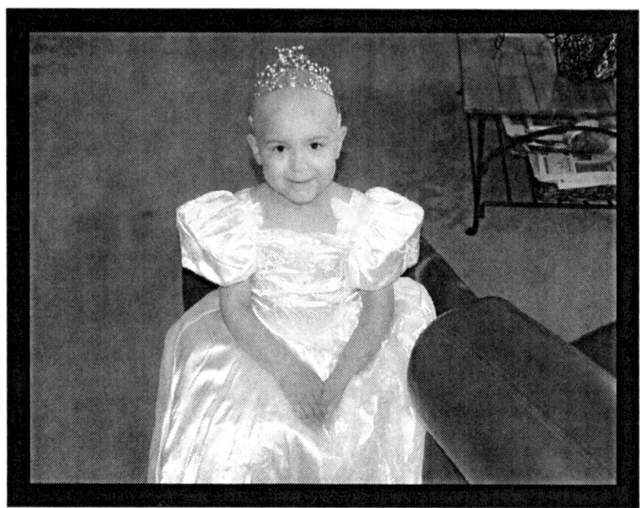

McKenzie in one of her many Disney Princess Costumes

Monroe did his best to work faithfully during these days. By now, he had been with Merit almost five years. He did what he could during chemo weeks from home. He would travel on weeks when we weren't doing chemo because chemo was such a twenty four hour demand. With changing I.V. fluids every few hours and administering anti nausea drugs, it took both of us to keep McKenzie taken care of. There were at least a couple of occasions when he had to leave and either I would finish up and de-access her port or he would remove the fluids a few hours early. Daddy was her favorite nighttime companion. So also when she was on chemo, he was so tired that it made working a challenge. But he persevered, as did we all. His boss and all the people at Merit were so supportive. He was always told, "Do what it takes to take care of your family." So many friends from Merit helped carry his workload. We are so thankful that

God placed him in a job where we would be helped by so many. I believe it helps Monroe to be the hard worker he is today because he wants so badly to give back to the company who helped us so much in those days.

Monroe also became the watcher of the insurance payments. It is no easy feat to keep an eye on what insurance will pay and what they won't. It's a confusing maze. Monroe became adept at knowing how to watch for how things were coded from the care provider and knowing what to ask the insurance company. He devoted many frustrating hours on the telephone trying to sort out this jumbled mess. Even two years later, we received a bill for around $30,000.00 from a hospital stay. Monroe was able to go to his Human Resources department at work who issued a letter reminding the hospital of their agreement to accept the amount sent by the insurance company at that time. We had certainly met our deductible by June of that year with millions of dollars of care already provided for our precious angel.

You might ask through all of this, "How do you explain what is happening to a two or three year old?" I admit, I've asked myself a few times what we told her. The child life specialists at both hospitals offered plenty of help in this area, but for the most part we handled this ourselves. Because McKenzie was so out of it at first and because she was so young, we kept it pretty simple. We told her that she had a "boo-boo" in her tummy and that it was making her sick. We needed to do all these things (take this medicine, change this needle, take all these "pictures" of your belly) to make that "boo-boo" go away. She never really bought it. Maybe she knew, deep inside, how it would go. Who knows? Maybe the pain had become so much a part of who she was that she didn't even recognize it as pain. Heaven knows she never complained of pain prior to diagnosis. So it just was to her. She didn't recognize her illness as illness because it had become all she knew of how she felt physically. I remember early on asking Dr. Patel when she would quit throwing a complete fit when they accessed her port. He said, "Oh, in a few weeks, it will become no big deal to her." She threw fits and cried every single time they accessed her port. She never embraced the value of the treatment. As a child, there was no way she could understand why we did all that we did, in our minds, **for her**, but in her mind, **to her**. Monroe and I worked hard to make sure that we were her comforters, not her medical staff. That was another reason it was so difficult to administer the chemo drugs and the I.V. fluids at home- because we became her caregivers, the people doing that **to her.** However, if we didn't do these things, then she would have to be hospitalized every single time a dose of chemo was administered. And the fine line between being parent and caregiver was walked because it was always better to be at home where she belonged, where she is loved. So we did our best to explain things to McKenzie and her life went on as normally as possible. She performed procedures on her dolls. She grew taller and matured. She did all these things under the cloud of cancer. Was she her disease? No. Did she completely understand it? No. Did I? No. Only God could completely understand who she was and the effects of the disease. He was her Creator and had a perfect plan for her life. He has a perfect plan for my life and yours, too. He did a great job of explaining it to her through us. He used us to love her and teach her about Him despite the disease.

Thursday, January 17, 2008 10:11 AM, CST

McKenzie had a good night last night and managed to sleep until almost 5:30 this morning. She continues to be happy, cheerful and full of energy. Today is a free day for her because we do not have any Doctor's appointments scheduled. On Friday, we will return to the Hem/Onc at 9:00 in the morning for more blood tests. So we are enjoying a quiet, non-medical day at home. We will update tomorrow after her appointment. Thank you again for meals, blood drives, prayers and kind messages. We appreciate EVERYTHING that is being done for McKenzie and our family. THANK YOU!!!!

Thursday, January 17, 2008 2:33 PM, CST

We are having a nice quiet day! No fever so far. Thank you for the prayers in that direction. We return to Dr. Patel's office tomorrow morning and that will be soon enough!

I realize now that I never posted the results of Caroline's x-ray. There was no fracture. We are praying now that the pain will dissipate. Thank you everyone for keeping up with us! Jeri

Friday, January 18, 2008 7:29 AM, CST

We are off to Dr. Patel's office. Pray she cooperates. We will let you know if we end up admitting. Y'all have a good day despite the cold and rain! Jeri

Friday, January 18, 2008 11:14 AM, CST

McKenzie is back home from the Doctor and it looks like we are doing well. My new saying is, "We are in good shape, for the shape we're in." I will not say that she cooperated, but it did only take 4 people to hold her down. So the good news is Dr. Patel will not have to add to his staff for this little MVP. For now we are home and looking forward to a quiet weekend. We will go back to the Dr. Mon., Wed., and Fri. next week for continued tests. Thank you again for the kind words, thoughts and out pouring acts of kindness. We will update as things progress.

Saturday, January 19, 2008 7:46 AM, CST

Good morning everyone! Well, it is Saturday morning and we are still at home! Thank the Lord! We had a fun family evening with a fire in the fireplace (our first in this house) and watching Ratatouille. Princess McKenzie is holding court at the breakfast table this morning. She can't decide if she wants oatmeal like Mo, a sprinkled donut, or just Chocolate "nilk". Don't tell her there is laxative in her "nilk"! Posting new pictures... Enjoy this beautiful sunny morning, Jeri

Sunday, January 20, 2008 5:07 PM, CST

Good Sunday afternoon to all of our family and friends! We continue to be blessed to remain at home with our sweet McKenzie! She has had a fairly normal weekend except for staying at home! She is usually on the go with us to sporting events, church, and shopping. She hasn't complained too much about being left behind, but of course she always has someone home to play with her and all of her new toys to play with! She got her nails done by Caroline today. She is now crashed on the sofa. I think the NFL playoff games put her to sleep! We return to Dr. Patel's office tomorrow morning. We'll let you know how that goes! Have a great evening and stay warm!!!!

Monday, January 21, 2008 9:04 PM, CST

Hi everyone! Sorry it's been so long since I updated. With the long weekend and the kids at home, it's been busy. McKenzie, too, is high maintenance these days. She may be a little spoiled, but oh well! We went to the doctor today and not much has changed. Her hemoglobin and platelets look good enough for her not to need a transfusion at this time, but her white blood count is at an all time low. We are glad that we have avoided returning to the hospital so far and we continue trying to shelter her from any "germ-y" situations. Please continue praying for her to stay away from any germs that would compromise her immune system further. Please also pray for strength for Monroe and for me. We are wearing down a little. I am fighting congestion/sore throat and we are both feeling a little down. Please hold us up in your prayers.

Tuesday, January 22, 2008 4:56 PM, CST

Well, McKenzie and I have had a pretty good day. However, while I was asking for prayer for Monroe and I to remain healthy it seems as though I should have also asked for prayer for the other children. Little Monroe went to the nurse at school today complaining of a headache. It apparently got worse and I'm told his cheeks were fairly rosy. My sweet mother in law has gone to pick him up around 1pm and will keep him overnight. He has no fever as far as we know, so maybe just a little 24-hour thing. We know that Fifths Disease is rounding his school, but his symptoms don't seem to fit. We've spoken to his doctor and unless he develops other symptoms, we won't take him in. We simply must keep him apart from McK. They were around each other as recently as 5am this morning when she woke up and went to get him up, too. This has become a pattern for her. She wakes up somewhere between 4:30-5:30am and goes looking for company, either Monroe or her daddy. Now you see why her daddy and I are dragging a bit! She has had a pretty good day. We were able to remove the last of the steri-strips that covered both her incision from the biopsy 2 weeks ago and the incision on her port. We have had our bath (a challenge on a good day, a nightmare on a bad day). And finally, Monroe and I were able to do her shot of immune boosting drugs. We go back to the doctor in the morning. I will keep you abreast of any changes...as the McKenzie turns... Tee Hee. I do feel a bit like a bad soap opera! Y'all pray for health of all. Thank you so much for all your support. Love, Jeri

Wednesday, January 23, 2008 1:47 PM, CST

Well we are back from the Dr. and McKenzie's blood counts have all started to move up. We are excited about the good news. However, now that the blood work is in order we will be going back to the hospital for additional tests. On Thursday morning she will have an Abdominal CT at Methodist hospital, and then on Friday back to the Onc.

These should be out patient procedures and we should not have to spend the night. McKenzie is doing better with the regular appointments and today it only took two people to hold her down. This is an improvement! Little Monroe is still in exile at his grandmother's house, however, we hope to get him back home tonight, and hopefully he will be back in school on Thursday. Yesterday I was reminded of on old Carol Burnet skit where they said, "As the stomach turns so do the days of our lives." We will keep you posted as the week goes on.

Tuesday, January 29, 2008 9:10 AM, CST

Doritos! That was the food of the day yesterday and already again today. Yesterday, McKenzie ate (8) 100-calorie packs of Doritos along with lots of other food! I figure the more weight we can get on her the better before chemo begins next week. Her appearance is much altered because of her hair loss, but I am not quite ready to send you all a picture. Her personality is NOT altered at all! She is just herself! She got a new ballerina outfit yesterday and slept in it! This morning she is Cinderella again. We talk a lot about wearing hats, but she is still warming up to the idea. The new one you are bringing, Tonya, will surely get her excited! Have a great day!

Wednesday, January 30, 2008 7:11 AM, CST

As you can see from the new photos, McKenzie maintains her spunky personality. She keeps us quite busy! She is asking a lot of questions such as when do we go back to the doctor, why do I have a baby head (no hair like a newborn baby), and what does the doctor say about me? We do begin chemo Monday and even though it will be outpatient at the doctor's office, I believe it is going to be a long week. We are expecting this 2nd round to be rougher on her. I pray for no nausea. I pray for patience and stamina for Monroe and me because with the chemo comes steroids and with the steroids comes a baby who stays awake 24 hours a day. We'll get to come home, sure, but we won't be sleeping! I guess God is preparing me by bringing all these things to my mind. Well, y'all have a great day!

Friday, February 1, 2008 6:50 AM, CST

Good morning everyone! Well, the break is over. I am a little sad because as long as we didn't have to go to the doctor this week, I could pretend that we didn't have to go back at all. Okay, dream over. We head back to Dr. Patel's this morning. I will have a better idea of what Monday's chemo will look like later today. Hopefully, we'll know what the rest of the week will look like as well. Monday will be the longest day, I understand. She seemed to be hurting a little overnight, but refused Tylenol. You can pray that McKenzie will cooperate this morning and that God's peace will prevail in my soul. With His Love, Jeri

Friday, February 1, 2008 8:03 AM, CST-Journal

Seek the Lord while you can find him. Call on him now while he is near. Isaiah 55:6, NLT

Jeri - this is the verse for today on KLOVE.com. I opened it up right before I read your update and I feel it is appropriate

- God is SO NEAR your family right now. There are so many people praying for McKenzie and for healing. There are also just as many people praying for you, Monroe, Courtney, Caroline and Little Monroe, too. God is NEAR, God is WATCHING, God is PROVIDING and God is STRENGTHENING your family. We prayed this morning at 7:15 for McKenzie and the whole family. We lifted up Dr. Patel and his nurses and all those who will be attending to McKenzie during her treatments. God is the GREAT PHYSICIAN. Love you, Cindy

Cindy L.

Monday, February 4, 2008 8:14 PM, CST-Journal

Oh Jeri,

I can't tell you the feeling I felt today when I showed up at Specht Elem. and the blood drive bus was PACKED full of wonderful people all there on little McKenzie's behalf. There was McKenzie's picture when you opened the door and there was standing room only. I had to fight back the tears for fear that people would think I was scared of the needle!! What a blessed family you are to have so many who love you. Kudos to the organizer of the drive.

I'm so glad this day is behind you- one day at a time... I'll pray for sound sleep for all and no nausea. Can't wait to see you and visit in person.

Love you, Angelia

Angelia T.
San Antonio, TX

<u>*Sunday, February 3, 2008 7:54 PM, CST*</u>

Hello everyone. Well, I have a very heavy heart tonight. I so enjoyed the weekend and didn't want tonight to come. But here it is. I know that the passing of time is a gift from God, but I wish that this weekend could have lasted forever. I am seeing signs that it is time to get back on the chemo horse. So now we load up and charge on. Please pray for strength again for Monroe and for me. She did not sleep well last night. But we have had a GREAT day today spent with everyone in our family who wasn't fighting the congestion crud. I am praying that she sleeps well tonight and that we do, too. She got a new Belle dress today (from Disney's Beauty and the Beast) and I will try to post some pictures of that tomorrow. I will update tomorrow if I get some time. Y'all pray for no nausea, sleep for all, and as always a CURE! Thank you. Jeri

Monroe

As we neared the end of our first break, it was very difficult to think about what was ahead. Jeri and I would learn to dread the five days of chemo. We would spend long hours at the doctor's office followed by sleepless nights of care for McKenzie.

During the nights of chemo, I would generally sleep on the floor in McKenzie's room with a bucket ready in case she would get sick. In addition to the chemo, she would be on around the clock fluids. She would carry a backpack with her pump and IV solution. The constant fluids would make her have to go to the restroom continuously. We would have little if no warning of the impending trip to the restroom. Between the vomiting and the running to the restroom with her backpack in one hand, it was an awful lot to ask of a not quite three year old to handle, as well as for parents of four children.

Then at 6:00 AM every morning, after a full night of sheet changing, night gown changes and trips to the restroom, it was once again time to get up and make sure Courtney, Caroline and Monroe were dressed and ready for school. Homework done, papers signed and out the door in time for the bus, or basketball practice or early morning tutoring at school. Once again, looking back, it was not anything Jeri and I could have done alone. God carried us on his shoulders.

Monday, February 4, 2008 7:53 PM, CST

Hello to all my wonderful family and friends! It has been a long hard day, but it is over! Once again, the passing of time is a gift from God! We had some rough periods of time today, but the worst was mainly due to McK's hardheaded attitude. She refused to go to the bathroom after two hours of fluids! Finally, we got her to go and then she took a really good nap. The rest of the day was just tiring because we were just sitting and waiting for the drugs to go in. We've been blessed with no vomiting and a tiny little bit of nausea so far. It is about time for another round of anti-nausea medicine, so I gotta go. Pray for sleep! Jeri

Tuesday, February 5, 2008 7:11 AM, CST

The vomiting began about 5:30am. We can give her more Zofran in about thirty minutes. Pray it ceases. Jeri

Also, thank you to Sally May (are you okay this morning?) who organized the blood drive at Specht Elementary yesterday.

Thank you to all who donated blood and also to those of you who tried (Blake, how's Jen?)! We are so touched by the outpouring of love on McKenzie's behalf!

Wednesday, February 6, 2008 5:17 PM, CST

Yes, we have a baby on steroids! McKenzie finds strength and insomnia in some of the anti nausea steroids they are giving her! She had day three of chemo today. Monroe stayed up with her most of last night and he squeezed in a little nap today. Marty, if you are reading, he was still taking work calls! She napped for almost an hour late this afternoon, but is awake now. That is actually a good thing because now we have a chance to get her to bed this evening. Pray for us as we distribute medications for the next few days and work to be accurate with the I.V. fluids at home. Y'all have a good evening. Talk to you tomorrow, my friends. Jeri

Monroe

LETTER TO MCKENZIE, FROM DAD-Personal Journal:

February 8th, 2008

Happy Birthday. You made it to age three. What a journey the last six weeks have been. Keep up the fight.

Friday, February 8, 2008 7:01 AM, CST

Well, yesterday afternoon was interesting. McKenzie wanted to go out in the backyard with her father and brother. I told her to stay put at the kitchen table where she was painting while I got her shoes and her mask. She said no and picked up her backpack to go get them herself. When I slipped on one of her hats, she got angry and threw her backpack onto the tile floor. One of the pumps for her IV started going off. I wasn't able to fix it, she broke it! So I got to drive her to the medical center to get a new one in 4pm traffic and then home in 5pm traffic. Also, about 5:30 she started vomiting in the car. Boy, that was fun. She has sworn she won't do that again on threat of a spanking. We'll see. We are headed into the office for day five of chemo today. I am really glad it's Friday! You have a good one.

Monroe

February 8th, 2008 marked McKenzie third birthday- a milestone for Jeri and me and a day that would not go unnoticed at our house. It was bittersweet to have reached her third birthday and difficult to think about how much she had already gone through, and knowing how much more was ahead.

Saturday, February 9, 2008 8:50 AM, CST

Good Morning everyone! Yesterday progressed without any real surprises. We finished treatment, had a good evening at home with family, and went to bed. She was up and down from about 1am on. Monroe again stayed with her and we removed her fluids about 3:30am. She is happy to be free from them this morning, jumping and climbing all over the furniture. Now we watch for traces of infection. Please pray that we have no fever and do not have to be readmitted to the hospital. Next this morning is a much needed bath- she hasn't had one all week with the I.V. fluid attached. Y'all have a good weekend. Talk to you soon.

Monroe

Everyday in the beginning of treatment would bring new challenges. We experienced peaks and valleys. One day we would finish chemo and think, oh, tomorrow will be better, she will be herself, she will be worn out and need to sleep. Jeri and I knew we needed sleep. However, for many, many days and months ahead we would continue to find that there was no "normal" pattern.

Sunday, February 10, 2008 3:23 PM, CST

Matthew 25:36 says "I was sick and you cared for me". I want to say thank you to everyone of you who have cared for us "while we are sick". You have showered us with gifts, brought food, sent cards, offered prayers on our behalf, sent emails and guestbook entries all in the name of Jesus. You are living out His love for us. Thank you for being the hands and feet of Christ for the May family. You continue to be a reassurance to me in a very uncertain time.

Now about McKenzie: we are having a problem with her sleep cycle. She really doesn't have one. She has slept for a couple hours in the afternoon yesterday and today. But, she really isn't sleeping at night. We had hoped that once the fluids were removed that she would be able to sleep better without having to go to the restroom every 30 minutes. That has not been the case so far. Last night, she did not get to sleep until after midnight, got back up at 4:45am, and then was back up before 7am. This is really hard on Monroe especially as she continues to prefer his care to mine. So please pray that she begins to sleep.

We plan on doctor's office visits M-W-F this week. I am praying fervently that the Lord allow her to remain fever free and at home. If she spikes a fever, we return to the hospital and this may delay the next chemo round. Please join me in praying against that. For many reasons, I need us to stay on schedule.

Talk to y'all soon. Jeri

Thursday, February 14, 2008 10:05 AM, CST

Happy Valentine's Day! My Valentine's Day gift was 7 hours of non interrupted sleep. She slept last night from 8:30pm until almost 5am. It was great. My mother laughed and said, "How much of that medicine did you give her?". I actually gave her both the Tylenol/codeine and some Benadryl. The doctor suggested that yesterday. I think we'll try it again tonight! I am thanking God for being 6 days past chemo and still no fever. Psalm 34:15 says "The eyes of the Lord are on the righteous and His ears are attentive to his cry." Thank you for being the righteous and crying to the Lord with me. I thank you, too, for sharing with me when I see you what is going on with you. I love being able to repay the favor and lifting you up in prayer in your time of need. We are all in this together! Sorry, a little High School Musical moment... Have a great day! Go kiss your sweetheart and hug your babies. Smile at your friends and ask them if they are on a diet before you give them chocolate!

Saturday, February 16, 2008 7:10 AM, CST

Good Saturday morning everyone. On Friday we went to the doctor and everything was about the same as Wednesday. Counts were a little bit lower but once again we did not need a blood transfusion and we got to go straight home after the appointment. So we are very pleased with the progress.

Last night was a very good night. McKenzie only got up one time and went right back to sleep. She even stayed in bed until 6:05 this morning. Wow, we feel almost normal.

We are planning a quiet weekend, other than the normal basketball games, church and an occasional birthday party to attend for one of the kids. So things will be busy as normal.

Monday we will visit the Bone Marrow Transplant Unit at Methodist Hospital to start preparing for the upcoming BMT procedure. As well as this we will have our regular visit to Dr. Patel. Please pray for McKenzie during all of these appointments, and for strength for Jeri and myself.

Thank you all for EVERYTHING that everyone is doing. We have upcoming Blood Drives at Monroe May Elem, and Floresville High school. We can not start to thank everyone who has contributed and who will contribute.

THANK YOU FOR ALL OF YOUR SUPPORT.-Monroe

Monroe

As we finished the second round of chemo, ten different doses in just over a month, we began to prepare for the next phase of treatment. McKenzie would need to go through a Bone Marrow Transplant (BMT). She would first have a procedure where a catheter was placed into her leg and her blood would be removed and placed through a machine to harvest her own bone marrow. It would be collected and stored for future use. Then her blood would be immediately returned. This is similar to how kidney dialysis is done. February 18th would begin the new phase of treatment for us all.

Monday, February 18, 2008 9:10 PM, CST

Sorry, guys. I thought I had updated this morning. Well, we went to Dr. Patel's today at noon and her counts were up slightly. That was good news because that will enable us to move forward with evaluating the response of the illness to the latest round of chemo. We will be going in Wednesday for a second bone marrow biopsy. The first one was done on January 7th in the same surgery in which her port was inserted. So she will be put under anesthesia for this procedure. We will also be having another CT scan soon, probably next week, but sooner if I can get them to move it up. I am anxious for results. Following our visit with Dr. Patel, we met with the Bone Marrow Transplant physician. We were both overwhelmed with the detail of the information we had previously received only in overview. It was hard to comprehend that this treatment will get more difficult as we move forward, not easier. We know that we are being carried by the hand of God. I am trying not to look forward too far down the road, but only focus on what He has given me to do today, this week, and about a month out. Maybe that was part of the overwhelming part- we were talking about things that were going to happen 3 and 4 months down the road. Anyway, please pray for us to receive good results from the bone marrow biopsy this week and to be encouraged by that. Pray that we do not get overwhelmed by knowing what is ahead. Pray for a spirit of cooperation in McKenzie. Thank you so much.

Wednesday, February 20, 2008 3:39 PM, CST

Good afternoon. We are home from the bone marrow biopsy. It was done in Dr. Patel's office. I am amazed what they can do in the office. They put her under, did the procedure, and we did recovery all in the office. It was exhausting because she was unable to eat before and was upset about that. Then, she had a difficult time coming out from under the medication at first. She fussed and threw herself around for about a half hour. Finally, she slept for a couple of hours and we were able to come home. We should have the results from this biopsy by tomorrow morning. I will post as soon as I can tomorrow. She is very energetic this afternoon. You can pray for strength for me because it doesn't look she is going to nap the rest of the day!

Friday, February 22, 2008 1:43 PM, CST

Hi everyone! We are home from the doctor's office and don't have to go back until Tuesday! And we received some very good news today in the form of the bone marrow biopsy. The bone marrow from the left side was 100% clear and the bone marrow from the right side was 99% clear. We thank the Lord for this good news. We will be going in on Tuesday for the CT scan to take a look at the mass and see how it is reacting to the chemotherapy. We will charge on with treatment as scheduled and thank the Lord for the healing He is doing.

A big thanks to all of the people who gave blood at Floresville HS today! You are so kind and we so appreciate it! Y'all have a great day!

Monroe

Life continued to move forward for us all. We had the normal illnesses and sicknesses fill our house as well as the ongoing battle of stage IV neuroblastoma. Courtney, Caroline and Monroe went to school, stayed involved in athletics and school activities. Courtney finished basketball season, Caroline was a patrol at elementary school and Monroe worked hard to be a first grader. Life marched on.

Monday, February 25, 2008 7:36 AM, CST

Well, we can't seem to catch a break. McKenzie's older brother, Monroe, came down with something last night. He has a headache, fever, and nausea. We will try to get him to the doctor this morning to eliminate the possibility of strep throat. McKenzie is on her way to my dad's house so that she can stay away from him at least for today. Please pray that no one else in the family gets this, especially McKenzie. I am praying that God will keep her in a little bubble of health. He is able. Thank you to everyone for your support and prayer. Walking in His grace, Jeri

Tuesday, February 26, 2008 5:42 PM, CST

Hello everyone! Thank you to everyone at Monroe May Elementary for the blood drive today! You truly make a difference.

Well, it was a full day for us. Little Monroe stayed home one more day; I think he will go back tomorrow. He tested negative for influenza today, so we are safe from that anyway. He hasn't run anymore fever this afternoon; I guess we are out of the woods.

McKenzie had a CT scan and a bone scan today. It was a long day at Methodist Hospital; McKenzie was not in a cooperative mood, but we got through it! We stopped by the doctor's office in between procedures and he said there was further shrinkage in the mass. More good news! I am seeing proof of God's healing power through the hand of the doctors. I will let you know if I hear results of the bone scan before Monday when we begin chemo again.

Y'all have a great evening! Jeri

Friday, February 29, 2008 7:27 AM, CST

Good morning everyone. Well, it was a long night-especially for Monroe. McKenzie was up every couple of hours. We had decided to try not giving her the Tylenol/codeine and Benadryl two nights ago and it went okay. We may have to go back to giving it to her tonight in order to get some sleep. It's hard because we just want her to be normal and it is difficult to accept that this is our "normal" for now. As we go through the day today with little rest, **please pray for us to be very patient with her**. *She requires consistent discipline and we* *both tend to be angry and reactive when we are tired. As always, we appreciate your support and prayers. Jeri*

<u>Sunday, March 2, 2008 9:07 PM, CST</u>

Hello my friends and dear family members! We have had a wonderful weekend. We went out on Saturday to Guadalupe State Park and walked around for an hour or so as a family. It was good to spend some quality time together. One of the older girls actually suggested it. Today, I went to church with the older girls and then we had family over this afternoon. It was very nice. Tomorrow, reality crashes in with the third round of chemo beginning. We will be at the doctor's office for about eight hours. At least we don't have to be at the hospital, right? We will come home with the usual assortment of pumps and I.V. fluids in a backpack. One prayer request is that McKenzie doesn't break any of the pumps this time! Another request is prayer that Monroe and I will have strength to endure the week, which requires three days of steroids used as anti-nausea drugs. Another request is for a spirit of joy. "Count it all joy, brothers" is what I need. Otherwise, the tendency is toward depression especially contrasted with the great weekend we've just completed.

Thank you to all who have been so generous and kind to us. The cards and words of support mean so much. You all are the body of Christ to me.

With Love, Jeri

Tuesday, March 4, 2008 7:18 AM, CST

Well, it was a good day yesterday, but a long night last night. She was sick a lot. She is sleeping right now, but as soon as she wakes up, we will head for the doctor for day two of chemo. Please pray she is not sick in the car- that is so miserable for her. Please continue to pray that Monroe and I will have strength to finish the week strong. Thank you and don't forget to count your blessings and praise the God of Israel today.

Wednesday, March 5, 2008 7:24 AM, CST

Another long night... She only got sick a couple of times, they are still messing with the formula of drugs trying to get them just right in order for her not to be sick at all. Today will be the third day of five days of drugs. We are looking forward to Friday more than you know. Please pray that she will remain non-combative and cooperative. Pray strength for Monroe and me. Thank you all...

Thursday, March 6, 2008 2:06 PM, CST

Well, God has carried us through the first four days of chemo round three and I know He will carry us through the next thirty six hours until we de-access her and are done for the week! This round is definitely tougher on her little body than the previous two. The doctor warned us that this might be the case. They are giving her more aggressive anti-nausea drugs this time, too, which are making her sleepy at different times throughout the day. She slept in my arms during the chemo dispensing this morning and she has never done that before!

We are watching T.V. now and she is just starting to show signs of a possible afternoon nap. Also, strangely enough, she wants mama today. That is very unusual. She is always such a Daddy's girl. I'll take it when I can get it. Thank you for your prayers and phone calls. They comfort me like nothing I can tell you. Talk to you soon, Jeri

Friday, March 7, 2008 5:43 PM, CST

Well, we made it through all five days of chemo. We anticipate de-accessing her tonight. She is in a horrible mood. She and I had a yelling contest this afternoon for about twenty minutes because her daddy had to leave the house and she didn't want me. And did I mention that she kept her daddy up all night last night?

Our other challenge is with McKenzie's big brother, Monroe. If you have been journeying with us for the last eight weeks, you know that Monroe has not been well and has come home from school sick a lot. Today, we finally got a diagnosis of bronchitis and a string of drugs for him. We are glad to finally be able to treat him and pray that this heals him quickly.

Please continue to pray for the strength of Monroe and me. We are really struggling and need some rest. Thank you, my friends and family. Please have a wonderful weekend. Hug your kiddos, go to church, praise God for your blessings. Even with all this going on, I can't tell you how blessed I feel. Jeri

Monroe

The weeks after the chemotherapy were rough as well. We continued to venture to the doctor's office every other day and do blood draws to check her counts. Once the counts dipped low enough then we had a constant concern over her having to be hospitalized due to infection.

Throughout the month of March, 2008 McKenzie got closer and closer to surgery and the Bone Marrow Transplant. Timing was very important and we had to make sure that the cancer was responding to the first three rounds of chemo.

We continued to pray and we continued to have many, many prayer warriors supporting us around the United States. God's arms stayed wrapped around our family during these months. He was there and present at our side and guiding our decisions for our little girl. He was also there for our older children. Day by day we got up and did what had to be done. There was just no other choice.

Friday, March 14, 2008 1:31 PM, CDT

Hello everyone! Well, we heard a new one today. McKenzie's counts are actually nonexistent. It is what is expected following the chemo round last week, but still sounds kind of strange. She is not acting or feeling much different although she is having some g.i. tract issues. But that is normal. We are scheduled to go in on Monday morning for a CD-34 test to determine if her counts are appropriate to do the stem cell harvest beginning Tuesday. I am not sure how to ask you to pray. I guess pray that we will be able to do the test beginning Tuesday and that they will finish by Wednesday morning so that she can go home. Her siblings are on Spring Break next week and we would like to spend some quality time with them on Thursday and Friday. Pray for strength for Monroe and me over the next week. Thank you, my sweet friends and family. Jeri

Monday, March 17, 2008 2:57 PM, CDT

We are back from the morning run to the doctor and the hospital. Today we had two different rounds of blood tests to prepare for the Stem Cell Harvest on Tuesday. Good news is she is healthy enough to proceed with the Stem Cell collection and will report to the Methodist Hospital bright and early on Tuesday morning. Did I mention we would need to be there very early? If all goes well we will spend one night in the hospital and go home on Wed. If things do not go well we will stay until Thursday. McKenzie will be in the PICU for her stay and will be in bed until the catheter is removed. I am going to request no visitors during this procedure other than family. We are not sure who will be allowed to visit, other than her parents. This will just be the **harvest of cells;** *the* **Transplant** *will take place at a later date. Please pray for strength and cooperation. This will be a tough procedure on her little body and require a lot of care from the nursing staff and patience for her parents.*

Thank you everyone for your continued prayers.

Monroe

Tuesday, March 18, 2008 7:16 PM, CDT

It's 7pm and we are sitting in the hospital room in the Hematology/Oncology Ward. She is just beginning to wake up after being under sedation most of the day. It has been very rough here today. She has screamed in protest since we woke her up at 5am to give her Neupogen shot and take her to the hospital. She screamed in protest when they gave her medication in pre-op, when she woke up in post-op, and throughout the day when anyone else touched her. They placed the central line in her groin first thing in order to be able to collect the stem cells. They were supposed to leave her sedated, but did not. They transferred us to the P.I.C.U. where they were to do the collection, but then it took an hour and a half to get her sedation from the pharmacy. It was extremely frustrating because she screamed for most of that time. When they finally got her sedated properly, they began the stem cell collection. The procedure took about four hours. Then we began the circus act of trying to get her transferred up to this floor. We got word about 5pm that they were able to collect enough stem cells that they won't have to repeat the process tomorrow and that if everything else goes well this evening we might get to go home late tonight. We removed the line about 6pm. She is still very groggy and having a hard time waking up, so we'll see. Thank you for your prayers and thank you to all who are helping with the other children. Please pray for her continued recovery and praise God that they were able to collect what they needed in one procedure.

Wednesday, March 19, 2008 2:21 PM, CDT

Today has been a fairly quiet day for McKenzie. She has stayed at home and enjoyed the doctor free zone, and after Tuesday this was a welcome relief. Her mood has been good and her appetite plentiful. She is down for a nap this afternoon and so far has not had any more ill effects from the prolonged sedation. Overall we are very pleased with the Stem Cell collection numbers and are hopeful this will serve her well when the transplant takes place in a couple of months. We are guessing the transplant will be sometime after the fifth or sixth round of chemo. We will venture to the doctor later this week to get an update on what is next. We are hopeful the rest of this week and next will be quiet as we prepare for the next round of chemo.

We are thankful for the quick recovery from such a tough day and we are thankful to about half of the staff we encountered yesterday at the Methodist Hospital. The Hem/Onc nurses and staff are outstanding and our first nurse in the PICU was very good as well. The rest of the staff and doctors left something to be desired. However, I am sure that most of them only enjoyed about half of our family as well. Luckily, Jeri is always pleasant to be around.

Anyway, thank you for the continued prayers and phone calls. We are in good shape for the shape we are in.

Monroe

<u>Saturday, March 22, 2008 8:42 AM, CDT</u>

Good morning everyone, I hope you are having a good Easter weekend. Yesterday McKenzie went to the doctor and he dropped a bombshell on us, instead of doing chemo the week after next we are starting Monday. This was not what we were expecting but, that seems to be the way our lives go most days. So on Monday we will begin the fourth round of chemo.

We will keep you updated as the week unfolds. Thank you all for your continued prayers and well wishes.

Monroe

Monday, March 24, 2008 7:39 PM, CDT

Hello everyone. Well, it's been a long day. Day one of chemo was rough. She had a worse than usual reaction to the steroids and threw a horrible fit. She was still pretty wired, however, and roamed the hallways of the doctor's office. We will try to do without the steroid tomorrow. The nurse (our favorite) was surprised at her extreme reaction. We weren't. She had just never reacted that way in front of anyone. Since she walked the halls all day and refused to nap, she was overly tired and really fought us while getting into the car and home. Now we are home and she napped through dinnertime. No big deal since she had three Hamburger Happy Meals today. She'll be fine. Pray for some rest tonight for us. Pray for peace to prevail and some encouragement. We are a little down. Jeri

Tuesday, March 25, 2008 8:20 AM, CDT

An extremely long night... The medication we gave her at 10pm wired her and she was awake and yelling until 2:30am. She did play Bratz dolls from about 1am until 2:15am. She was also seeing things like bugs crawling. I don't think we'll try that medicine again. I know that the Lord my God Himself is fighting for us. I know that Jesus my High Priest is interceding for us. I know that you are, too. Thank you. Pray for a better day and a better night tonight. Jeri

Thursday, March 27, 2008 6:34 AM, CDT

Good morning everyone. We are on day four of round four today. Yesterday went well; McKenzie only got sick once. She is such a little trooper. She slept through most of the morning's treatment and then was awake throughout the afternoon. She loves it when her brother and sisters get home from school. She talks often of what she will do when she gets better. I know that my God is powerful to save. I believe that He is healing her. Talk to you soon. Jeri

Thursday, March 27, 2008 9:22 PM, CDT

One more day of chemo for this round- we will finish the week tomorrow with the final day of this round. She seems to be doing well. She has lots of energy today and only slept a little this afternoon. I am hoping that means she will sleep well tonight.

Many of you have asked, "What's next?" Well, after this round of chemo we should have 1) a round of scans as soon as her blood counts recover- usually a couple of weeks barring any infection. 2) Surgery in a few weeks to remove the mass-finally! She will be recovering for several weeks from the surgery. 3) Next will be round five of chemo. 4) Radiation 5) Bone Marrow Transplant and then some other things. So, we still have a long road ahead. I appreciate the support of so many family and friends. Please continue to keep us in your prayers as we walk this long road. We love you all. Jeri

Friday, March 28, 2008 2:48 PM, CDT

We're home from chemo! She is doing well. She slept through most of the dispersion of the drugs this morning. That was good. She had a pretty good night last night, but **she has a nasty sounding cough and a stuffy nose. Please pray for this to go**

away. Dr. Patel says to expect admission to the hospital this week; I told him that we would pray against it.

Also, her hemoglobin was low this morning which indicates that a blood transfusion will be needed Monday if this count does not return to a more normal level. Please join me in praying that God will spare her this four-hour procedure on Monday.

Thank you everyone. Jeri

Monday, March 31, 2008 9:38 AM, CDT

Praise the Lord we made it through the weekend without a hospital admission. Monroe has taken her to her appointment this morning and will call me to come if a blood transfusion is ordered. We have so many people praying that it will not be needed, but if it is God's will then okay! Thank you all... Jeri

Also, I added some spring pictures of McKenzie this morning. Enjoy!

Tuesday, April 1, 2008 9:51 AM, CDT

McKenzie continues to struggle with a good night's sleep because she coughs continually. We tried another new cough medicine, without much success. Since she struggled to sleep, so did we. Please pray for strength for Monroe and me as we go about our usual work schedules today. (Him out and about, me at home with McK) I am praying that this congestion goes away soon. I don't want her in the hospital with an infection.

God has carried us this far without that burden and I pray that He spares us that burden this week.

On the lighter side, Happy April Fool's Day. I woke up to find a raisin in my toothpaste (thank you, Courtney) and the milk in the milk carton had been turned green. She better watch out the rest of the day. All of you should go play a little trick on someone you love. And if you want to know the history of April Fool's Day, call me or email me. Courtney left each of us a copy at the breakfast table! Y'all have a great day! Jeri

Wednesday, April 2, 2008 7:57 AM, CDT

Good morning everyone! Thank you all for the very practical suggestions for treating her cough. I am considering them all and will talk to the doctor about some of them this morning. We go in this morning for what I hope is a routine appointment. I am praying that I am not surprised with a blood transfusion or other delay, but that we can come home right away.

The night was a little better. She was only up three times and was able to go right back to sleep each time. Whether her cough was better or whether I was so tired that I just went to sleep and didn't hear her remains to be seen (or heard, ha ha).

I hope you all have a blessed day! Jeri

Friday, April 4, 2008 9:13 PM, CDT

Well, the day we were dreading came tonight. When McKenzie woke up from her nap this afternoon, her fever began rising. We called the doctor and headed into the hospital by 6pm. She is resting comfortably right now and watching a movie. But she is just not herself. She just doesn't feel good. So please pray for quick healing. Pray for some sleep and for this awful cough to go away. Thank you all. Jeri

Monroe
LETTER TO MCKENZIE, FROM DAD-Personal Journal:
April 5, 2008-Methodist Hospital

Over the last two months you have continued to have an eventful journey. You have been through four rounds of chemo, multiple CT's, a Stem Cell harvest, and a couple of blood transfusions. Wow and the journey continues. We are back in the hospital because you have a fever that is difficult to contain. Last night you spiked 104 degrees, this morning you are doing better. You are resting, you have had some cereal and your fever seems to be under control. You continue to fight and you hang on with everything you have. Unfortunately, I believe that the worst may still be ahead. The end of this month you will undergo surgery to remove the tumor. This will be as long at eight to ten hours followed by a lengthy hospital stay. Then you will have another round of chemo and then you will undergo the Stem Cell transplant. This will take place back in the hospital where you will have "Heavy Chemo and Radiation." You are going to have to be VERY TOUGH to get through all of this. I love you, keep up the fight.

Monday, April 7, 2008 3:57 PM, CDT

Good Afternoon! Hope everyone has been enjoying this lovely spring weather. I will enjoy it more once the oak has completed its bloom! Oh and of course I will enjoy it more once we are not stuck in the hospital! We are still awaiting results from this morning's CT scan. I expect Dr. Patel any time now and will let you know as soon as I hear something. She is sleeping now and has been for a couple of hours. Her cheeks are rosy and I will be talking to him about whether it is a reaction to something or effects of the fever. She has not really run fever for the last couple of days, so I would be surprised if it were that. We'll see. Thank you to those of you bringing meals this week. I have adjusted the calendar for the next two weeks and will do so for the last week of April as soon as I have an idea about surgery scheduling. That is something else I am waiting to speak to Dr. P about. Thank you everyone for your continued prayer support and website postings. I love reading your words and thoughts. Talk to you all soon. Jeri

Monday, April 7, 2008 9:46 PM, CDT

Late breaking news! We are home! Dr. Patel came in about 7pm and said, "Do you want to go home?" We said YES! It took a while to get here, but we are here now! I will update with details tomorrow, right now I want some sleep! Jeri

Sunday, April 13, 2008 7:40 AM, CDT

Good morning everyone! Well, we have seen a few of you out and about with our other children. Some of you have guessed that things must be going well because we haven't been posting much! I think that is funny, but true. When we are not in crisis with McKenzie, we tend to get busy with our other children and forget to keep you updated on her progress!

McKenzie is doing well. Her counts as of Friday were okay. The biggest holdup right now is her sinus congestion. The doctor says that we could not do surgery with this much congestion in her head because if she were intubated for six to eight hours (like she will be) the congestion would move into her lungs and turn into pneumonia. Therefore we wait. Because the oak pollen is still so high here in San Antonio, she is still congested. I am too! I think it really is almost finished, but it is still high. We don't have to go back to the doctor until Wednesday and I am praising God for the break!

We went to the lake house yesterday for the day and McKenzie discovered her swimsuit! I hadn't intended for her to go swimming and she didn't, but she sure does love her swimsuit and won't take it off! I will get a picture today and try to post it. If I do, be sure to note the matching shoes!

As a final note, the reason we ended up coming home from the lake house without spending the night is that my mother fell and broke her ankle. She feels so silly and bad that everyone ended up coming home on her account. But, I wanted to be home and close to her to help her. She will see an orthopedic surgeon tomorrow about surgery. Would you please pray for quick healing and minimal pain for her?

Well, that's everything! Sorry about the long posting and talk to you soon. With Love, Jeri

Monroe

No family goes through just one thing; life runs fast and continuously pushes on around us all. Our lives continued at mock speed. During one of the weekends McKenzie was feeling good, we tried to slip away to Lake LBJ. Lake LBJ was our home away from home and provided our family with much solitude and peace. Most times we were there we could relax and push our problems to the side at least for a little while.

On one particular weekend we went up on Saturday morning and tried to get a few things done quickly around the house and then head out on to the water. I had just finished mowing the yard and getting cleaned up when I noticed Courtney running to the kitchen to get some ice in a zip lock. That is never a good sign around our house, so I began to question what was going on. She informed me that Jeri's mom, Meemaw, had fallen while playing Ping-Pong. When I arrived in the back of the house, I found Meemaw laid out on the floor with an anklebone stuck in a way I was sure that was broken.

We quickly put her in the car rolling her in an office chair to the driveway and headed for Marble Falls Emergency clinic. Sure enough, after an x-ray and a quick exam, it was determined that she had a break in two or three places. The weekend was over and we headed back to San Antonio. The following week, it was determined that Thelma, a.k.a. Meemaw would have to have surgery and be in a wheelchair for eight to ten weeks.

Escape to the Lake- Bald Head and All

Wednesday, April 16, 2008 7:27 AM, CDT

Good morning everyone! So much is going on with us this week. I don't know where to start. Along with continuing to try to get McKenzie's congestion under control, we had my mother's broken ankle surgery yesterday, and little Monroe has strep throat. He is quarantined at his grandmother's house. Monroe is not feeling his best either, however; luckily he is out of town. So the good news is that McKenzie may not have been around them enough to get it. Me and the other girls? Well, time will tell. So things are a little more crazed than usual around here! But, you know even with the dark cloud that is following us around, I feel blessed. I have the ability to follow the Lord wholeheartedly. I choose to follow

Him through the valley. It's better than walking through the valley alone! He will guide us through all this and into a pleasant place. I truly believe that. And I believe that your prayers are part of what carries us! So thank you! McKenzie is standing in the family room dancing right now. She is so full of life! She is begging for blackberries with whipped cream- one of her new favorites. She is so precious!

Have a great day! Jeri

Monroe

Life moves on, things change, and bad things happen to good people. Whatever phrase you would like to use, they are all true.

At the end of April 2008, we continued to face many, many tough decisions. As we began to prepare for surgery, we suddenly decided we did not have the confidence in our surgeon that we desired. After more prayer and discussions, Jeri and I decided we would need to seek another opinion from another surgeon.

Our initial thought was that we would use the surgeon that had placed McKenzie's port-a-cath and performed her biopsies in January. However, after meeting with the surgeon, we decided that this was not in the best interest of our daughter.

Monday, April 21, 2008 5:32 PM, CDT

Hello everyone. We met this afternoon with the surgeon. Currently, we are looking at next Tuesday, April 29th for surgery. We will know more later in the week and we will update you as soon as possible. Jeri

Monroe

LETTER TO MCKENZIE, FROM DAD-Personal Journal:

April 24th, 2008-San Antonio, TX

We are on the verge of having surgery for the removal of your tumor. The good news is that it has reacted to your first four rounds of chemo. We met with the surgeon on Monday and have decided to get a second opinion. We are anxiously awaiting the meeting with the next doctor. I have traveled to Phoenix this week and am headed home on the plane tonight. It is truly amazing that everywhere I go, I run into people who know your story and want to know how you are doing. You are an amazing little girl and people love you even though they have never even met you. We love you as well and we want to see you through to the cure. It is tough from day to day and yet we know that God is carrying you and our whole family on His back through this time. The next several months will be as tough as the last. Hang in there and fight. It is all that any of us can do.

Jeri

It was Jesus alone that kept us fighting to get through this tough time in our lives. He alone was our reason for getting out of bed during those dark days.

Thursday, April 24, 2008 4:21 PM, CDT

Hello everyone. Well, it's been a very frustrating day. We are no closer to an answer to the question of timing or choice of surgeons for McKenzie's surgery. Dr. Patel assures me that it needs to be next week because her counts are quite recovered.

He says he will call me today with a plan. **Please pray for a confident decisive plan of action that Monroe, Dr. Patel, and I can all agree upon.** *Thank you. Jeri*

Thursday, April 24, 2008 8:35 PM, CDT

The decision has been made to postpone surgery at this time. Dr. Patel consulted with the surgeons and it appears that it would not be possible to remove the tumor at this time. The course of action will be to move ahead next Tuesday with a heavier dose of chemo starting on Tuesday and going through Saturday. We are frustrated and discouraged with the news; however we will forge ahead with this plan of treatment. As always we appreciate your prayers, kind words and thoughts. May God bless you all and your families. Monroe

Friday, April 25, 2008 8:30 PM, CDT

Hi everyone. Well, it's been a difficult last 24 hours for me. I was very disappointed at the news that the tumor was not currently removable. I want that thing OUT of my baby! I know God has a plan and I am crying out to Him to tell me why. His answer is to soothe my soul. He has done that through His Word today and now with an incredibly beautiful thunder and lightning storm. We've been sitting out on the front porch watching the sunset and the storm blow in. It is gorgeous. I may even have to post you a picture on the website tomorrow. McKenzie is running around playing. She is being a little toot because she didn't take a nap today, but it's almost bedtime now! Y'all can pray for me to continue to be soothed and encouraged. Thank you.

Monroe

So with the delay of the surgery, we were forced to go back to chemo treatment. McKenzie began five solid days of chemo and around the clock fluids. Jeri and I were frustrated, sad, and beaten up. It would not be the last time we faced disappointment.

Wednesday, April 30, 2008 6:36 AM, CDT

Today will be day three of chemo round five. We will have two more days after today. She is sleeping more this time. She is also getting sick a little more often. The doctor has told us that each round will get progressively more difficult on her and that has proven to be true. Pray for strength and endurance for her and us. Thank you, Jeri

Friday, May 2, 2008 6:55 AM, CDT

Hello everyone! It has been a long, hard week. Monroe and I are both a little down. Today is day five of this chemo round. We have added another drug this week to be more aggressive. It runs twenty-four hours a day along with the fluids we already came home with. The worst part of that is that we usually de-access her sometime late Friday night so that she can sleep better. We won't be able to de-access her until the chemo drug runs out sometime Saturday morning. The doctor said to expect more nausea with the additional drug, but praise God we really haven't seen that. She did have more nausea the early part of the week, but we didn't start the new drug until Wednesday. Either way, we are almost done with chemo this week and will be glad when it is finished as always.

We have had the additional challenge of having two of our other three children sick this week. Courtney had a little virus the first couple days this week and little Monroe came home sick on Wednesday afternoon and stayed home yesterday. Everyone should be back in school today and we pray they make it through the day.

A final update for you all: we will be seeing a different surgeon on Wednesday, May 14th. This one says that it may be possible to remove the mass. He cautions (this all through Dr. Patel) that the surgery will be long and involved. We don't have a date for that surgery yet, but will let you know as soon as we know. Please begin praying for God's perfect timing, perfect team of doctors, and no complications. I will be praying, too, for them to be able to remove it all. One other prayer request and that is the rebounding of her blood counts following this round of chemo. If she gets an infection and is hospitalized, it simply delays the process of surgery.

Sorry for the long posting. Hope you all are doing well. Jeri

Monroe

We did, from time to time, have a good bit of news come into our lives. My sister, Kate, and her husband, Russell, had been working for over a year to adopt a child from China. In May, they finally got word that they would be able to go and pick up their baby boy. Our family was very happy. Even McKenzie was excited at the fact that she would be getting a new cousin.

Saturday, May 3, 2008 8:13 AM, CDT

Good Saturday morning everyone. We are anxiously awaiting the final drops of medicine to go through the port so that we can, as McKenzie says, "take the tubes out." I think she is going to react like lion released from her cage as soon as she is set free. She has already chosen the Princess outfit to put on as soon as she is free.

A quick bit of good news: We heard this week that McKenzie is going to be getting a new cousin. Her Aunt Kate and Uncle Russell got word this week that their adoption has gone through and they will be making a trip to China in the next couple of months to bring home a bouncing baby boy. Congratulations to Russell, Kate and big brother Rusty. We are happy for you.

I hope you all have a good weekend and enjoy some quality time with your families. -Monroe

Sunday, May 4, 2008 8:20 AM, CDT

Good Sunday morning everyone! Well, chemo round five is behind us. It is always good to get that done. McKenzie came running up the stairs yesterday morning after Monroe de-accessed her saying, "Look, Mommy, no tubes!" She feels free. We do, too. She slept over at Meemaw and Grandpa's house last night enabling Monroe and me to go to church together and spend an evening at a 40th birthday party with some of his high school friends. It was great to get out and see some friends we hadn't seen in a while. Hope y'all are enjoying your weekend, too. Tomorrow we go to Dr. Patel's and begin Neupogen shots to help her white blood counts to recover. I am praying to stay out of the hospital from infection. We'll see and let you know how it is going. Talk to you all soon. With Love, Jeri

Tuesday, May 6, 2008 4:13 PM, CDT

Good Tuesday Afternoon Everyone,

We went to the doctor yesterday and as we expected McKenzie's counts were down. She got a Neupogen shot yesterday at the Dr. and then another one at home today to help boost her white cell recovery. At this point, all is stable and we will plan on seeing the new surgeon next week on the 14th. Please pray that McKenzie's counts recover quickly and we avoid the hospital this weekend or early next week.

Thank you everyone for your continued prayers.-Monroe

Wednesday, May 7, 2008 6:00 PM, CDT

Hello everyone! Well, McKenzie had a blood transfusion today. Monroe took her to her to her regular appointment at Dr. Patel's this morning and her white blood counts were almost non-existent and her hemoglobin was pretty low. We were not expecting that one- we should have known- and we had to do some juggling to get the other children taken care of. Dee Dee to the rescue! Meemaw and Grandpa are coming to sit with McKenzie and her brother so I can catch some of Caroline and Courtney's strings concert tonight. We are so blessed to have all of them near.

Anyway, McKenzie may be facing hospitalization soon. Her fever was rising earlier this afternoon, but they gave her a mega dose of a Tylenol like drug prior to the transfusion. We will need to watch it carefully tonight. Please pray for God's perfect timing in this matter.

Thanks for all the continued prayers. Jeri

Monroe

As the school year came to a close, the end of the year commitments increased. Courtney was finishing eighth grade and Caroline was finishing fifth grade. It was exciting and challenging times for both of them as well as Mom and Dad trying to keep up the pace. Without the help of Jeri's parents and my mom, there was no way we would have been able to keep up.

Thursday, May 8, 2008 10:32 AM, CDT

Good morning everyone. Today I am writing to you from the Methodist Children's Hospital. We had a restless night. McKenzie was up a lot not feeling well. She ran a low-grade fever (99.9 to 100) all night. This morning it went up to 100.4 and we headed for the hospital. She is kind of quiet, not really in a bad mood, but not in a good one either. She is watching Annie and wants to hold my hand so I am typing one handed! Pretty talented, huh? Well, you can pray for quick recovery and for the hours to go quickly around here. I have plenty to do, but I feel bad for her. Of course, she will sleep a lot I think. We'll keep you posted. Jeri

Friday, May 9, 2008 8:59 AM, CDT

Go Spurs Go! Well, they won! And more importantly, Happy Birthday Dad! Today is McKenzie's Grandpa's birthday! We won't tell his age, but he is a wonderful grandpa to her and all of his grandchildren!

Now about McKenzie- she is doing pretty well this morning. She slept much of yesterday and then not much last night. Isn't that just the way it goes?! The fever is better under control this morning. She spiked up over 102 last night, but is cool this morning. Of course, she is always "cool", but you know what I mean. She has discovered the remote control on her bed and is busy turning on and off the lights, up and down the TV volume, and up and down the bed! We are glad to see a little spunk. Keep up the prayers! Jeri

Saturday, May 10, 2008 7:14 AM, CDT

Good Saturday morning everyone from the Methodist Children's Hospital. We had a quiet night, we only got up a dozen or so times. The nurses came in all night long, and then to top it off, since McKenzie was exhausted and asleep, at 6:00 AM they made her get up and stand on a scale to take her weight. Hospitals are so relaxing.

Dr. Patel informed us yesterday that we should plan on being here for a while, possibly through next Friday. This was not the news we were expecting, but by now Jeri and I know the only thing we can really count on is the unexpected. We will keep up updated as the week goes on.

Right now we are watching Madeline for the one-thousandth time.

Got to go, we have to make the journey to the restroom.

Hey dads: don't forget Sunday is Mother Day.-Monroe

Sunday, May 11, 2008 12:19 PM, CDT

Happy Mother's Day, everyone.

We are on day 4 at the hospital with no end in sight. Her counts are still low and we cannot go home until they begin to recover. Last night was another long night with little or no rest at the hospital. McKenzie received 4 different antibiotics that ran throughout the night. **Hospitals are not a restful place**. *She continues to ask when are we going home, and the hard part is we do not have an answer.*

We will keep you posted as we get news. Take care and have good day.-Monroe

Monroe

And always, when we thought that we could not have any more excitement in our lives, God would once again tell us "Oh, yes, you can handle more." He was always right, we never quit, and neither did McKenzie.

Tuesday, May 13, 2008 9:40 PM, CDT

Hi everyone! Jeri here. Much has happened in the last day or so. Some good, some bad. Okay, McKenzie had a heart ultrasound and a bone scan today. She has an MRI scheduled tomorrow morning. This is all in preparation for surgery. We are tentatively scheduled for May 27th, the Tuesday after Labor Day. The surgeon has given us much to be concerned about, but believes they can get most if not all of the mass removed. The caution comes because there are two major arteries feeding several organs involved. It seems like good news that they are willing to move forward with the surgery, but it is extremely scary. It will be a very long surgery. We can begin praying for the surgeons now.

Our day was further complicated when our eleven year old daughter fainted following some vaccinations and suffered a concussion. At one time today, we had two daughters at Methodist Children's Hospital. It was not good. Our older daughter is home now and recovering. You can pray for continued healing for her.

I will tell you more about the upcoming surgery as we learn more and as time allows. I am headed for bed now. Sleep well and thank you as always for the support you provide.

Wednesday, May 14, 2008 6:18 PM, CDT

Hello everyone! Just a quick update- WE ARE HOME! Monroe talked them into letting us come home. I'll give you more details later. Jeri

Monroe

As we settled back into a brief routine from the early May hospital visit, we all began to focus on the surgery ahead. Jeri and I knew that the surgery was very serious and would take a great deal of skill and precise coordination with the surgeons performing the procedure. The tumor had been reduced in overall size; however, it still spanned across McKenzie's abdomen and was attached to all of her major organs.

The surgeons would have to dissect the tumor from her spleen, liver, lungs, aorta and kidneys. The surgery would take about eight hours. We also were planning on a lengthy stay in the hospital, best-case three weeks, and worst case up to six weeks.

As we got closer and closer to the surgery date, our emotions were filled once again with the unknown and concern about what the future would hold.

Wednesday, May 21, 2008 8:44 AM, CDT

Good morning everyone! Today is Wednesday and we are still enjoying a "normal" week. Her favorite movie this week is "E.T.- the Extra Terrestrial" and we are watching it now. We don't have to go back to Dr. Patel's office until tomorrow. McKenzie is still fighting the congestion a little. You can pray that it is completely clear by Tuesday. You can also pray that Monroe and I will have wisdom in knowing exactly what to tell McKenzie about the upcoming surgery. She already hears us talking about it and I want to prepare her without frightening her. I don't want to tell her too early so that she worries about it, but I don't want to wait too long either.

I have heard of at least two groups of friends that are gathering on Tuesday morning to pray during McKenzie's surgery. I am so grateful for these and would love to hear of others of you that decide to do the same. I will be praying for steady hands and clear thinking of all medical staff. I will be praying for the mass to be calcified enough to simply pop off the arteries and be completely removed. I will pray for no complications following surgery and speedy recovery. Most of all, I pray for God's will to be done.

Thank you all that have signed up for meals and those that have brought them recently. I added one day next week and will add them as we see how long her hospital stay will be.

Have a great Wednesday! Jeri

Monroe

Once again, we retreated to Lake LBJ for solitude before the surgery. We spent Memorial Day at the lake, on the boat and playing with the kids in the water. McKenzie was strong and as happy as we had seen her in a long time. She had no idea of the storm that would be ahead. Jeri and I tried to remain focused on the day and not worry about surgery. God was with us that weekend and we all seemed to relax and enjoy each other. Courtney, Caroline, and Monroe, all played together and spent time with McKenzie. They too knew that the risk of this surgery was high and that the many things could happen. What stood in the back of my mind was that this could be the last weekend we were all together.

Saturday, May 24, 2008 6:58 AM, CDT

McKenzie is having a good weekend being a "normal" 3 year old. She is spending time with her brother and sisters. I have talked to her a little about the upcoming surgery and it went well. I tried to be very casual about it and she received it that way, too. She is sleeping late this morning; unfortunately her brother was not able to! Many of you have notified me of your prayer groups praying for McKenzie and I sure do appreciate it. Y'all have a great Memorial Day weekend! Jeri

Monroe

The weekend came to an end quickly and the day of surgery rolled around and we headed to the hospital. The plan was for McKenzie and me to go to the hospital on Memorial Day evening and check in. It was difficult explaining to our three year old why we needed to go home from the lake and head to the hospital. She did not feel sick and she did not like the hospital. But on Monday May 26th, 2008, we packed up and headed to the Methodist Children's Hospital where we would spend a large amount of our summer. Ready or not, we moved ahead, trusting that we were in God's will.

Surgery

<u>*Monday, May 26, 2008 6:51 PM, CDT*</u>

Good Evening All,

We are headed out to the Methodist Children's Hospital tonight to check in for Surgery in the morning. We are planning on her going in between 8-9 in the morning and the procedure will last between five to eight hours. Jeri and I will do our best to update the website as soon as we know something.

McKenzie will be going from the OR to the ICU for twenty four to forty eight hours after the surgery. So we would like to request NO FLOWERS OR GIFTS at this time, but as always we appreciate ALL Prayers.

Thank you all for your prayers and support. -Monroe

Jeri

When McKenzie was first diagnosed, I assumed that we would do surgery immediately to remove the tumor. I assumed that because that was what I had experienced with the people I knew in the past that had cancer. They would remove the tumor, and then do chemotherapy. That was not the case with this disease. Because the mass was so large (10cm x 12cm) and apparently not encapsulated at all, surgery was not the first line of treatment. First came the chemotherapy in an effort to shrink the mass (not tumor because it was not encapsulated) to a surgically removable size. Throughout our five monthly rounds of chemotherapy, we had C.T. scans to periodically check the effectiveness of the drugs in shrinking the mass. I was encouraged early on by the fact that the mass was shrinking. Finally, came the day when we were told that the mass was small enough to attempt to surgically remove it. The general size of the mass in May was 4cm x 6cm. I say "general size" because the mass was intricate, having woven itself throughout McKenzie's little abdomen. It wound around organs and arteries. We prepared for surgery with the doctors. A surgical team was chosen. We filled out paperwork and spoke to the insurance company to pre-approve the procedure and subsequent hospitalization. The surgery was scheduled for the Tuesday following Memorial Day. We spent the Memorial Day weekend at the lake house thinking that we might not be there again for a while. We were right. Looking back, I could never have been prepared for the surgery or what would follow. I could not have known what was coming any more than I could have predicted her initial diagnosis. I think I viewed the surgery as the beginning of the end of treatment.

Monroe went to spend the night with McKenzie at the hospital the night before so she would be ready for the early morning. I met them there in pre-op that morning along with my mom. McKenzie recognized that something was going on by the unusual route her hospital stay was taking. Also, she knew by now how to work "the system" of parents and grandparents. So when Meemaw came in she was determined to have Meemaw stay and not allow her dad to come back in. She knew that Meemaw would do all within her power to keep McKenzie happy and out of pain. At first, we tried to let her stay, but as soon as the nurses tried to do a procedure to ready her for surgery and it became apparent that McKenzie was looking to Meemaw to get her out of it, Monroe had to come back in. He was the brave one who went with her into the Operating Room and waited until she was drifting off to sleep. I think it is one of the hardest things to do to hand your baby to a nurse and watch them walk down a hall headed for surgery. I've had to do it too many times and I think it's one of the cruelest things a mother has to endure. So I was grateful they let Monroe go with her. He met us in the waiting room and we made good use of the waiting room for ten long hours.

Monroe

On Tuesday morning, McKenzie and I headed down from the fourth floor to the second floor. With her in my arms, I carried my precious baby back from the Pre-Op room to OR4 and laid her on the table. She screamed and yelled and kicked because she was so frightened. I helped to hold her down until the anesthesia was applied and she settled down. Then with a kiss on the forehead and a bracelet that she had worn on her wrist, I left and went to the waiting room for what would be a very long, long time.

I was met at the waiting room by Jeri, my mother, Jeri's parents, my cousin Blake, my Uncle Jim, my Aunt Nancy, and several other friends. We all began our wait, to see what would happen next.

Jeri

We knew the surgery would be long, but were not prepared for that length. The original estimate was four to six hours. We had many friends and family visit us that day. Some brought us lunch, some brought us dinner. It was an excruciating wait. Every few hours we would receive an update from the nursing staff. We heard details of how things were going and estimates on how much longer the surgical group expected surgery to continue. It was discouraging when, after four hours into the surgery, they came and told us they were just beginning to work on removing the mass.

Tuesday, May 27, 2008 12:58 PM, CDT

Hello everyone! Well, we don't know much yet. We know that she has been in surgery for four hours fifteen minutes and they have yet to begin actually removing any of the mass. She is fine as far as we know. It looks like it will be a long surgery. Y'all keep praying, I feel it. I know you already are! Thank you. Jeri

Tuesday, May 27, 2008 5:08 PM, CDT

Okay, eight hours, eighteen minutes later and we have what I think is good news. Dr. Patel just came out and he said that it looks like they got it all. We are cautiously optimistic. They are beginning to close now. We are waiting to hear from the surgeons and get their opinions. They will plan to keep her intubated overnight tonight and sedated. She has an epidural that will stay until at least tomorrow to help manage pain. We are nearing the end of today's adventure in surgery and will begin the adventure of recovery. Recovery will be the next long road to walk down. Thank you all for your continued prayers. I will update you more as we know more. Jeri

Monroe

The hours and hours of waiting for the surgeons to complete their tasks, the five months of chemotherapy and many, many long days and nights agonizing over what was the best course of action for McKenzie had paid off. The doctors were confident they had done a good job and that the cancer had been removed from our little girl's body.

Jeri and I were very relieved and anxious to see McKenzie as soon as possible. However, nothing could have prepared us for what we would see when we arrived in the PICU at the Methodist Hospital.

We were taken through two electronic double doors to one of the saddest places I have ever been. Nurse and doctors standing and moving around a very quiet main room with twenty to twenty-five smaller rooms with sliding doors off to the sides. In each of the rooms to the side was a child. Their ages ranged from newborn to teenager and all of them clinging to life and trying to fight a good fight.

When we entered our little McKenzie's room, we found our daughter on a ventilator, with I.V.'s in both hands and both feet, tape across her eyes and tubes coming out of her abdomen. She could not move, she could not talk, and she did not respond. The oxygen machine forced her to breathe and the heart monitor beeped in the background. The room was about twelve by twelve and there was barely enough space to walk around the bed. Without the machines, McKenzie would not be able to breath on her own.

Jeri

Again, when they came out and said it was finished, I felt relief as though this were really the beginning of healing. They said she wasn't awake yet, but that they were moving her to the Pediatric Intensive Care Unit. So our friends and family went home for the night and so did Monroe. That first night in the P.I.C.U. was really weird, even for a hospital stay. We were in a small curtained area with breakaway walls. McKenzie seemed to get a great deal of attention with many doctors and nurses coming and going. She was not really awake yet. There was only a single reclining chair and very little light. They gave her breathing treatments through her breathing tube. She seemed to get a bit agitated with those. But, otherwise there was not much movement on her part. Her incision was very large. She struck a pitiful pose with no clothes on, only a pull-up. Her little baldhead lay so still on the pillow. She had so many tubes and wires coming out of her. She was extremely puffy and swollen. Her fingers were like balloons. It was hard for me to see. But she was my beautiful baby then as always.

Tuesday, May 27, 2008 9:30 PM, CDT

Well, after 10 hours in the O.R., we have access to our baby again. The surgeon agreed that they were able to remove all diseased tissue that they could see or feel. They took 4 lymph nodes and her appendix. She is resting comfortably in the

PICU right now. The staff here is getting to know what is being called her "strong constitution". This group seems actually to listen when I tell them she needs strong doses of sedation. They are monitoring her constantly both on the monitors and in person. There seems to be at least one person in the room at all times and often 3-4 people checking on her. She is receiving blood transfusion tonight. Her hemoglobin is a little low. It is truly God's hand in allowing them to remove the complete mass. I thank Him for answering the prayers of His people. I am blessed to have all of you "storming the gates of Heaven" on our behalf. I pray you all have a restful night. Jeri

Wednesday, May 28, 2008 7:09 AM, CDT

Good morning all. McKenzie has had a rough night, but she is holding her own. Her night nurse calls her spunky. Of course, we knew that. We have had difficulty maintaining the balance between keeping her asleep so that she won't pull on her tubes and keeping her vitals stable. Her blood pressure went down and her heart rate went up around 5am, but both are more stable now. She has two I.V. poles and more tubes going in and out than I can count. She has also had a temperature and we have been addressing that with antibiotics and ibuprofen. Please continue to pray for her recovery and the wisdom of the staff members who care for her so diligently. Oh and of course, pray for endurance for Monroe, me, and the other children. You have my thanks and my love as always, Jeri

Jeri

I wanted nothing more than for her to sit up and start arguing with me. But she didn't. Monroe and I returned to our 24-hour on, 24-hour off schedule.

Monroe

As a parent, it was extremely difficult to look at our child and have much hope of recovery. As Christians, all we could do was what we had done for the last five months and that was, once again, remember our faith in God and know that He would walk through this recovery with us, no matter how difficult.

Wednesday, May 28, 2008 8:05 PM, CDT

Good Evening Everyone,

It has been just over 24 hours since McKenzie came out of surgery. We are still in the PICU and she is still on a respirator and receiving more medication then you can imagine. The nurses and the doctors are amazed at her strength and her ability to function with very high doses of painkillers. Our evening nurse just told me she has never seen anyone be able to **answer questions** *after that much pain killing medicine.*

Today Jeri and I are feeling that many of our prayers have been answered, in order to get us to this point. However, we also know that McKenzie still has a very long journey ahead. She has won several battles and yet the war goes on. We are still planning on being in the hospital several more weeks and then we will go home for a couple of weeks, and then come back for the stem cell transplant, more chemo and radiation. So this is not the end, we are somewhere in the middle. Therefore, your continued prayers are very important. McKenzie is fighting hard, and this gives us all hope and encouragement to continue our around the clock efforts.

Thank you all for prayers, meals, child care, phone calls, rides to practices, emails, text messages and general support.

We appreciate you ALL.

May God Bless Each of You,-Monroe

Monroe

While we were in the PICU, we talked to her, read to her, prayed with her and sang to her. We played her favorite music "Sleep Sound in Jesus" and we waited. We asked that only grandparents and immediate family come and see her. The days were long; however, the nights were even longer.

Thursday, May 29, 2008 4:20 PM, CDT

Hello everyone. Jeri here. It's my night in the PICU so I thought I would catch you up on what is happening with McKenzie. She is stable. They are attempting to wean her from the drugs that "paralyze" her. She is still sedated, but able to wake up more and move more. They say that is in anticipation of removing the ventilator soon. They say she will need to be off of that medication in order to soon begin breathing for herself. But then let me clarify "awake". Awake for her is startling and moving her arms more. She opens her eyes slightly and looks for me. At one time today, she held onto my hand when I started to move away.

She had some oxygen saturation issues this afternoon which told the intensivist that she is not quite ready to come off the ventilator, but obviously that time needs to come in the next couple days. We were also told today that the epidural will need to come out tomorrow. That has been a source of pain control for her. We will deal with that tomorrow, though!

She is still having fluid balance issues. That is something you could all begin praying about for me. The surgeon stopped by today and said that we should see improvement in that area soon, but we have not seen it so far. She is so puffy and swollen. She is being given medication to help with this issue, too.

So, there aren't a lot of changes, but a couple of slight ones. Please pray that she begins to recover.

Jeri

The other children occasionally came to see her. Dr. Patel stopped by every once in a while. But as time went by, it became apparent that McKenzie was less and less an interesting case to the doctors and nurses of the P.I.C.U. We would often go without an assigned nurse for half a shift until someone was called in or pulled from another department. As hours turned into days and days turned into weeks, the routine grew frustrating. We were caught in a bad cycle. McKenzie was not beginning to even try to breathe on her own. It seemed that she could not because the anesthetics were so strong. But they could not turn them down because she was not breathing on her own. It was a "Catch 22" situation. They continued the breathing treatments and that remained the only times she displayed any of her usual spunk. At least twice she pulled out her breathing tube from her throat. She did that once when I was there and once when Monroe was there. The time she did it in my presence was one of the scariest times of my life. The breakaway walls were removed, all the lights were turned up, and a team descended on her. They were breathing for her and performing CPR. We almost lost her that day. Monroe said it was the same the day he was there.

Friday, May 30, 2008 9:12 AM, CDT

Friday morning here. It's been a rough night for McKenzie. And about 30 minutes ago, she pulled out her ventilator. She had 8 people working on her and they have it back in. But I need everyone to pray right now for her oxygen saturation level to stabilize. They have her stable, but please pray for recovery to improve. Thanks, Jeri

Saturday, May 31, 2008 7:24 PM, CDT

Hi everyone! I hope you are all enjoying your weekend. It certainly feels like summer out there! I want to give you an update on McKenzie. It's not much of an update. She is still completely sedated and not breathing on her own. She is still completely relying on the ventilator. The only change is very slight. We may be seeing a very slight change for the better in her fluid balance. Her little face does not look as much like a prizefighter as it has. Her fingers are more like sausages than balloons this evening. I am trying to put a positive spin on all this by thinking that she is healing more while she lies so still. Who knows! God knows. I believe that He is still in charge of her little body and will work this all for the good of those who love Him and are called according to His purpose. So keep praying and have a nice evening. Jeri

Sunday, June 1, 2008 8:47 PM, CDT

Sunday evening here at the Methodist. McKenzie is still in the PICU and it looks like she will stay another day or two. We are starting to see the fluids move, which should help with her breathing. This afternoon we have also seen her wake up at least four or five times and be very active. When she wakes, she is frightened because she cannot talk and we have to keep her restrained. Jeri and I hope that the ventilator can possibly be removed on Monday, which will help.

We have spent five full days and this will be night number six, in the PICU. We are ready to get out of here back up to the fourth floor. The recliner that we take turns sleeping on is not very comfortable. We both feel like the move to four will be a welcome change.

Progress is slow and we pray that the morning will bring marked improvement for our little Princess. Thank you all for continued support and prayers.

Also please pray for strength this week for Jeri and myself. It is the last week of school and our other three children have very busy weeks as well. One day at a time, I keep reminding myself, one day at a time....

Thank you Dee Dee for the relief at the hospital over the last week. -Monroe

Monroe

Just over a week after the surgery, we began seeing little glimmers of hope. However, we were not out of the woods yet and we continued to make very, very slow progress. Jeri and I were not sure we would ever be able to take her home. It was very difficult to sit and watch day after day.

Jeri

Even now, as I read over our journals from those days, I feel an oppression settle over me. That was the general feeling, oppressive, which from under we felt we couldn't move. Many days into this routine, we had one of the intensivists suggest something new. He suggested a drug that we would add to her sedatives. This drug was currently only used for up to twenty-four hours at a time and recommended by the manufacturer to be used only for seventy-two hours at the most. So we would add this to her other drugs and then wean her from those. Then we would slowly wean her from this one as well. Anything was worth a try. I already felt like we had lost her. My greatest fear was that she would never wake up or if she did, she would not be our same McKenzie. So we agreed to try it. But, after a full week, nothing had changed. I believed and so did Monroe that we had to get her off the sedatives. We had to see if our little girl was still in that shell. We finally convinced Dr. Patel and with his pull in the hospital began weaning her from the drug. He is my hero. At first, there was only a blank stare from her beautiful brown eyes.

<u>*Tuesday, June 3, 2008 3:26 PM, CDT*</u>

Oh my goodness! What an outpouring of love and prayer for our family! Don't let anyone tell you prayer doesn't work. Almost as soon as I posted that cry for encouragement prayer this morning, we had two different doctors come with encouraging news, I think she took a couple of breaths over the ventilator, and I saw McKenzie awake enough to communicate with shakes/nods of her head that she didn't want her legs covered up. Then after I left Monroe read her favorite book, Fancy Nancy, and she got real agitated when he finished. He asked her if she wanted to hear it again and she was able to nod yes! So thank you! I know it will continue to be a rollercoaster ride, but God showed up and worked in His timing just when I needed Him to. I give Him the glory. He is healing her and caring for my emotional needs along the way. Thank you for "storming the gates of heaven" for Monroe and me yet again. With much love and gratitude, Jeri

Monroe

<u>LETTER TO MCKENZIE, FROM DAD-Personal Journal:</u>

June 4, 2008

You had surgery on May 27th and it lasted for ten and a half hours. The good news is your doctor thinks he was able to remove the tumor. Since surgery, you have been in the PICU. This is day number eight. Progress has been very slow. Yesterday we saw a little light at the end of the tunnel. You took a few breaths on your own, and you responded to me reading your favorite book, <u>Fancy Nancy</u>. We are attempting to bring you off of so much medication and hoping that you will begin to breathe more and more on your own. It is very slow going. Today, your brother and sisters get out of school for the summer. We hope that you are able to enjoy some of the summer with us. We still have a long road ahead. There are literally thousands of people praying for you to get well. Your web site has over forty-one thousand hits on it so far. Mommy and I are amazed at the outpouring of prayer and kindness towards our family. So many people love you that have never even met you. Hang in there, Precious. I love you.

My one concern is that the doctor has made a very serious mistake. You were on an experimental drug for five days. Currently the FDA claims that this drug should not be used longer than twenty-four hours. The effects have been that everything seems to be slowing your recovery to a snail's pace. None of us knows what to do next.

Wednesday, June 4, 2008 9:26 PM, CDT

Hello one and all. We've been watching and waiting for our little fighter to come up for air (literally!) for 9 long days. She has officially shown up! She is waking quite often now and is breathing over the ventilator often, too. Each doctor that looks at her says tomorrow looks like a promising day to extubate her. She is adjusting her legs and torso position to her own satisfaction and if we move her, she moves back. It is all very small movements, but it is progress and that is good. Keep praying, God is listening and healing. He is good.

Thursday, June 5, 2008 6:36 AM, CDT

Good morning everyone. Okay, we can really use some prayer cover this morning. They will begin around 7am seriously weaning her from the sedatives in anticipation of removing the ventilator. Please pray that she will just remain calm enough for them to accomplish all that needs to be done prior to extubation. As soon as we get over this major roadblock, we will rejoice! I will let you know later today if it happens or not. Jeri

Thursday, June 5, 2008 8:24 PM, CDT

It has been almost 10 hours since McKenzie was taken off of the respirator. So far she is doing well. Dr. Patel came in today and explained that the 6-hour mark and then the 24-hour mark are significant times to watch. So we have passed the first benchmark and will continue praying that we get through the next one.

She has smiled several times today and earlier she received a visit from Courtney, Caroline and Monroe. She seemed glad to see them all, and they were glad to see her.

Dr. Patel also shared that if all goes well we could go home by early next week. Also, he felt that, on Friday, we would most likely move back to the 4th floor. So we are making progress.

Unfortunately, he brought some discouraging news as well. He said we would begin the next phase of Stem Cell Transplant, and chemo within two weeks of being discharged. So we will check back into the hospital within a couple of weeks of going home. He also said to be prepared for a long stay of three to six weeks for the next phase. This was a lot of information to absorb and not exactly what we wanted to hear today after a long week and a half.

One day at a time, one day at a time.

Please continue the prayers for strength for all of our family: Mom, Dad, Sisters, Brother, Grandparents and all those who help to provide us strength and support on a daily basis. And continue your prayers for recovery and healing for McKenzie. Thank you all!-Monroe

Friday, June 6, 2008 11:05 AM, CDT

McKenzie has passed the 24-hour mark off of the ventilator and her breathing is holding steady. During the night and into this morning she developed a fever. For now we are treating it with Tylenol. Please pray that in does not get worse.

At least another 24 hours in the PICU. Time moves slow. Last night was night number 10 in the PICU and night number 11 in the Hospital. I only wish we got Hilton points for our nights, McKenzie would be Platinum. -Monroe

Sunday, June 8, 2008 8:21 AM, CDT

Good morning everyone. It's Sunday now. There is not much change in McKenzie's present state. Monroe was with her overnight last night and he says she is a little more active this morning than yesterday. Maybe that is a good sign? We don't know. Only God knows what is going on in her little baby head. **We did have a CT scan yesterday and have some new information from that. Her brain is fine as far as they know- they have ruled out the possibility of stroke. Praise God. However, they found a different problem. Her complete spleen and half of liver are not receiving blood supply. They do not want to go in surgically at this**

time to correct this for obvious reasons. She will lose the spleen, but Dr. Patel says that the liver in children this age will regenerate. They are attempting to address the issue with medicine. *So another hurdle is set up before us. We know that God is the only perfect runner Who can clear that hurdle. As you can imagine, Monroe and I are tired of running and jumping at this point in the race. 24 on and 24 off at the hospital is no way to live life for the two of us or for our other children. But as always, it appears that only the wisdom and healing of God's powerful hand will get McKenzie out of that hospital bed. As Mr. Webb put in his guestbook entry, "Jesus, we need your healing now." With my love and thanks to all of you, Jeri*

Jeri

Our next move was to get her moved up to the fourth floor where the Hematology/Oncology patients were treated. I felt like it was familiar territory and familiar staff and Dr. Patel could regain control of her care there. She was still only breathing with the help of the machines. She showed spunk when the breathing treatments were given, but otherwise was still lifeless. We kept working to get her off of the breathing tube, weaned from the sedatives, and moved to the fourth floor. Finally, the day came! We had her moved upstairs and she was placed in one of the isolation rooms. She continued to fight the breathing treatments, but it was great to see her fight return. She couldn't speak. Whether it was from the breathing tube remaining in her throat so long or simply from weakness, we'll never know. We waited for her to begin eating and started with only clear liquids. She progressed to popsicles and applesauce.

She was not allowed to leave the hospital until she could have a bowel movement. We began walking her slowly. At first, it was just standing, and then taking a step or two. Then finally, we had her doing laps around the nurses' station with all of them cheering. The day she simply refused to take the breathing treatment, I knew she was still in there. It was hard to tell, but it felt like we might actually get our baby back.

Sunday, June 8, 2008 8:21 PM, CDT

Words cannot truly describe the emotional roller coaster that our family has been on over the last two weeks. We have sat by McKenzie's side day and night praying that God's will be done. We have not received the answers that we desired, yet we still know that all is in God's hands, and answers ARE being given.

Today we were able to get McKenzie moved back to the 4th floor. She is still unresponsive. However, we are told that her overall health is improving. She is on antibiotics as well as a drug called "Methadone" to help her with the withdrawal she is experiencing from being on high doses of medication for such a long period of time.

We are hopeful that she will return to herself very soon. It is extremely difficult to be by her side and watch her in this condition.

While in the hospital with her last night, I watched Apollo 13 with Tom Hanks. At one point in the movie he is asked if he was ever scared flying. He has the line "You never know what events will transpire, in order to get you home safely." We have no idea what the next step will be, however, one day we will all be delivered home safely. We just have to live our lives as the events transpire and trust in God.

Thank you for your prayers. Monroe

Tuesday, June 10, 2008 2:02 PM, CDT

Hello and good afternoon to all of my beautiful family, friends and prayer warriors. You all are totally God's people doing what God's people ought to be doing. You are storming the gates of heaven (as Angelia says) for McKenzie and for our entire family. Thank you. We continue to see teeny tiny baby steps in McKenzie's recovery. Let's see: she has stood and taken a couple of steps twice today, she has slapped a respiratory therapist who was trying to give her a breathing treatment, she has worked with PT to kick a balloon and squeeze it between her knees, she said a few words with the speech therapist (when really encouraged to do so), she voluntarily said "okay" to Meemaw twice on the phone, and gave Grandpa a real smile. She had a visit from Courtney who did her nails and played violin for her. She also had a visit from Aunt Kate before she leaves for China. She had a visit from Dr. Patel and one of the surgeons. Whew! It's been a busy day for a little girl and all before 1:30 in the afternoon! She is resting now. I asked the occupational therapist to come back later if possible and the pca who wants to weigh her, too. She got to see Dee Dee last night and will get to see her later today, too. I know it sounds like she is doing incredibly well, but I want to caution you guys to be realistic. We are pushing her pretty hard. She is not just voluntarily doing most of this. Monroe and I both expected her to bounce back on her own more. So please don't think we are out of the woods yet. Okay, this next part is a little more graphic. Skip over it if you are squeamish or don't care to hear the yucky details. She still has a tube that runs from her stomach out of her nose that removes stomach secretions. Partly, we are getting her up and down more trying to get her g.i. tract moving. Literally, we need to see some bowel movement. They are waiting to see that before they will let her begin to taste and swallow. She is still on i.v. nourishment and fluid. So specific prayer requests include bowel movement (all you mothers out there understand this!), continued progress in physical, speech, and occupational therapy, and continued healing internally. We will have ct scans again tomorrow. Also pray for cooperation during that procedure. Whatever we do, we don't want to have to sedate her! (That is a joke, we won't sedate her!) Please pray specifically for Monroe as he attempts to resume a somewhat normal work schedule this week. Pray for stamina for me and endurance in keeping schedules moving for the other children. As always, I so appreciate the love and support of each one of you. Jeri P.S. Sorry for the long posting!

Jeri

One sweet memory I have of her recovery on the fourth floor is Courtney coming to play violin for McKenzie. Courtney has played violin from age 6. She has gone through many phases of practicing passionately or prioritizing other activities as more important (academics, sports, hanging out with friends). But this year of McKenzie's treatment, playing violin became an outlet for Courtney's emotions. She would rehearse for hours on end especially if she had a contest or audition approaching. It was so good for her to turn her raw emotions into a positive outlet. Of course, McKenzie had grown up hearing music pouring out of Courtney's room. McKenzie would sit and listen. She often played a little American Girls Dolls violin standing beside Courtney while her sister rehearsed. It was so cute to see. One day while McKenzie was recovering from surgery, Courtney asked if she could bring her violin to the hospital to play for her. I don't remember if we requested permission from the staff or not, but play she did. We chose an hour late in the morning when the fewest patients would be sleeping and she played for quite a while. It was a beautiful sight for the proud mama of two such special girls. I think McKenzie really enjoyed it and we had several comments from the staff of how much they enjoyed it, too. It was a special moment I will treasure forever.

Friday, June 13, 2008 6:44 AM, CDT

> *Good morning everyone. Well, it was a quiet night. We did have one major triumph last evening. McKenzie did have a bowel movement! I know, I dislike being so graphic, but I got a little excited about it. I was thinking, too, that years from now she will be mortified that I shared with the world that one night in June 2008 she went poopy! Oh well. I am just happy that I am able to think that she will survive to be mortified years from now. I have to share that many times over the past few weeks I wasn't so sure. God is good to let us have this precious baby for this long. We have some hurdles to clear today. I will share more later, but please pray that McKenzie will continue to improve and that she will be at*

home soon. As much as we love our 4th floor Hematology/ Oncology unit, there's no place like home. (Can't you just hear my heels clicking and see my blue gingham dress?) Love to all, Jeri

Monroe

It became increasingly obvious to Jeri and me, as we stayed longer and longer in the hospital that we might not be able to go home with the same child we had entered the hospital with. McKenzie had not bounced back. When we got her to the fourth floor, it was almost like she had regressed to being a one year old. She needed help with everything. Her speech was limited, her bathroom habits were not regular, and she had very little control. We worried that, perhaps, something had happened to her brain during the long surgery or the long stay in the PICU. In the back of my mind, I began to imagine what it would be like if we never did get to take her home. On top of everything else, there was a new problem that we had not shared with our family and friends.

Friday, June 13, 2008 9:18 PM, CDT

I am writing tonight as a really tired woman... Please pray for us. Monroe and I are barely holding it together. We are tired and stressed. We are tired of being stressed. We are stressed out about being tired. We just want our baby girl back the way she was before the surgery. We have one major problem that I haven't shared with you all. McKenzie is having vision problems. The doctor says that the vision is actually working fine, but the brain is not processing the vision. We can't, they say, do an MRI at this time to find out exactly what is going on because we can't sedate her. Besides, they really don't think there is anything to be done but wait and hope that she returns to normal. You know, that alone would not be the end of the world. But to pile that on top of all that going on in her little body is just too much to handle. We just want to scoop her up and bring her home. We want our family jigsaw puzzle put back together again. We are miserable this way. Please pray for this to end soon. We know that God will not allow us to be tested past what we can endure, but it sure feels like we can't endure anymore. As always, thank you for your prayers and support.

Jeri

I don't know to this day what Dr. Patel had to do to get her released because we were told it would not be allowed, but Monroe and I were convinced that she would heal so much better at home. So one day, Monroe called and said he was busting her out. There was no sweeter sight than him carrying her into the house at last! She was still so weak, still not speaking, and barely eating. But she was home! And so began the long road to real recovery.

This was a real low point spiritually for me. I did not feel capable of drawing any closer to God. I felt like I was stretched out bare before the altar face down. But, Jesus picked me up, held me close, and drew me closer. Somehow, my faith was strengthened.

Monroe

Finally, I could not take being in the hospital any longer. I have a strong dislike for all things cancer. My father passed away with pancreatic cancer, my grandmother with melanoma, my uncle with leukemia, and we have watched other family member battle breast cancer and prostate cancer. I do not like oncologists or hospitals! So finally after three weeks in the hospital and little recent improvement, I talked Dr. Patel, the one oncologist in the world that I trust and respect, into allowing us to go home.

My thoughts are that, with rest and with family and McKenzie being in her own room, she would improve more quickly than being in the hospital. And, worst-case scenario, we could always bring her back. So, after much discussion and a few threats, I informed the medical community that McKenzie and I would be checking out on Saturday morning. We did not get a bill under the door and a noon check out time, but we did get out!

LETTER TO MCKENZIE, FROM DAD-Personal Journal:
June 14th, 2008

Good morning, my sweet baby girl. We are beginning day number twenty in the hospital and things are progressing at a snail's pace. You have been up and moving around over the last two days and we are happy to see you walk. You are going to the bathroom regularly and you can hold liquids down. But the thing that frightens your mother and me is that you are not the same spunky little girl that we checked in with three weeks ago. You are not mentally sharp and you seem to have a hard time seeing and looking at people or television. We are still very concerned for you. We hope that things change soon.

Saturday, June 14, 2008 10:00 AM, CDT

I have three words for you: SHE'S COMING HOME! Yes, Monroe is busting her out of the Methodist Hospital! She is not whole. She is not complete. But she is all mine (thanks to God Who gave her to me!) and she will be home with her family. I think that will speed her healing like nothing else. Thank you for your prayers. I will keep you posted as things progress. Jeri

Jeri

From that point on, McKenzie had horrible nightmares. For the rest of her life, she rarely slept through an entire night without screaming for her daddy or me. Monroe and I slept at first on the floor in her room, then graduated to a recliner, and finally moved a second twin bed into her room. We tried many different things to ease her sleeping patterns- warm milk, Benadryl, and finally, a sweet little sleeping pill that Dr. Patel prescribed. That helped somewhat, but a full night's sleep was rare for McKenzie and rare for us.

Monroe

Over that same weekend, we got some great news from China. Everything had gone well and my sister and brother-in-law were the proud parents of an 18-month-old baby boy. Billy Wilson would be our newest member of the family and we were all anxious to get to meet him as soon as possible.

Monday, June 16, 2008 7:57 AM, CDT

Good morning everyone! The best news today this morning is that Monroe's sister, Kate, and her husband Russell have gotten their new baby Billy! Well, it has been a rough weekend with McKenzie, but better than being at the hospital. She is still not herself, although we do see glimpses of her now and again. She continues to have difficulty seeing, but I want to believe her vision is improving. It is hard to tell. Right now she is looking at pictures with Monroe, her brother. The worst part right now besides the lack of vision returning is the night time. She cries all night. She appears to be working out her anxieties by crying in her sleep. It is a constant whimper. She wants only Mama. The wanting Mama part was cute at first, but now not so much! Some of you have asked about bringing her favorite foods to the house. Because we busted her out of the hospital a little earlier than the doctor's were ready for, she is not on a regular diet yet. She has been having clear liquids only and finally added applesauce yesterday. Today, I will try some soft vegetables in her broth or maybe a porridge made with grits. The doctor said either one would be a good next step, but I can't decide which one she would dislike the least. She is enjoying popsicles and really loves chicken broth. Anything else would be too rough on her liver and pancreas. Both were beat up pretty bad during the surgery and are still healing. Well, now she is drawing with Monroe. Like I said, we see moments of hope. Please continue praying for her internal healing, her improved vision, and for endurance for Monroe and me. Thank you all. Jeri

Jeri

Surgery was a turning point in the way I viewed her treatment. My optimism was tainted during that process. Perhaps God used that to prepare me for what was to come. I was never quite as sure after that that we would have her forever. It scared me almost more than her original diagnosis. I pondered the question of her mortality deep in my heart. I questioned decisions about her medical care. Monroe always had and I was finally coming over to his way of thinking. I would not "cross over to the dark side" of viewing her medical care almost as torture for a while yet, but my way of thinking was definitely changing. I was not quite as optimistic as I used to be. Just like that long ago night at the lake house, I glimpsed what it would be like to be without McKenzie. But when she survived the surgery, my faith was strengthened.

Stem Cell Transplant

Jeri

So we brought our sweet baby home and walked the rocky road to recovery. As we suspected, she flourished in the comforts of home. She began eating slowly and doing a little more each day. We visited Dr. Patel regularly and he began whispering in our ears about Stem Cell Transplant. Back in March of that year, we had completed the Stem Cell harvest. The protocol called for an autologous stem cell transplant. This was one that would use McKenzie's own cells rather than those of a donor. There was less chance of rejection of the cells that way. So, she had been anesthetized and had a catheter inserted in her groin area. She was kept sedated while they removed the cells and spun them in a process called apheresis. This collected her healthiest cells (she'd already had three rounds of chemo at that point) and saved them for later transplant. Monroe and I began to question the wisdom of subjecting McKenzie to this upcoming process. You see, not only would they be transplanting the harvested cells, but also they would be subjecting her to "mega" doses of chemo prior to the transplant. We had seen five rounds of chemo (they were HORRIBLE) and almost lost her in the surgical process. Neither of us could imagine what "mega" doses of chemo would be like and we weren't really sure we wanted to follow through with this considering the high risk of losing her again. We kind of just wanted to lick our wounds and crawl away like a dog after losing a street fight. Although we hadn't actually lost the fight of surgery (they said they removed everything they could see or feel of the disease), we felt pretty beat up and this procedure was due to take place in just over a month. We just wanted some time with our baby to recover physically and emotionally. That was not to be. We were instructed by Dr. Patel to go and visit with the transplant doctor, who would be in charge of the transplant team. We visited his office where we had been before for blood transfusions. Monroe and I went alone. I left that visit with two things: 1. More knowledge of the stem cell procedure itself. It sounded horrible. They talked about how the chemo they would administer would completely shed all cells lining her gastrointestinal tract beginning with her mouth. They would call her transplant day "her new birthday" because the chemo administered would take her body to such a low point that it became like new birth. 2. An understanding that if we decided against the transplant we could be actually sued for neglect. This above all else made us angry. This was our daughter, we felt, and our decision. This poor little girl had been subjected to so much. Technically, she was already in remission, so why do this? We agonized over the decision. We spoke with Dr. Patel during our regular appointments. He so understood and explained, too, that without the stem cell transplant there was no doubt the cancer would return. So we eventually decided, very reluctantly, to move forward with the procedure.

Monday, June 23, 2008 10:04 AM, CDT

Good Monday morning everyone. Sorry to have not written through the weekend. We took a little family outing to the lake house and tried to forget about the realities of having a three year old with cancer for a while. She is doing amazingly well. I attribute it to the healing hand of God and your prayers. Let me give you some specifics. Her incision is healing well. Her vision seems to be improving (although it is sometimes hard to tell with a three-year-old.) Her appetite is good. Her spunkiness is evident. Her blood counts and liver enzymes are, according to the doctor, looking good. Over the weekend, we had some ups and some downs on nighttime sleeping. When she wakes up screaming and we can't get her to stop with any amount of comforting, it's bad. I was up with her for about an hour and a half at one time Friday night. She did sleep at her grandmother's house on Saturday night and I got a full night sleep in the same bed as my husband! You may think it sounds mundane, but it is the first time in over a month for me! Last night we were back at home and she did pretty well. She slept most of the night until about 5:30 this morning when she woke up and cried for me. So overall, she is doing well. She does tire easily and complains about the heat outdoors, but don't we all? That would be normal of anyone recovering from surgery as major as hers was. We are enjoying having our little girl coming back to us.

I take her back to Dr. Patel's office tomorrow for blood counts. I will let you know how that goes. Also, Monroe and I will be meeting on Thursday with Dr. Patel without McKenzie to begin talking about the stem cell transplant. That would be the next step. As you can imagine, Monroe and I are a bit gun shy about doing anything else to our baby. Please begin praying for us that we will get the information that we need to hear and make a wise decision. We rely heavily on Dr. Patel's advice and knowledge of statistics on McKenzie's condition. Once again, I am praying for God's wisdom in deciding on the best course of action for McKenzie.

Thank you all for coming along beside me in this journey of prayer and love for our little McKenzie Jo. With Love, Jeri

Friday, June 27, 2008 4:57 PM, CDT

Happy Friday everyone. It is a busy day as always here at Casa de May. I think summer is supposed to be more relaxed, but with three busy kiddos at home from school and a three-year-old fighting cancer it is anything but relaxed around here!

Well, Monroe and I met with Dr. Patel yesterday afternoon to get some more information about the stem cell transplant. The description he gave us is pretty serious. He also gave us some pretty grave statistics about the results of choosing not to do the transplant. We honestly have wondered if choosing quality of life for now would be better than risking losing her during another procedure. I've got to tell you- this is one of the toughest decisions I have had to make in my life. I am asking all of you to pray Psalm 143:8 for me, "Show me the way I should go..." I know that God is showing us.

Let me clarify the "quality of life" we are experiencing right now. I believe McKenzie's vision has recovered pretty well. Physically, she is feeling pretty strong. She wants to do normal kid things like go to the park, swim, and jump on the trampoline. We have taken her to the park, but she was worn out in about ten minutes. She goes onto the trampoline with other kids, but is tired of the heat in about five minutes. We haven't tried the swimming pool yet, but we may soon. Her greatest challenge (and ours) is nighttime sleep. She has been sleeping great during the day sometimes up to three hours. However, she has great difficulty going to sleep at night. Last night it was after midnight when she finally allowed me to sleep. When I woke up at 4:30am and tried to move to my bed, she screamed. Monroe tried to comfort her, but as always lately she refused to let him stay with her. We then went back to sleep and again at 6:15 when I tried to get up and leave, she woke up and screamed. Today, I have a new game plan- no nap! Sounds reasonable, right? We'll see. It's 5:20 now and she is a little fussy, but still awake. I am going to attempt to keep her awake until 8pm. We have tried Benadryl at bedtime with no result. Last night, we began something Dr. Patel suggested- melatonin. It obviously didn't help last night, but he says it may take up to three days to take effect. I hope it will take effect soon and that no naps will help her get her days and nights corrected. Well, that is all I can think of right now.

Once again, sorry for the long posting. As always, thank you for the prayers. Please continue praying for us as we contemplate the expected challenges of the stem cell transplant. We know that God is carrying us in the palm of His hand. With Love, Jeri

Monroe

After meeting with Dr. Patel, Jeri and I were even more confused as to what was in the best interest of McKenzie. I was amazed at the statistics that he shared with us. After all that she had been through and all the pain and suffering she had faced, she still had less then a 50% chance of a cure. This was difficult for Jeri and me to comprehend. The time, the energy, the fights to access her port, the watching and waiting, all for less than a 50/50 chance that she would be cured.

We were both very low at this point and very wary of putting our little princess through even more pain and suffering. And on top of everything else, we needed to make a decision over the weekend.

In the end, we decided as we had before, that we must choose life. After prayer and long talks, we both came to the conclusion that there really was no other choice; we had to keep pushing. So, we agreed to move ahead with the next treatment. We had to have faith that God would see that she survived this procedure, too.

Tuesday, July 1, 2008 6:45 PM, CDT

Hello everyone. Well, it's Tuesday now. I can't believe I haven't updated the website in so many days. I am not so vain to think you have all been sitting around checking your computers, but I have had several friends ask me what was going on. A combination of the older children being out of school (and keeping me running) and a series of technical challenges with my computer has kept me from updating. Anyway, here is what is happening with McKenzie: she continues to recover. We saw Dr. Patel today and her blood counts are fine. Her sleep schedule is improving a little. I am not sure if that is due to the melatonin we have been giving her or if it is due to keeping her awake all day and letting her have no nap. She is ready to go to sleep by 8 to 8:30 every evening. She is still waking two to three times at night. She cries for me and will not let Monroe stay with her. I am getting some sleep in my own bed at least in the first part of the night. We work hard all day to keep her awake. We take her to the pool, to the store, read her books, dress up, and watch all her favorite movies. It has been fun for her to be a normal kid with a normal white blood count.

It looks like that won't last long. Monroe and I have made the decision to move ahead with the stem cell transplant. With the odds against her being cured at all without it, we chose to allow the medical team to continue acting as God's healing tool. We will be talking soon to the transplant team and will let you know when we have some firm dates on the calendar. It is going to be a very long process. We will be in the hospital four to six weeks. That will seem an eternity for Monroe and me to be apart and for the children to always be away from one of us. It will most likely take up the rest of the summer for the other children. I need to thank all of you who have called or emailed and had the kiddos to do things with yours. That has been most helpful and will continue to be so as we head into this most difficult phase of treatment. Thank you, too, for all of the wonderful meal support. We are so grateful for your kindness and good grief, if you are willing to brave 281N or Bulverde Rd. anytime close to dinnertime, you are a true friend! I will let you know as I have more specific prayer requests, but for now simply pray for our family to keep healing emotionally so that we are at our best when we head into the hospital. Pray that God will ward off depression. Pray that we make the most of every moment- with her and with each other. I will update some pictures in the next day or so. If I don't get back to the computer before Friday, Happy Independence Day! With Love, Jeri

Monroe

We tried to make everyday and every event count! Whatever lay ahead in her fight, we did not want to have any regrets.

Sunday, July 6, 2008 5:28 PM, CDT

Good Sunday Evening Everyone,

Just a quick update: McKenzie and family have had a great 4th of July weekend. We ventured to the lake and we all had good time. Grandparents, cousins and aunts and uncles spent the 4th together and McKenzie even stayed up late to see the fireworks over the water from the boat. She swam, did water balloons, and got to be a regular three-year-old for a while and this afternoon she went to her cousin Rusty's birthday party and got to meet her new cousin, Billy. We are thankful for all the weekend events.

This week, we will have a doctor's appointment with Dr. Patel and begin to prepare mentally for the coming weeks. Please continue your prayers for sleep. She still wakes often and can only be comforted by Jeri. Jeri needs strength and rest and so does McKenzie.

Thank you all for your continued prayers and support.- Monroe

Monroe
LETTER TO MCKENZIE, FROM DAD-Personal Journal:
July 10th, 2008

We are in between treatments right now and you have been out of the hospital almost 3 weeks. Next week we will begin meeting with the transplant doctor to prepare for the Mega Chemo and Stem Cell transplant. Your mother and I are very worried about this next phase and are both dreading what is ahead. Dr. Patel told us to expect 3-6 weeks in the Hospital and this scares me to death. The good news is that over the last couple of weeks you have begun sleeping through the night and you have been able to return to some of the fun things you used to love. You have been swimming, to the lake, to the movies and yesterday you even were able to have Drew's little sister Haley over to play. These are all huge blessing. We were not sure we would ever be able to return to "normal life". We love you very much and want you to be cured. Time will tell. Be strong and know that you are loved.

We believed that every procedure brought us closer to healing and the normal life we so desired.

Friday, July 11, 2008 2:53 PM, CDT

It is Friday and we have made it through another week. Jeri has ventured to Lubbock this weekend to pick up Courtney from Orchestra Camp at Texas Tech and they will be home tomorrow. Hopefully she can get a little rest tonight..

We had a doctor's appointment on Thursday and counts were good. We will meet with the Stem Cell physician on Tuesday of next week to confirm plans for the Transplant. So, for now we are all just enjoying being away from the hospital and having normal summer days.

McKenzie is sleeping much better during the nights and this is truly a blessing, so thank you all for your continued prayers.

Take care and have a great weekend. We will update again next week after the next round of doctor's appointments. -Monroe

Monday, July 14, 2008 8:24 PM, CDT

Hi everyone. It's Monday evening and I wanted to give you all an update on the plan for the stem cell transplant. We met with the BMT team today. No big surprise really, but here is the game plan. I will take McKenzie in tomorrow for some blood work and a quick examination. I am also supposed to take a urine sample that we are having a difficult time obtaining this evening. Then we will admit her at the Methodist next Monday evening. She will have 4 days of continuous chemo drugs, more than she has ever had. Three days following the chemo, they will give her the stem cells that were collected last March. Then we will continue to stay in the hospital until she has a white blood count, is eating, and not vomiting. It may be 2 weeks, it may be 4 weeks. So that is the big picture. I will continue to fill you in on the details as we go. We have not really told McKenzie much. She knows she will have to go back into the hospital, but she doesn't know when or for how long. Please pray for us as we prepare her and her brother and sisters for this possibly long process. Pray for strength and for God's best outcome in the procedure. Please pray for Monroe and me as we prepare to be away from each other only seeing one another in the hospital daily when we shift change. Thank you my friends. Talk to you soon, Jeri

Monroe

Once again, we all had to prepare mentally for what was ahead. It took a great deal of coordination with family and friends to keep the home front running well and all the parts moving. Courtney, Caroline and Monroe had to be taken care of. Jeri and I knew that a new school year was just around the corner. Courtney would be starting her freshman year at Johnson High School, Caroline would be starting Middle School at Tejeda, and Monroe would be moving into second grade.

So, one of the many challenges, during this hospital stay, would be getting everyone ready for the new school year, as well as spending twenty-four hours a day with McKenzie. Oh yeah, and I had to work. My company was very understanding; however, they did expect me to continue to run my region.

We all learned to expect the unexpected, and with that in mind, just took things one day at a time.

Jeri

In between the decision to move forward on the stem cell transplant and checking into the hospital, we had a little bump in the road. McKenzie spiked a fever and went on four days of I.V. fluids and antibiotics. This set back the transplant a week. Also during that week, we had difficulty with her top port access. It was decided that if the top port didn't work when we went in for the transplant that a central line would have to be surgically implanted. That was a worst-case scenario for us considering the difficulty we'd had waking her from anesthesia following surgery. So we began to pray that the top port would cooperate enough to get us through the transplant.

Thursday, July 17, 2008 4:47 PM, CDT

To quote the movie Apollo 13, "Houston, we have a problem." McKenzie began running fever last night. We went in to Dr. Patel's office today and her white blood count is way up indicating an infection somewhere. She has had a runny nose lately, but clear. We did blood and urine cultures and should know more specifics by tomorrow. He has put her on I.V. antibiotics for three days and we are carrying around a backpack with fluids for at least forty-eight hours. And the worst part is that **transplant will be delayed at least a week.** *I will let you know more as we find out.* **Jeri**

Monday, July 21, 2008 7:38 AM, CDT

Hello everyone. Happy Monday! Well, we made it through the weekend. Monroe barely escaped the weekend! He stayed home with the younger children while I took Courtney to Georgetown, TX for a basketball tournament. That would normally not be so bad for him, but with McKenzie on I.V. fluids it made it extremely difficult for him. The fact that McKenzie continually cried for me didn't make it any easier either. Anyway, she received four days of I.V. antibiotics and fluids. We go back into the doctor this morning to see what the next step is. I will let you know something as soon as I know something. Pray for God's perfect timing in regard to the stem cell transplant. Thanks and have a great week! Jeri

Monroe

So after another temporary setback, we once again prepared for "mega dose chemo" and the stem cell transplant. We had no idea what was ahead. Looking back, that was a blessing most of time; ignorance is not always a bad thing.

Friday, July 25, 2008 3:42 PM, CDT

We went to see the doctor today and what a praise we have, McKenzie's port worked as it should. The office was able to get a blood return, so we are good to go on Monday.

On Monday afternoon, Jeri and McKenzie will check into the hospital and on Tuesday morning McKenzie will begin ninety-six hours of "mega dose chemo." She will finish this on Friday afternoon and then on the following Tuesday she will receive her Stem Cell Transplant. We are planning on being in the Hospital a minimum of three weeks.

So the good news is that McKenzie is healthy enough to be admitted to the Hospital.... (Ha, Ha)

Have a good weekend, and we will begin updating next week as we begin the next phase of this journey.-Monroe

Monday, July 28, 2008 6:39 AM, CDT

Well, today is the big day. We will admit to the hospital this afternoon. We haven't told McKenzie yet. We just really wanted her to sleep well and have as much a normal day as possible. She spent the weekend with her grandmother at the lake and we went up yesterday and took her for a boat ride. She has a friend coming over this morning to play. So pray for us to be break it to her in just the right way and that she will not take it too hard. Pray for us all to be strengthened as we go into this procedure which we hope will be our last big one. Thank you all my dear family and friends, Jeri

Jeri

We checked into the hospital with the expectation that we would be there at least three weeks. The procedure itself would only take about a week, but she would need to stay in the hospital until her white blood count appeared, she was eating, and not vomiting. Of course, with her white blood system being wiped out completely, she was in complete isolation. She could have no visitors except us, her parents, and maybe her siblings and grandparents if they were completely healthy. We did manage to sneak in a couple cousins and aunts and uncles, but family only. We praised God when both ports worked. They began the chemo drugs on a Tuesday and finished on Friday. She experienced very little nausea at first because they had begun to figure out what combination of drugs worked with her and occasionally listened to us about which drugs had ill effects on her. I often got the feeling that the medical staff in general was not used to dealing with intelligent, educated parents. It seemed that most parents just went along with whatever they said or did. I guess we were exceptional and I know McKenzie was an exceptional patient. It was difficult to entertain her for that first week. She didn't feel all that bad and certainly didn't want to stay in bed and just watch movies.

But, as time went on, she declined. Just as they had predicted, she began feeling awful. She received the stem cell transplant on Tuesday, August 5th- her "new" birthday which happened to fall on my brother's birthday. She continued to go downhill. She didn't speak because everything in her mouth, throat, and everywhere else hurt. She didn't communicate except when she cried. She spiked a fever and had to have heavy antibiotics. She was fed intravenously. She was on all kinds of monitors- heart, pulse/oxygen saturation, and blood pressure. It was so hard to watch. The new cells were supposed to start building her back up, but it was an extremely slow process.

Tuesday, July 29, 2008 11:02 AM, CDT

Good morning everyone. Well, we have begun the chemo. We arrived yesterday afternoon and were admitted and put on I.V. fluids. The first room they put us in was very small. I asked for a bed for Monroe or me (whoever is here on any given night) and they said they would be glad to bring one in, but they would have to remove the chair from the room. That would be uncomfortable to only sit on the bed for the whole month that we plan to stay, don't you think?! Fortunately, a larger room became available. Unfortunately, we had to move at midnight! McKenzie fussed through the move, but we finally got her settled. She slept until about 7am (after being woken up at 4am to take her vital signs, of course!) and then we began chemo about 9am. So far, she has shown no signs of nausea. Thank you for your prayer cover. I was going to tell you, too, that she woke up yesterday morning at home and asked me if she would be able to play with her friend before she went to the hospital. I never really had to tell her that we were coming. I guess we had talked enough about it that she already knew. She has been in a good mood this morning and is now getting a bit fussy. She is hungry for her favorite foods like always- pineapple and popcorn. So please pray for continued no nausea and fortitude for her. Pray for strength for Monroe and me. Thank you with love, Jeri

Wednesday, July 30, 2008 9:47 PM, CDT

Hello everyone. Well, it has been an okay day with McKenzie. She has had a little more nausea today than yesterday. She did have a pleasant surprise when her sister, Courtney, visited today. She is her usual spunky self. The staff is working hard to find creative ways of getting her to cooperate. She does her best, but having your vital signs taken every four hours, taking oral medications when you are vomiting, and having your bodily fluids measured is not fun! Unfortunately, with this type of heavy chemo, we have no choice but to keep a close eye on her blood pressure, temperature, and pulse/ox. If one of those areas fluctuates slightly, it could indicate a major problem in her little body. We believe that God is enabling her to sail through this, but we must take every precaution. Bill Cosby's "Little Bill" off Nickelodeon has become her new favorite show. We watch it over and over again. I guess it is better than "Annie". I finally was able to convince her this evening to change nightgowns after three days. As soon as she did, the nurse brought in her medication. I walked across the room and she squirted the pink medicine all over herself- in her hair, on her clean nightgown, on the wall, and all over the bed. It was another mess to clean up, but kind of funny. Well, she is watching TV and is comfortable right now. I am hoping for a little sleep soon. Pray for that for me tonight and for Monroe tomorrow night! Pray for no more nausea than we've seen so far. Pray for strength and endurance for the family. Thank you and good night. With Love from Jeri

Thursday, July 31, 2008 6:12 PM, CDT

Good Evening Everyone,

We just finished another viewing of "Little Bill" the preferred video for this hospital stay. Miss McKenzie has had several visitors over the last two days: Cousin Billy and Uncle Russell, sisters Courtney and Caroline, Grandmother Dee Dee and Uncle Blake. This seemed to make her happy. So, thank you for coming by.

The nausea has continued, however, the medical community seems pleased with her progress, her counts and her general well being (there is a contradiction in terms).

Our biggest challenge is to keep her happy and cooperative. She has to take some oral medication and this is always a challenge. The other challenge is what to do with a three year old, trapped in a small hospital room, when she does not always feel bad enough to stay in bed. Fun and games... Childlife Services brought us window paint so we are decorating the hospital one window at a time.

At this point, we have to let the drugs take their course then see how her body will react with the new stem cells. IV's, chemo drugs, and stem cells, stuck in a Hospital with no discharge date in site. There might be a country song in there somewhere. I will work on it....

Take care, hug your children, kiss your spouse, and be thankful for all you have. -Monroe

Saturday, August 2, 2008 2:09 PM, CDT

Hello all. Well, it is Saturday afternoon. As Monroe says, "we are in good shape for the shape we are in.". The last time she was sick was 10am yesterday morning. I began praying earnestly about that time that God would allow her to have no more nausea. He has answered my prayer and those of all of you praying, too! Thank you. Last night, my mother slept over with McKenzie giving Monroe and I a night at home together and each of us will get two nights in a row in our own bed, too! This morning when I walked in, McKenzie had decided that she wanted cheese pizza and was sitting here eating for the first time in a couple of days. So far, that has at least stayed down for a few hours. I see that as a good sign. She is officially done with the chemo drugs. The doctor says they will continue to knock her blood counts down over the next several days. Right now, she is pretty exhausted and is resting. She also got to do glitter with one of the child life team members this morning and they had a lady bring in a certified visiting dog to pet. Please continue praying for no nausea. Please continue praying for Monroe and I strength and endurance. Thank you! Jeri

Monroe

My grandfather, who was also named Monroe May, always had a way with words. One of my favorite sayings that he used was "I'm in pretty good shape for the shape I'm in." I always liked this phrase coming from a diabetic, partially blind man who had lost his wife to cancer, son to cancer, granddaughter in a car wreck, and was the last living member of his family. The man had lived through a lot and still managed a positive attitude and an active life. I learned a lot about living from all of my grandparents.

Monday, August 4, 2008 8:28 AM, CDT

One week down, and this morning McKenzie is planning her exit strategy. She has decided she will wear her bow dress, white sandals and ride in my truck. As soon as we get home she will play dress up, jump on the trampoline, and then watch "E.T.". We have been discussing this since late yesterday afternoon and she has thought it ALL OUT. I just keep telling her soon, soon.

Tomorrow, we will do the stem cell transplant and then wait and see what happens. The doctor keeps telling us that the road ahead will be rough; Jeri and I are hoping for the best and preparing for the worst. I would like to think that it will not be as bad as everyone says. Time will tell.

Today's schedule is movies, followed by movies, and maybe if we have time we will watch a movie. Oh yeah, and probably make a trip to the restroom.

Take care and have a good day. We will keep you posted. Monroe

Tuesday, August 5, 2008 6:36 AM, CDT

Good Morning! Today is the big day- the stem cell transplant. McKenzie is not really aware that anything of consequence is happening. One of the nurses mentioned last night that we should have a party like a birthday party for her and McKenzie looked at her and then me strangely. To her, it is just another day in the hospital. She just wants to go home. We had the traumatic weekly needle change last night. That is always hard. I would do anything to take her place. She is sleeping still this morning. We had a pretty quiet night. Thank you all for your constant prayers and support. I feel connected to each one of you because of the phone, the email, and this website. The day is dawning outside. Pray for us and I will pray for all of you, too. Go out and make it a great day! With Love, Jeri

Tuesday, August 5, 2008 7:08 PM, CDT

I wanted to share a couple of things from today. First, the transplant went well and was over in about an hour. It was just like getting a blood transfusion. The doctor spoke with Jeri and me and explained that from here on it is a matter of waiting for McKenzie to recover from the chemotherapy from last week. He said the fastest he has ever had a patient recover is in nine days from the transplant. So that would be one prayer request: Pray that she breaks the record.

The doctor also warned us that the days ahead might be challenging with discomfort, infections, diarrhea and nausea. All this is caused from the chemo. So, we are prepared for the worst. However, we are praying for the best. So, the second prayer request would be that McKenzie sails through the next seven days with as few complications as possible.

Finally, just a funny story to show that McKenzie is still herself: This afternoon the doctor walked in the room, right after she had gotten sick in the toilet. She looked at him and told him he could go ahead and empty the potty and then leave. We all laughed. Then she finished the conversation by telling him he was free to go and we would call him if we needed anything else.

The girl still has spunk. -Monroe

Thursday, August 7, 2008 11:33 AM, CDT

Hello everyone. I am struggling with what to tell you all about how McKenzie is doing. I could say she is okay and you would all rejoice and she kind of is okay and you should all rejoice. But, I don't want you to get the wrong idea. She isn't laying here feeling okay, she feels awful. She is running a mild fever- 99 degrees or so. It is not severe enough for them to begin the heavy-duty antibiotics, but the doctor says he thinks the fever will increase and we will have to do that in the next twelve to twenty-four hours. Her mouth hurts because she has Mucusitis, but once again her case is mild. She has barely a white blood count, but they expect that to go away, too, within the next twenty-four hours. She just generally feels awful. But, everything is going as expected. She is functioning well for a transplant patient. She is monitored constantly for fever, increased blood pressure, and pulse/ox levels. We are working to try to get her some reasonable rest at night, but so far that is not happening. Please continue praying for her to begin recovering as soon as possible. Please pray for Monroe and me because we are beginning to feel the effects of balancing her needs, the needs of the other children, and our own needs. Thank you, With Love, Jeri

Jeri

We understood that she needed constant monitoring of her breathing and heart rate, but struggled to see why the nursing staff could not allow her to sleep when it was apparent to us that rest would only help the healing process. It became a battle between the night nursing staff and us, especially Monroe. He begged them to allow her a little more sleep when her monitors showed nothing amiss, but they were indignant. They insisted that they must have further vital information. We spoke to supervisors, but nothing helped. We so loved the day staff, but came to dislike the night staff. It was just another reason to pray for her to recover quickly and get home to rehabilitate.

Friday, August 8, 2008 1:50 PM, CDT

Hello everyone. I don't even know where to start today. I guess I will start with McKenzie's condition. She is doing okay. Just like yesterday, don't think she is sitting here having a party, but she is stable. Everything that the doctor expected to happen has happened. Her fever continued upward late yesterday so they did begin the heavy-duty antibiotics. Her heart rate was elevated today, so they are monitoring it carefully. She feels pretty cruddy. She is not eating or drinking. She is receiving nutrition intravenously. Her white blood count is non-existent. Her platelets are very low today and she will be receiving platelets (just like a blood transfusion) in a few minutes. So please continue praying for her body to recover from the chemo.

The next part is hard for me to write. Monroe and I are both **very frustrated** *with some of the care that McKenzie is receiving. The frustration that we feel is with the night staff caring for her seems unwilling to let her sleep. Yes, I know many of you have faced similar situations while hospital bound yourself or with a loved one. There is no rest for the weary, so to speak. We have tried asking the staff to let her sleep, but they are adamant that they must continually wake her for different reasons. We have even tried speaking to supervisors to no avail. The one woman we have spoken to for the last two days is unyielding. She badly wants us to "understand their position", but is unwilling to be flexible. Monroe and I are past trying to reason with them. We have spoken to the doctors, but they are no help either. The day staff is incredible, but the night staff, while proficient, is deficient in flexibility. When someone is sick, what do they need more than anything? Rest is the best answer I can think of. Monroe is questioning our decision to proceed here at Methodist instead of further considering St. Jude's or another facility. So please pray for us. Pray that voicing our concerns will not further make the situation worse. We don't want to be a target of the nursing administration; we just want our daughter to get some rest enabling her to heal. Please continue to pray that she will heal quickly so that we can go home! Thank you all, Jeri*

Jeri

We had considered other care facilities. We had many friends and family members who suggested that we, at least, explore other treatment options. We had been in contact with St. Jude's to compare treatment protocol. It was identical to the protocol we were following. There seemed no reason to uproot her from her hometown to follow an identical treatment, so we continued our current course.

Monroe

LETTER TO MCKENZIE, FROM DAD-Personal Journal:

August 9, 2008

It has been a rough last two weeks. You finished your chemo last Saturday and then on Tuesday, August 5th you received your BMT treatment. Since then your counts are low, low, low and you have been very sick. In addition, on Thursday night you spiked a fever and are now on antibiotics. You do not feel good. It is so difficult to watch you have to go through all of this. I hope and pray that as you grow up, you will have very little memory of any of this. Last night, Meemaw stayed with you and I know that you appreciated her being here. Dee Dee comes by almost very day to stay with you while Mommy or Daddy goes to grab something to eat. You are loved by all. You have had almost 60,000 hits on your web site and people continue to shower you in Prayer. Hang in there; I have to believe that you will turn the corner soon.

As a father, there is no way to prepare your heart and mind for the battle of cancer with your child. Fathers are supposed to protect and take care of their children and do all that they can to defend them. The things McKenzie was forced to do and withstand with very little understanding of why was almost more than I could take. I loved my daughter, but watching, waiting and caring for this sick little girl, took a toll on me to my very core.

Sunday, August 10, 2008 2:16 PM, CDT

Hello everyone. It's a quiet Sunday afternoon here in the hospital room. That is kind of nice. In between McKenzie feeling nauseous or heading to the bathroom, I am able to watch a movie or read a book quietly. I wish I could give a good report on McK's progress, but we really have not turned the bend yet. Last night about 9pm, her oxygen saturation level was dropping so they did a chest x-ray. They saw spots on her lungs, but are not calling it pneumonia. They are treating it as they would pneumonia with antibiotics and trying to administer oxygen. She really hates the oxygen. They like it when she gets mad because she tends to take deeper breaths and that improves her oxygen saturation level. They are monitoring her very closely and trying hard to keep her comfortable. That is difficult because of the nausea and the sores in her mouth. The only bright spot is that I think we are seeing the diarrhea less often and of course the big bright spot is that we are not in the PICU. Okay, you can call me "Pollyanna". I wear the title proudly. Please keep praying for her to begin the road to recovery. I must believe that today will be the worst day and that tomorrow we will begin to see improvement. Either way, I know that God has His Mighty Hand on her. He loves her so much. He loves her more than I do. It's hard to believe, but I hold to that Truth. May He richly bless you all on this beautiful sunny Sunday afternoon and through the night. With His Love and mine, Jeri

Jeri

We watched her for twenty days lay in that hospital bed before we saw any significant rebound of her white blood count. Around the nineteenth day, she whispered a few words and slowly began to sip water an ounce at a time. We watched her survive possible pneumonia with spots on her lungs and treated her with more antibiotics. We watched them give her the hated IPV breathing treatments again and watched her fight every step of the way. We watched her receive transfusions of blood and platelets. We watched her precious hair fall out AGAIN. It was agonizing for her and for us.

Somewhere around the eighteenth day, the top port again quit working. We talked them into working without it as the only other option was surgically implanting a central line.

Tuesday, August 12, 2008 1:38 PM, CDT

It looks like today is the day we have been waiting for, McKenzie actually has a White Blood Count! Although it is still low they are not using the term "false positive" any longer. She has still had to have a blood transfusion and platelet transfusion today, however, I am encouraged that she is finally starting to move in the right direction.

However, please realize that she is not doing cart-wheels across the floor or leaping off the bed. She is however, speaking softly and moving around more than she has in the last two weeks.

Everyday brings new challenges of things we knew to expect, however still do not like to see. Yesterday McKenzie began loosing her hair again. It had grown quite bit in the last two months, so it is no fun watching it fall out again. She is still as beautiful as ever even with no hair.

We are not out of the woods yet, however, maybe we are no longer running deeper into the forest.

Thank you for all the continued support.-Monroe

Wednesday, August 13, 2008 8:14 AM, CDT

GOOD MORNING EVERYONE! Psalm 33:1 says, "Sing joyfully to the Lord, you righteous; it is fitting for the upright to praise him." Well, this morning we definitely have something to sing joyfully about (and McKenzie is sitting "upright" from time to time). MCKENZIE'S WHITE BLOOD COUNT IS 1.7! Yeah!!!!! She is still not turning cartwheels as Monroe says, but we are definitely seeing improvement. She is drinking water an ounce at a time. She is finally talking and even singing along a little to Annie. We do still have a challenge with fever and high heart rate. Oh and I do have one big prayer request: **As of Monday evening, McKenzie's top port has not been working and I would really like everyone to pray that we are able to reposition the needle today and get it working.** *She will not lay still for it, but it must be done. So, we are obviously not walking out of here today. But, you can pray that she begins eating a little bit and that would speed things along. Thank you all so much for your support and prayers. With Love, Jeri*

Monroe

LETTER TO MCKENZIE, FROM DAD-Personal Journal:

August 15th, 2008

It is very early on Friday morning and it is my night at the hospital. This is day nineteen in the Methodist and your mother and I are very tired. As you know, we take turns spending the night and on the nights at the hospital there is really no sleep. The nurses come in and disturb you CONSTANTLY so we are all weary from the disruption. McKenzie, I just want you to jump out of bed and get moving. It is so frustrating to sit and watch you lay in bed. You are beginning to talk a little more and most of your stats seem to be improving. WE love you and look forward to seeing you jump on the trampoline and play. I miss having you at home as well as being at home with the family. This is so hard on so many levels. I hope we have done the right thing for you and for the family.

Friday, August 15, 2008 1:47 PM, CDT

Wait! Stop the presses! This just in! McK may get to go home tomorrow! Yes, Monroe called me this morning to say that the doctor was making plans that way. So far, she has been disconnected from all I.V. fluids and has been walking around the Hematology/Oncology Unit to regain her strength. Also, her brother and sisters came to visit today! She sat up and laughed and talked with them. The girls colored a picture with her. We all ate lunch in front of her in hopes of encouraging her appetite. That didn't work except she did eat half a pretzel. She mainly needs to be drinking and drinking and drinking. The appetite will return. Her white count did not decrease today as they expected, but rather jumped up to 8.6! She did not need platelets as expected, but even if she needs them tomorrow, that should not stop us from going home. Right now, she is watching Annie and sleeping. I still maintain that rest is her best medicine for now. She will recover so much quicker if we can get her home to her own bed and sofa surrounded by her family and her pets. Her hair is gone with the exception of a couple of tufts. Monroe is threatening to shave the rest. We'll see- only if she wants to. I think it will fall off when I can get her home and into the tub for a thorough bubble bath! She does still have eyelashes and eyebrows, but I am not determined that she will keep them. **So please pray that she keeps drinking and drinking and drinking. Pray that no fever creeps up and that she keeps moving around well. Pray for protection from viruses as her immune system is still compromised and will be for some time.** *Thank you my wonderful friends and family. With Love, Jeri*

Saturday, August 16, 2008 1:09 PM, CDT

Praise God from whom ALL blessings flow... McKenzie came home today after twenty days in the hospital. We are all celebrating her arrival and are so excited to see her IV Free.

We have been challenged to keep her drinking clear liquids between now and tomorrow morning. On Sunday morning she will have to go back to the Methodist for some blood work, and if all is still well we will be free from the BMT unit.

We are still not sure what is next, however we are rejoicing in today's blessing.

We will keep you updated. Monroe

Monroe

This time when we brought our baby home, I had a new sense of hope. McKenzie had survived the harshest treatment there is for her disease. She had endured six rounds of chemo that was thirty different treatments. She had gone through a stem cell harvest and transplant, she had spent almost three months out of the last seven and a half months in the hospital, and countless blood draws. And the good news was that she was now officially in remission and we had one week to prepare Courtney, Caroline and Monroe for the first day of school. It was time for more changes to be made. But the good news was she came home!

Jeri

On the twenty-first day, we praised God as she was able to go home! We knew she again had a long road to recovery, but there was no place where she ran that race better than at home surrounded by those who loved her. We began strongly "encouraging" her to drink fluids constantly. It was a difficult battle to fight with a strong willed three-year old. But, as always, it was that iron clad will that got her through. We let her try anything to eat that sounded appealing. She would often try something and then spit it out, even all her old favorites. It was finally three weeks post transplant when I was actually able to report that she was slowly beginning to eat and gain strength. Her blood counts took FOREVER to rebound, or so it seemed. It made me happy when Dr. Patel began to talk of "now that treatment is complete and she is in remission" we would do this or that. The older kids went back to school and we began to think about McKenzie even attending preschool that fall. Very slowly, life began to inch back toward normal, or at least, our new normal. It would be a false reassurance, but we would not know that for a while.

Monday, August 18, 2008 12:24 PM, CDT

Greetings from rainy San Antonio- yes! I said "rainy"! We are getting some much needed rain here today! We had a pretty good weekend with McKenzie. Of course, getting her home was a wonderful part of the weekend. I had to take her back yesterday to the hospital for counts and fluid balance check. That was very hard- she did not want to go! However, she did not need fluids so after a couple of hours of waiting, they were able to de-access her and we came home. She is asking for different types of foods, but is taking a taste of things and then spitting them out. Nothing tastes good, she says. So we just keep trying whatever she asks for. We also have to force her to continue to drink, drink, and drink. She is back to needing someone to sleep in her room with her. That is understandable after having someone in the room with her for three weeks in the hospital. Last night, she did go to sleep by herself (I was standing there, but she just fell asleep and then I left) and she slept for a couple of hours before waking up and crying. She actually let Monroe comfort her and stay with her. That was nice for me to sleep in my own bed. She still seems so fragile, but I guess that is to be expected. Please continue praying for her recovery. Please pray that Monroe and I will be strong for her and the other children as we make our way back to "normal" lives. McKenzie will return to Dr. Patel's care tomorrow. We will let you what is next as soon as we know...Thank you for your continued prayers. With Love, Jeri

Jeri

The rain San Antonio received offered relief from a long drought. It was symbolic of the drought we'd been enduring emotionally. We had little hope, but the rain helped.

Monroe

LETTER TO MCKENZIE, FROM DAD-Personal Journal:

August 19th, 2008

Today, we went back to Dr. Patel and found out what is next. You have survived through the worst and most aggressive treatment that is available for Neuroblastoma and have come through it amazingly well. We went home last Saturday Aug. 16th and now we will wait and see what is next. McKenzie, you have beaten the odds to this point and now we will hope and pray that all of the knowledge of the Dr. has been correct and that a cure will turn to reality. Only time will tell. Over the weekend we contacted Make-A-Wish and the plan has been set in motion to get you your trip to Disney World. Your journey is not complete and will continue for months and years ahead. We will take it one day at a time and love you, and Courtney, and Caroline and Monroe as we always have. Your have brought the family together in ways none of us could have imagined. We are still committed to getting through this the best we can and keeping our family intact. Fight, fight, fight, and don't let the red-eyed monster win. I love you McKenzie.

- Diagnosis- Stage IV Neuroblastoma, with cancer in the bones.
- Five rounds of chemo- each round four to five days long with I.V.'s at home around the clock.

- Side effects of vomiting and diarrhea over and over again.
- Five trips to the Hospital.
- One surgery for port placement and biopsy.
- One surgery lasting 10 ½ hours for removal of the tumor.
- Two weeks in the PICU for complications.
- Mega-dose chemo for four days around the clock.
- Bone Marrow Transplant for bone cancer.
- Countless CT scans and bone scans.
- Countless blood draws.
- Countless antibiotics.
- Over 95,000 hits on your website.
- Prayers around the world.
- One more day with your family- **PRICELESS**.

You are a walking miracle. Thank you, God, for McKenzie.

Wednesday, August 20, 2008 4:47 PM, CDT

Hello and Happy Wednesday everyone! Just a little update on McKenzie- I will try to keep it short. We went to see Dr. Patel yesterday morning. Her white count is 3.4- not bad; definitely all her own body's producing. We will still need to keep her protected from "germ-y" places (we are not taking her out in public yet) and "germ-y" people (please don't come to visit if you have the least sore throat or runny nose). She did not need platelets or blood. That was good. What she does need is to begin eating. She is drinking liquids pretty well, but still really not eating. She is extremely skinny looking right now. I think she has grown a little taller and overall has lost a few pounds. Her little arms and legs look like twigs. She will mention things that sound good and we get them as fast as humanly possible. But then she will make some excuse about why she doesn't want it- it's too hot or cold or whatever. She has taken a few bites of different things, but it isn't much. **Please pray that she will begin eating regularly soon.**

Now the good news: Dr. Patel says that technically she is in remission. There is no known disease in her little body. We will be giving her 4-6 weeks to completely recover from the transplant and then we will do some scans to double check. **Please pray that she has no evidence of disease when we do those scans.** *Also, this fall, Dr. Patel says that she will be able to begin reentering normal kid situations like preschool.*

So, some good news, some bad news here. Please keep us in your prayers. Thank you so much. Jeri

Friday, August 22, 2008 10:04 AM, CDT

Hello everyone. Friday today, Happy Weekend. Are most of you getting your children ready to start school next week like we are? We got to go to a pep rally last night for the new high school where Courtney will attend. Monroe and I can't believe we are old enough to have a high school age daughter! McKenzie got to go stay with Meemaw and Grandpa while we did that. Even Meemaw was not able to talk her into eating... We are still jumping up and getting whatever she asks for, but she will just take a bite or refuse it after we do. She has had some nausea and the doctor is putting her back onto Zofran for that. At least she is still drinking fluids well. **Please continue praying that she will begin eating soon.** *With Love, Jeri*

Wednesday, August 27, 2008 10:13 AM, CDT

Hello everyone! I may be lengthy today, so if you have lots to do, come back to me later, okay? I am sorry I haven't updated in the last few days, but of course school has begun and I have been trapped under a load of heavy paperwork. If you have a child in public school or have in the past, you know what I am talking about. There are so many papers to fill out and return! I am doing that for all 3 of McKenzie's older siblings, so I have been quite busy! We have also attended multiple open houses and emailed a few staff members. McK is glad to have the TV to herself now that they are gone all day, but I think she is missing them, too.

Now about how she is doing: First, the praise- she is eating! She began on Saturday to ask for things and then actually eat some of them. She is not winning any pie eating contests, but she is taking a few bites at a time and even ate most of a peanut butter sandwich yesterday! She is so skinny! I want to do my best Italian grandmother voice and say "EAT!", but she will at her own pace. Also, praise about her activity level- as she begins to eat, she has more energy to be up and about. For so many days, she just lay on the sofa and slept. It was depressing to see her that way. But as you guys can see from the new pictures that I posted, she is starting to move around more. Just like the pie eating contests, she is not winning any marathons, but she does have some short periods of time when she is actually energetic. Then she crashes. Yesterday, I actually took her to the Disney Store with Meemaw to get her new Ariel the Little Mermaid costume. She got so excited that she got sick in the car on the way home and then came home and slept for two hours. But, it was worth it. The only thing she didn't get was the red wig and only because they didn't have one! I will pick one up soon, don't run out and buy her one!

Now, for the "not as good" news: we were at Dr. Patel's office yesterday and her counts are not recovering yet. Her white count is the same as last week and her platelets and hemoglobin were okay, so it is really not bad news. But her "gran" was 0.9; it is still just slowly beginning to recover. **Please pray that her counts will begin to recover in a mighty way over the next week.** *I can accept that it will take time; I just don't want her to regress. She wants to do so much more, but her little body is holding her back! She is laying here next to me watching "Little Bill". She is begging to play with a friend, but doesn't have the energy to get up off the sofa. She is still not sleeping really well at night. Some nights she sleeps by herself until 2 or 3am; other nights it is only until 10:30pm. Monroe and I still take turns going in and sleeping in the extra twin bed in her room. At least we are blessed to have an extra bed! But there is nothing like getting to sleep all night in your own bed.* **So, please pray that she will soon begin sleeping all night without crying for us.**

Okay, next I am going to do some theologizing. I give you permission to skim, skip, or just dive into some of my inner thoughts. I still question God as to why He allowed this to happen to us. Yesterday, I found part of His answer. It is in 2 Corinthians 1:3-11. Here it is: "Praise be to the God and Father of our Lord Jesus Christ, the Father of compassion and the God of all comfort, who comforts us in all our troubles, so that we can comfort those in any trouble with the comfort we ourselves have received from God. For just as the sufferings of Christ flow over into our lives, so also through Christ our comfort overflows. If we are distressed, it is for your comfort and salvation; if we are comforted, it is for your comfort, which produces in you patient endurance of the same sufferings we suffer. And our hope for you is firm, because we know that just as you share in our sufferings, so also you share in our comfort. We do not want you to be uninformed, brothers, about the hardships we suffered in the province of Asia. We were under great pressure, far beyond our ability to endure, so that we despaired even of life. Indeed, in our hearts we felt the sentence of death. But this happened that we might not rely on ourselves but on God, who raises the dead. He has delivered us from such a deadly peril, and he will deliver us. On him we have set our hope that he will continue to deliver us, as you help us by your prayers. Then many will give thanks on our behalf for the gracious favor granted us in answer to the prayer of many." Just like Paul, I feel as though God has comforted me the whole time of our cancer experience. He has done so in part, so that I can comfort those who walk these steps behind me and beside me. There is one, sweet Lori, who has been used by God to comfort me because she has walked in my shoes. There is another who has been a comfort to me because she has shared with me some things to expect along the journey, sweet Kristi. Although she and I have never met, she has encouraged me. Now it will be my turn to encourage others. Also, the struggles have built endurance, patience, and hope in me. My trust in the Lord is strengthened in the struggle. You all know how we despaired even unto death. We shared with you how down we were many times. And you prayed for us. Your prayers often carried us. For that I cannot thank you enough. He has delivered us and will deliver us. And He will deliver you, too, through whatever dark valley you cross.

Okay, that burden has been on my soul to share with you. Now I have done it. Email me or call me if you want more. I would love to share with you, but my computer is about to rebel. I will update again soon. With Love, Jeri

Follow Up

Jeri

After that, life became almost idyllic. We went from being a family with a little girl with cancer to a family with a little girl with her hair growing in. McKenzie did go back to preschool that fall. She was on a new drug (new to us) called acutane. I knew something was up with this new drug because the pharmacist (with whom I had become very good friends) acted like she was handing over nuclear weapons when I went to pick it up. She asked something about a pregnancy test and I reminded her that McKenzie was only 3 years old. I called Dr. Patel's office and they said they would take care of it. Now I know that acutane, being exclusively used to treat acne, causes horrific birth defects if one gets pregnant while on it. We'd been told McKenzie would never have children of her own; the chemo drugs would render her sterile if the surgery hadn't permanently damaged her internal organs enough. She also would have been a candidate for radiation if the surgery hadn't beat up her internal structure. The radiation would have definitely prevented her from having children. Now that

I've had a teenager on acutane for acne, I realize the hoops through which Carole at Dr. Patel's office had to jump to get the medication for her every month. The medicine only came in capsules which McKenzie could not yet swallow. It is an orange liquid in the capsule so daily I cut open the capsule and dropped the liquid into orange juice for McKenzie to drink. We slowly returned to our lives as normal with the exception of regular visits to Dr. Patel's office.

McKenzie maintained her colorful personality. She loved to dress up and wear outfits that didn't match. It drove me crazy, but after coming so close to losing her, I tended to let her wear whatever she wanted- at least around the house.

Monroe and I continued sleeping in the extra bed in McKenzie's room often, but even sleep came easier eventually. That only happened with sleep aids, but it did happen.

The kids all returned to their fall activities and McKenzie right with them. We went to BSF and preschool. We attended football games, basketball games, and orchestra concerts. It was normal with just a little less hair.

Thursday, September 11, 2008 8:32 AM, CDT

Good morning from the projected path of Hurricane Ike! Only God knows whether we will even get any rain from this coming storm, but I have been very impressed with the advanced planning of the school district and cities. I am heading to the store this morning to stock up on supplies- just in case! I'll see y'all there. McKenzie is doing okay this morning. She continues to battle the stomach aches and the gas. I walked into the house last night from Caroline's open house at school and I thought a bomb had gone off- a stink bomb! McKenzie is just unable to contain it and I wouldn't want her to. But the rest of us are suffering! We keep the candles lit and the ceiling fans running, but it is still awful! Even 7 yr. old Monroe is complaining about it, but I think deep inside he is proud of her. She is even besting him! The hard part of last night was that when I came in, she was asleep on the sofa. I brought her jammies down and was getting ready to change her and thought I would slip her into bed easily without really waking her. However, when I went to take off her shoes and started changing her, she woke up and began wailing. I mean she was really upset. She began screaming about being in the hospital. Apparently, she was dreaming that she was in the hospital and that someone was waking her up to do something to her. She screamed and screamed for "Mommy". I picked her up and held her and kept saying, "McKenzie, I am here". It took her about 45 minutes to get calmed down. She didn't recognize that it was me for a long time. That was really hard, it just broke my heart. She finally got back to sleep only to wake up a few hours later. Monroe took care of her and I was able to catch up on sleep a little. She is very needy this morning- she wants someone sitting right with her every second. So, **please pray for her emotional security to right itself. Please pray for strength for Monroe and me so that we can be the parents we need to be for her. Pray that we also parent the other children as they need us to. Pray for her physical comfort from the stomach aches. And pray for limited devastation from Ike while still sending us a little bit of rain! Thank you all, Jeri**

Tuesday, September 16, 2008 9:07 AM, CDT

Good morning everyone! Well, I only have a few minutes to write. Miss McKenzie is very demanding these days. Monroe and I are trying desperately to return to normal life, but she really isn't. The best way I can describe her right now is EXTREMELY needy. Here we are 6 weeks post transplant and we have still been sleeping in her room with her every night. She has been unable to go to sleep by herself. During the day, she wants to change clothes constantly, change T.V. shows constantly, eat constantly, and wants a playmate (us) constantly. Okay, I've been gone for 10 minutes and back again because McKenzie just had a very bad stomach ache. That is normal, just the kind of thing I am talking about. Usually about once an hour her stomach hurts and we run to the bathroom. This may go on for a while or we may not go back for a couple of hours. Right now, she is resting on her bed because this last round was pretty bad. I mean it seems reasonable if you consider the fact that her entire abdomen has been pushed around by the tumor, and then beat up surgically, then hit with chemo again and finally not having eaten for 3 weeks only to begin again. It is bound to take some time to become "normal" again. And then again, maybe her G.I. tract will never be normal again. Many of you have said to me how glad you are to see her doing better. Praise God that there is no known disease in her body right now. She is doing some normal things like go to church and go to some friend's houses. But, she is far from "normal". I am weary of our new "normal". But, I truly believe that as Psalm 37:24 says, that God will uphold me with His hand. Even though I am stumbling around, I will not fall. We go back to Dr. Patel's office next week and we are supposed to start the retin-A treatment then. It will be an oral medication. So here are this week's prayer requests: **Pray for strength for Monroe and me. The other children are feeling it, too. Pray for a spirit of cooperation in McKenzie as we work to get her to sleep in her own bed by herself. And a spirit of cooperation in taking the oral medications at home. Pray for her to be protected from germs- she is displaying cold symptoms. Pray for relief from stomach aches. Pray for the cancer to not return.** *Thank you so much! With my love, Jeri*

Thursday, September 18, 2008 11:05 AM, CDT

Hello everyone! It's Thursday now. Well, McKenzie and I spent most of the afternoon yesterday at the doctor's office. Dr. Patel said that she would get sick and unfortunately, he was right. I took her to church for a couple of hours yesterday morning and when I picked her up, she was crying and complaining that her ear hurt. Since she has been displaying cold symptoms, I was not too surprised. She has had a cough and a runny nose. I called the doctor's office and they said to bring her in right away. We went and when they checked her white blood count, it was elevated. Dr. Patel examined her and thought perhaps her eardrum had burst because she had a little trail of something coming from her ear. They gave her some antibiotics through her port and also a prescription for some. We were there for a while and got home just barely in time to begin picking up the other children from the bus stop and school. Thank you, Eve, for being willing to intercept little Monroe at the bus stop and Christie and Meemaw for helping to get the girls to and from church last night for their church activities. Psalm 10:17 says, "You hear, O Lord, the desire of the afflicted; you encourage them and you listen to their cry." Thank you, all my family and friends for bringing my cries before the throne of God. You encourage me with your willingness to be the hands and feet (and tires) of God. He knows our desires and He will answer them. On the good news front, McKenzie did go to sleep the last 3 nights by herself. The first two nights she basically cried herself to sleep, but last night she told me she wouldn't cry. She went to sleep okay, but then woke up several times overnight and cried. I think her ears must be still hurting. Here are a few prayer requests: **Please pray for a willingness on McKenzie's part to take her medicine. Please pray for her to be relieved from pain and to sleep well. Please pray for me to look for the joy in mothering her through this needy time. And as always, pray for this disease not to recur. Thank you, with love, Jeri**

Jeri

I know people were praying for us, but even if they weren't, it comforted me and strengthened my faith to voice my requests.

Monroe

By mid-September, McKenzie had been out of the hospital almost a month. We were all home and trying to get back into a routine. I was traveling again for my job and Jeri was left at home to try to keep the home front going strong. Courtney had started her freshman year in high school, Caroline had begun sixth grade in middle school and Monroe was in second grade. Dr. Patel was encouraging us to get McKenzie enrolled in a mother's day out program back at Coker Methodist Day School. Jeri and I were reluctant because she still seemed so fragile. But McKenzie was ready and wanted friends to play with. We decided to enroll her two days a week for a couple of hours.

Friday, September 26, 2008 2:41 PM, CDT

Good Friday afternoon everyone, we wanted to send out quick update before the weekend. McKenzie continues to improve a little bit everyday. She is in a good mood most of the time and seems to be getting some of her stamina back as well. This week, Jeri took McKenzie to see Dr. Patel on Monday and her counts were all good and her ears have cleared significantly from the ear infection.

On Wednesday, we began the experimental drug to help continue the prevention of returning Neuroblastoma cells. The drug is a challenge to get McKenzie to take because she cannot swallow a pill. We may be forced to go to shots twice a day, however we are really hoping it does not come to that.

We continue to try to get into a normal swing of life with work, school, after school activities and all the things that have had to be on hold for many months. The other children are doing well so far in school and seem to be happy to have everyone back at home.

We appreciate the continued prayer, cards and well wishes. I know that there are many of you with your own bucket of rocks and we are praying for you as well. Thank you all for your support, and may God bless you all.-Monroe

Monday, September 29, 2008 6:49 PM, CDT

Hi Everyone, Monday evening here. We went to the doctor's office this morning. We have found that actually the new medicine we are taking does not come in a shot form and that capsules are our only recourse. Thank you, Gretchen, for the jelly idea. I may try that this evening as I really don't like trying to dissolve the gel from inside the capsule. It is messy and difficult. I am also concerned about some of the side effects that go along with this medication. I am not concerned even about the side effects that McKenzie may experience, but rather the side effects that our other children may experience later in life if this medication were to get into their bloodstreams. With mixing it in a cup with a spoon and then washing these items in our dishwasher, we don't know if all of it comes off. We are working on using all disposables, but taking capsules would eliminate any problems in my mind. Dr. Patel assures me that the other children cannot be affected, but I don't think there is anyone (except the Only One) that can give us the assurance I seek. I will just have to trust that He will hold all of these circumstances in hand. Our other challenge right now is again in McKenzie's sleep habits. She is going to sleep by herself and most nights at a reasonable bedtime (unless she gets too much of a nap in the car on any given day). Our problem is that she is screaming in her sleep several times a night. I think it started when she had her ear infection, but just never went away. He checked her ears today and said they were fine. She usually just screams for a few seconds and then gets quiet, but sometimes it goes on for an extended period of time. It always wakes us up and we only go into her room if she keeps it up for more than a few seconds. However, the constant waking is really rough on Monroe and me. We both feel sleep deprived. Monroe is suffering from frequent headaches, while I just lack clear thinking and motivation to complete my usual tasks. I often just feel like I am walking around in a fog. It is a lot like having a new baby in the house- that is the feeling. We both just so strongly desire to have our household "normal" again. We know that we are blazing new trails trying to find our new "normal", but it's got to be better than this. So please pray that we will begin to get some quality sleep soon! I do know that, as always, God is carrying us. Thanks for all your continued prayers. Oh, we asked Dr. Patel about upcoming scans. He says we will do the next round after she has had two rounds of this new medication. We take it two weeks on, two weeks off, so that will be in about five weeks. Talk to you all soon. With Love, Jeri

Monroe

As McKenzie grew stronger and our lives grew busier, we seemed to wait longer between our posts on Caring Bridge. Those that followed seemed to know that this indicated all was well with our little princess.

Tuesday, October 7, 2008 9:24 AM, CDT

Hi Everyone! Wow, I am just realizing how long it has been since I updated you on McKenzie's progress. I am so sorry! Life is back to being very busy at the May house. As most of you know, McKenzie's older sisters and brother keep us running fast with school and church activities.

Throw McKenzie's illness into the mix and boy, do we run! McKenzie's oldest sister, Courtney, is running Cross Country for Johnson High School and gearing up for basketball season. More importantly, she is in varsity orchestra at Johnson, too. Caroline is in choir at Tejeda and is trying the academic U.I.L. team. Both girls are very involved in church choir and youth groups. Little Monroe is playing Upward Flag Football through church this fall and his reading is really clicking this year. McKenzie? Well, she keeps me running, too. We had a doctor's appointment yesterday morning. Her white counts were slightly low for some unknown reason. She is finishing the first two weeks of her new preventive drug study. She actually swallowed her capsule yesterday morning, but that is the only time. She couldn't get it down last night or this morning and had to drink it in the juice. Thank you for all of the wonderful suggestions on the capsules. She wants badly to go to preschool and the doctor says she can so I am going to start looking at that. I really just want to send her on Fridays and most Mothers Day Out programs have a 2 day minimum. That is something you can pray about for me. Please pray that I will be able to get her into the right program. Please keep praying about her sleep schedule as we are still having challenges with that. The sleep aid the doctor prescribed has helped us get a few night's sleep, but we are still having some difficult nights like last night when she was up most of the night. I am rejoicing at every day that God gives us with McKenzie. I am praying for His will to be done in her life- whether He allows us to keep her for the next 60 years or only for today. None of us know the number of our days, but God knows the number of our days and the number of hair on our head (in McKenzie's case, every hair she will have again someday!). He loves us so much and blesses us with every good blessing in our life. We only have to thank Him and offer Him every heartbeat for His service. Sorry, I digress! But, I am feeling excited about life today and pray that you are, too. Bless God by loving Him today and be excited about what He has given you! With Love, Jeri

Jeri

As soon as I posted this, the Mother's Day Out program staff at Coker Methodist let me know they would love to have her back even for one day a week- another answer to prayer.

Thursday, October 16, 2008 10:21 AM, CDT

Hello everyone! Happy Thursday! We are doing well. McKenzie and I are home today for a change. We have had a busy week mostly with the other children, but she certainly keeps me running, too. We went to Dr. Patel's office on Monday. Her counts were up slightly, but nothing of concern to them apparently. I say "them" because Dr. Patel has a new partner in his office who was blessed to examine our precious McKenzie this week. It was a bit frustrating for Monroe to have to "start over" with McKenzie's diagnosis and introduce another doctor to her case, but he survived. I don't know how the doctor came out, but Monroe made it through. We are currently on our two week break from the preventive drug we've been taking and will begin again next Wednesday. Good news! McKenzie's hair is coming in ever so slightly. We've been watching recently because we thought we saw a "5 o'clock shadow" on her head. This morning, I think I actually see little hairs growing on her head! She got a new wig this week. It is Dorothy from the Wizard of Oz. She is planning to be Dorothy for Halloween. She has the dress and the ruby slippers, too. I will post a picture as soon as I can get her to hold still for one. Mothers' Day Out went well last week and she is looking forward to going back tomorrow. She also got to go out to lunch yesterday with a friend from the Bible study we are doing at church. They were so cute playing and eating at one end of the table while the adults talked at the other end. I can't tell you all how grateful I am for God carrying us through the last ten months, for your prayers, and for your encouraging words. Please continue praying for McKenzie to be disease free when we go for scans in November. With Love, Jeri

Tuesday, October 28, 2008 8:32 AM, CDT

Psalm 103:2 says "Praise the Lord, o my soul, and forget not all His benefits." I am praising Him this morning because one of the benefits in my life is His healing of McK's little body. She is doing well. We saw Dr. Patel yesterday and everything looks good. Her counts are in line. We have our scans scheduled for November 14th, so please pray that 1) they find no new disease and 2) the scans go smoothly. She must go fasting (not an easy thing for a 3 yr. old) and they will be putting her under anesthesia. She knows we are going for "pictures" soon, but we haven't begun talking about anesthesia again. We had so much trouble with anesthesia in May/June surgery that I don't even want to think about it. McK woke up screaming at 5:18am today. She woke up her sister, so please pray for Caroline, me and McK to make it through the day without falling asleep.

She has about a week left on this round of her medication. We are just mixing it in the orange juice and not trying to have her swallow the capsules. We'll get back on that horse sometime in the near future. McK had a fun weekend. She got to go to a birthday party for one of her friends at a public place pizza. She had a blast. Dr. Patel fussed a little over this because Chuck E. Cheese is such a dirty place, but it was worth it. She loved it! We have decided that when her birthday rolls around again, she wants a Barbie cake just like Maggie! She is looking forward to trick or treating on Friday. The plan is to wear her Dorothy costume. I will post some pictures if all goes as planned. Well, that's about it. Y'all go out and make it a beautiful fall day.

Monroe

As the months went by since the Mega Chemo treatment and the stem cell transplant, we began to settle into a normal routine. McKenzie gained strength and was able to do many things. We tried to celebrate the new things that she got to do as milestones. Jeri and I were very thankful for each birthday party she attended, each day she got to go to school, and each family event she was able to be a part of. We had no idea what the future held, but we tried to make the most of every day. With the approaching Holiday season, we were hopeful the news would continue to be positive.

Monday, November 10, 2008 5:17 PM, CST

We are a go for CT Scans on Friday at Methodist Hospital. Needless to say Jeri and I are anxious about what will be found, however, we are confident that God will carry us through whatever is ahead.

Please pray for McKenzie to be peaceful on Friday morning. We will head to Dr. Patel's first thing, and then we will walk over to the Methodist for the scan. At this point Jeri's biggest concern is about how McKenzie will handle the anesthesia. For me, I am anxious about what we will find. At least we both get nervous about different things....

Thank you all for continued prayers and we will share the results as soon as we can.

May God Bless You All.-Monroe

Friday, November 14, 2008 1:47 PM, CST

Well, thank you for all your prayers. God has answered so mightily today! MCKENZIE IS CANCER FREE ACCORDING TO THE SCANS! As many of you know, I was more concerned about the anesthesia than about the results of the scans themselves. Well, a funny thing happened. When we went into the pedi prep & hold area, they asked if we wanted to do the scans without anesthesia. McKenzie was kicking up a stink about having to do anything at all. She was crying and fussing and totally would not listen to reasoning. There is one lady in CT that we have worked with before and she talked McKenzie into going down to CT and watching a little computerized cartoon about the procedure. Monroe took her and by the time I finished paperwork with the nurse, they had her convinced to lay still so that that they could do it without anesthesia. So she did! I sat on the table (which I call a magic carpet) with her and we were finished by 10:30am! Monroe and I took her out for pizza, shopping at the mall, and grocery shopping. Dr. Patel called at 1 o'clock and said that everything looked great! We are so grateful that God has healed her and maintained her disease free state! He is so good! Thank you all again for praying for the procedure and the outcome! With Love, Jeri

Monday, November 24, 2008 8:33 AM, CST

Yesterday in church, our minister challenged us this Thanksgiving to be thankful for our blessings as well as our challenges. Over the last 11 months, our family has faced a huge challenge. Looking back I know that God has used this to help us all grow as a family, as parents and as husband and wife. We have always loved all of our children, however, through McKenzie's illness we have been challenged to look at life and family in new ways.

This Thanksgiving, take time to express to those around you how thankful you are for who they are and what they have meant in your life. Also, Psalm 107:1 states "Give thanks to the Lord for He is good, His love endures forever."

Enjoy the miracles of your life. We are all surrounded by them each and everyday.

Thank you all who are continuing to read this for your support and prayers. We are blessed as a family by your support.

Happy Thanksgiving, -Monroe

Monroe

As Thanksgiving turned to the Christmas season, McKenzie continued to feel better. She was even able to perform at her school for the Christmas program. I, of course, was there with video in hand, to catch every moment. I sat and cried almost uncontrollably throughout her performance. It was a day I will never forget.

Saturday, December 6, 2008 9:12 AM, CST

This week we visited the doctor again and all blood work continues to look good. McKenzie also finished another round of her experimental medication. She continues to be filled with energy and a strong spirit of joy.

On Friday, she was even able to perform with her Mother's Day Out class singing Christmas Carols. What a true pleasure it was to sit and watch her, knowing what she had been through the last 11 months.

We continue to be encouraged by life and are trying to enjoy each and everyday of the Christmas Season.

Thank you all for your continued prayers and cards.

May God Bless you all in this most Holy of Seasons. -Monroe

Tuesday, December 16, 2008 7:57 AM, CST

Good morning everyone! Merry Christmas! Ready or not here it comes! We are busy getting ready for Christmas at our house. The gifts are mostly bought, but I haven't started wrapping. As you can see from the pictures, we've been to see Santa. McKenzie instructed him on all the things he is to bring her. It was quite a list. I work constantly to help her understand that Christmas is the celebration of Jesus' birthday and that Santa helps us celebrate. Sometimes I think she gets it and sometimes she is sure it is all about what she is going to "get". I am telling you, she is a typical little girl! I pray that we all "get" the true meaning of Christmas this year. Jesus came to save us and save McKenzie He did this year!

Please say a little extra prayer for McKenzie today. She is fighting a cold. We saw the doctor yesterday and he gave her an antibiotic. So she should get better soon, but the cough and the nose are a challenge. When she sneezes, stand back! And I was just glad she didn't cough or sneeze on Santa! We go back on her preventive drug study tomorrow. We do two weeks on and two weeks off. I will try again this round to have her swallow the capsules. We could use a little extra prayer there, too.

Well, have a great day! Stay warm! With Love, Jeri

Saturday, December 27, 2008 7:10 AM, CST

Good morning everyone! McKenzie had a great Christmas! I posted several pictures from our various Christmas celebrations with family. In reflecting, I am, as always, thankful to God and you for your prayers that we have this great time with her. As we head into New Year's Eve, Monroe and I are looking forward to saying a big goodbye to 2008 and truly ringing in a new year. We are realistic in knowing that she may not always stay in remission, but you can bet that we are going to celebrate her life in thanks to God for every day we have with her! It has changed us, this experience with cancer. It has changed her, our family, and I think many of you. God used an ugly situation for the good of those who love Him. 2008 may live in infamy in our minds, but we are looking forward to the new adventures of 2009! Please come and walk with us through our new adventures! I'm sure we will need your prayers then, too! We'll be praying for you, too. With much love, Jeri

Jeri

Life in remission was a happy time, but it certainly had its' challenges. From diagnosis, I had faith that God would heal her and He did. Eventually, I would realize that my faith would need to be in His saving grace alone rather than in His healing of McKenzie. But, first, He gave us the gift of more happy times with her.

Make-A-Wish Trip

Monroe

In early September, I decided that McKenzie was doing well enough to apply for a Make-A-Wish trip. Make-A-Wish is a wonderful organization that grants special wishes to children that have faced a life threatening disease. All through McKenzie's illness, I had promised we would take her to Disney World Florida when she felt better. I was determined to make good on my promise.

I really had no idea what you did or how to get the process going, so I went online, found the website, and began filling out the information. It was simple! Make-A-Wish of course does plenty of checking with the doctors to find out the exact information and condition of the child and there are a lot of questions that must be answered before you ever find out if you are a qualified candidate for the program. I was determined to get her qualified. She had been through too much and come too far not to make this dream come true.

Jeri

When McKenzie emerged from the stem cell transplant, she was called officially in remission. I believed she would outlive all of us. So it kind of bugged me when Monroe started talking about contacting the people from the Make-A-Wish Foundation. I really didn't see the point in rushing to do something special for McKenzie because I wanted to remain positive in my belief that this chapter in our life was closing. We still saw Dr. Patel on a regular basis, but those visits went from twice a week to weekly and then monthly. Dr. Patel, too, thought it was a good time to pursue McKenzie's wish. She was, after all, fairly healthy and it would be a good reward for all of the awful things she'd had to endure over that year. So, his recommendation was made and we began the process.

Lori McGrath's family had been on a Make-A-Wish trip to Disney World that she said was over the top. Lori's neighbors, the Clarke's, had also been on a Make-A-Wish trip to Disney World and loved it. Both Lori and Kristi volunteered as Wish Granters for Make-A-Wish and encouraged us in the process. I call it a "process" as it really is a special journey. First, either a doctor or parent must instigate the paperwork. The doctor must confirm that the child does indeed have a life threatening illness. Then you get to meet with a Wish Granter and they discuss with the child their wish. With a child as young as McKenzie (three at the time), it can be confusing to ask them what they wish for. She mainly wished to be left alone. But she loved Disney movies and costumes. We had to remind her what Disney World was and show her pictures of our family Disneyland trip the year before. She was easily convinced. She wanted to go to Disney World! Time with her family would be a wish come true that we would be unable to fully appreciate for quite a while. So she told her Wish Granters- Lori, Kristi, and a new friend named David- that she wanted to go on a magical trip to Disney World and McKenzie's wish was granted. This was all in early October 2008. We were to give the Make-A-Wish Foundation two dates that would work with our family calendar and they would let us know when space was made available. You see, all children that wish for a trip to Disney World with Make-A-Wish end up staying at a place called Give Kids the World Village. It is located in Kissimmee, Florida within a thirty-minute drive to the Disney parks. While the village is large, it cannot house all of the children and their families who want to come. So there was quite a wait list apparently. We were told that it would most likely be Spring Break before our family could be accommodated. We were a large group with seven people- our immediate 6 plus Monroe's mom, Jane. McKenzie invited all of her grandparents to come, but only Jane was able to join us on the trip. As I said before, I was in no rush to take the trip because I felt we had a full life left with McKenzie to take her wish trip. So we began the long wait. McKenzie lived for each day alone and I did, too. I treasured each day I had with her. Each day was a blessing from the Lord. I still treasure each day He gives me with my other three children. My experience with McKenzie's cancer taught me that along with so much more. And it has become one of my passions to remind my friends to treasure each day with their children- even on those days when their children are being more than challenging. They all act that way from time to time and those days with McKenzie were especially challenging. She had become quite spoiled and demanding through her treatment. She was sure the world revolved around her. She would brook no argument from her brother and sisters. She didn't always get her own way, but she always demanded it. Following her stem cell transplant, she struggled for many months to sleep. Even more than the surgery, the stem cell transplant awakened restlessness and a terror in her that we worked constantly to quiet. She often woke screaming in the night and we worked to help her sleep peacefully for months. We worked to undo the damage that the stem cell transplant had inflicted on her general appearance. She took a couple of months to begin eating normally and she was so skinny. Her little arms and legs were like twigs when she came home. Nothing tasted good at first and we moved heaven and earth to get any food that she expressed even the slightest interest in. But bite-by-bite, she began gaining strength and so did our family. These were the months when we toiled to regain normalcy in our family. McKenzie was attending preschool one day a week and the other children were busily entrenched in their schoolwork and activities. So I was glad to wait for the Make-A-Wish trip for as long as it took. I got a call a week or two before Thanksgiving with the news that Give Kids the World Village had opened several new villas and would be able to accommodate us by Christmas vacation for sure and even by Thanksgiving if we wished. We made the decision to wait until Christmas break. I began to get really excited about it! You know, I've always been a very blessed woman. When I was a little girl, I had the love and security of my parents, the assurance of salvation since I was young, and the material blessings of a middle class family. But, looking back at this trip, I can really now see how blessed I truly am! Despite our adversity, God has tucked into little pockets of my life moments, weeks even, of such fun and happiness that just thinking about it makes me want to burst. That week of our lives was such a week. I had no idea what was coming- either on the trip or long term, but I knew that the trip would be fun.

Friday, October 10, 2008 7:51 PM, CDT

Good Friday evening from the May house. What a week, between politics, the economy, work, school activities and flag football, it has been a busy week. I know many of you have all had interesting weeks as well.

I wanted to share two exciting events that blessed our family this week. The first event took place Tuesday evening, and I am truly humbled by this experience. On Tuesday night, we had a visit from the **Make-A-Wish** *foundation. Kristi, Lori and David visited McKenzie and asked her what her wish was. And to no surprise she requested a trip to Disney World, with her parents, her siblings, and her grandparents. And it looks like her wish will be graciously and generously fulfilled. It was truly a unique experience to sit with Kristi and Lori who are each mothers of daughters that were granted similar wishes as well as with David, who has been a "wish granter" for years. What an amazing experience and what an amazing organization.*

I would like to ask if there are any organizations or schools that would like to be a partner with **Make-A-Wish,** *for McKenzie or other children like McKenzie, to please contact the May family or log on to: www.makeawish.com*

This is an amazing organization and they do amazing things for children and families going through terrible illnesses.

Thank you, Make-A-Wish. We have already been blessed by your Foundation.

Second, I want to share that McKenzie went back to Coker Methodist Mothers' Day Out this week. When we contacted Coker MDO early in the week, they were so excited about having her back. That made us feel like God was pointing us in that direction. So, for the first time in 10 months, our house was quiet today. Everyone was in "school". McK went about 6 hours to her "school" and loved being able to play with other children her age for the first time in a long time. This was a huge blessing and not one we were sure she was ready for. However, she came through with flying colors. Praise the Lord, he provides us all with a "strength that surpasses all understanding."

Well I hope you all have a great weekend, focus on the positive and not on the economy or the elections.

May God Bless you all. -Monroe

Monroe

As we got closer to the holidays, we began to have more and more excitement about the Make-A-Wish trip to Disney World in Florida. McKenzie had asked all of her grandparents to be a part of the trip. She was very anxious to go and meet all of the Fairy Princesses. We were excited to have a child once again cancer free and feeling good.

The Make-A-Wish organization does an outstanding job of organizing and arranging the trip. We began with an in person interview at our house, where McKenzie was asked what she wanted. She wore her white "Giselle dress"(from the Disney movie Enchanted), complete with white shoes and a tiara. The tiara looked especially stunning, due to the fact that McKenzie still was without hair.

During our initial meeting, we had to give several dates of availability for the trip. Our first choice was to leave on the 28th of December and return on January 3rd of 2009. We hoped that we would spend New Year's Eve in the Magic Kingdom and say "goodbye" to a rough 2008 and "hello" to a fantastic future and exciting 2009. January 3rd was significant because it would mark the one-year anniversary of McKenzie going to the hospital.

Our second choice was Spring Break of 2009. I was not as excited about this date because I was concerned that anything could happen over the next five months. With the severity of the cancer, I wanted to go sooner rather than later.

Tuesday, December 23, 2008 8:10 AM, CST

Good morning everyone! As we prepare to celebrate Christmas, we are reminded daily how blessed we are! McKenzie is mostly well today! She has been fighting a cold and is on antibiotics, but is doing fine. Her brother had the flu for 4 days and we managed to keep her from getting it so far. Hand wash, hand wash, hand wash! Not so easy for a 3 year old to understand. But, so far, so good. Please keep her health in your prayers.

We are soon to be blessed with a trip to Disney World from the Make-A-Wish Foundation. You can catch McKenzie in her new t-shirt on the photo page. She is watching a video on TV right now about the parks and is so excited! It's a major ordeal with so many of us going, so please pray for travel ease and safety, too. Traveling with kids is never easy and I want to be sure we don't forget anything. We'll post plenty of pictures when we get back.

Thank you all for your continued prayers! Jeri

Jeri

So we celebrated Thanksgiving and Christmas that year with special gratitude for the life of our baby girl. We had no idea how long we would have her. I mean, which of us really knows how long we will have our loved ones? We must be grateful always for those close to us, but that holiday season was especially poignant with all we'd been through. Most of what the children received as gifts was geared toward the trip. McKenzie received several Disney costumes and clothes with the Princesses on them. The older children received Disney Dollars- gift cards to be spent at the Disney parks and travel games to play on the plane trip.

A couple days after Christmas, we had McKenzie's Wish Party. Her Wish Granters (who all now felt like good friends like Lori who already did!) brought dinner and a giant cake to celebrate. We were told to invite anyone we wanted- especially friends and family who'd been pertinent to her cancer battle. We felt a little strange inviting people to celebrate the fact that we were taking a trip to Disney. But we invited family close to us and even some friends that McKenzie had recently made at preschool and in her Bible study class at church. It was a fun occasion, especially for McKenzie. It was like a birthday party; there were gifts for McKenzie and she even blew out candles on the giant cake. We still had our Christmas decorations up, so it was kind of a cross between a birthday party and a Christmas party!

We left the next day. Arrangements were made for the pets and bags were packed. Farewells were said and we all got on the plane. Getting through airport security with McKenzie was an experience. With her port still in place, she lit up the metal detector like the Fourth of July. She, accompanied by her daddy, was individually screened after that. It was difficult to explain that we were not trying to smuggle explosives onto the plane using our three year old. We made it through and headed for Florida. Another Make-A-Wish volunteer met us on the other end of the flight. She helped us locate our baggage and directed us to the rental car desk. Before we left her, she even gave us the exact change we needed to get through the several tollbooths on the trip from the airport to the Village. We were very impressed with the attention to detail. We still had no idea of the pampering we were in for. This was just the tip of the iceberg. I don't even remember that woman's name, but I will always remember her fondly. It takes so many volunteers to put together all the pieces of a trip like ours. And we were just one family with one sick little girl. God bless all of those like that woman who are just a small piece of the puzzle that is the giant network of the Make-A-Wish Foundation.

Monroe

When we arrived at GKTW Village, we checked in to an incredible complex of villas and amusement park type atmosphere. McKenzie was welcomed like royalty and we were all treated like conquering heroes. After a brief introduction and tour, we were taken to our own private two-bedroom two-bath condo complete with full kitchen and den.

Our first order of business was to go to the heated pool. It had been a long day and we wanted to take a swim. It was late December, so the kids were anxious to jump into the pool and say they had swum outside in winter.

As we spent time at the pool, we became increasingly aware of many of the families and special children that we were surrounded by. Some kids were in wheel chairs, some had large families, some were rich and some were poor. This place and these families all had a common thread: their children had faced a "life threatening illness" and survived.

After the pool, it was late and we realized we had not eaten. We went back to our villa and remembered we could order pizza until ten at night. I ordered two pizzas for us to share. When they arrived, I asked how much I owed. The answer was "zero"; everything at this wonderful place was taken care of. I could not even tip the delivery driver. I was blown away by the generosity.

The next morning we headed to Epcot Center in Disney. We had 5 days of fun ahead and we were determined to make the most of every day. McKenzie had decided to wear her Minnie Mouse outfit that had been a Christmas gift a few days earlier. She was complete with mouse ears and yellow shoes. She was quite a sight; her mother was determined to make sure that McKenzie got what McKenzie wanted.

As we entered Epcot, I remember a large array of emotions taking over. We had arrived at a destination we had all dreamed about for the last twelve months. The year had been horrible; McKenzie had suffered so much as well as the rest of our children. I wanted it to be a magical trip. I wanted to make this count. I knew what the past looked like and we had no idea what the future would hold. So for today, we would celebrate the positive and love the moments. It was as close to perfection as I could imagine.

Jeri

That brings me to the small detail of the financing of this trip. We had no idea before we went on the trip of all that we would be treated to, but after we began doing mental calculations of the cost. It was overwhelming. We were a pretty blessed family who, if we had stretched, could have afforded a trip to Disney World. But just like the MasterCard commercial said, this trip was priceless. We found out later that a distant friend of the family with a philanthropist's heart helped make that trip a reality for us and we are forever grateful. There were many families staying at the Village that could have never afforded such a trip. We saw many families with sick children less able than ours. We began seeing what a "high functioning" sick child we had. I can't say enough good things about the Make-A-Wish Foundation for caring so kindly for those brave souls and their children. We still try often to give back to those two wonderful organizations- Make-A-Wish Foundation and Give Kids the World Village. They gave so much to us and when God blesses us (which He does often) and prompts us to give back, we often direct our blessings to one of these.

When we arrived at the village, we sat through a short orientation and then climbed onto a golf cart for a tour that ended at our villa. All of the employees and volunteers at the Village had great energy and our tour guide was no exception. She took us to our villa and showed us around inside. There were two bedrooms and a sofa that pulled out. There was a full kitchen with a small table and two full bathrooms. There was a driveway for our rental van. There was everything we could need or want plus gifts for McKenzie. The gifts that arrived daily for her included stuffed animals, t-shirts (for all the kids), and games. At the end of the week we even received a disc of pictures taken with her around the village with Mickey Mouse and many other Disney characters. The kids were excited to swim at one of the Village pools so we headed over. The pool was completely accessible with a waterproof wheelchair for those children who needed it! We felt blessed again that our daughter was as highly functioning as she was. After dinner, it was off to bed to rest up for our big adventure.

We decided to spend our first day in Disney World at Epcot. McKenzie dressed in her new Minnie Mouse costume. She was in a horrible mood as we entered the park. Many of you know that I am a picture-taking freak especially on family vacations. The older kids are often caught with a sour look on their face simply because they recognize that Mom has the camera out AGAIN. But this time McKenzie was just plain cranky. While Monroe picked up a stroller for her, I tried several times to get a good shot of her at the beginning of our grand adventure. It was no use. All I ended up with were several frowny pictures of her! Oh well. As was so often the case, this became the theme of our trip. The rest of the children, Monroe, and his mom are all smiling in the pictures while McKenzie (if she even agreed to be in the picture) was frowning. We had a great time anyway!

We toured Epcot the first day, Disney Hollywood Studios (DHS) the second day, Animal Kingdom the third day, and park hopped to Magic Kingdom throughout all the days! It truly was a magical trip! We rode so many great rides and saw so many great shows! We ate so many great meals! I really can't say enough good things about our time at Disney World on this trip. It was absolutely priceless. Looking back now, it was perfect timing; God's perfect timing.

However, it was some of our less than perfectly magical moments that provided for some our most humorous memories. When a Make-A-Wish kid is granted a trip to Disney World, they are given a button to wear when they arrive. The button identifies them as a Make-A-Wish recipient wherever they go. One of the most important functions of the button is that in the Disney parks it serves as a Fast Pass. Anyone who has been to Disney since the invention of the Fast Pass knows that this takes you the front of the line. That is important because in Disney parks there can easily be a 45-85 minute wait in the standby line for the more popular rides. Another key is that not every ride or attraction has a Fast Pass option. Some you just have to wait for or not ride them at all. Not so for Make-A-Wish kids. With their button, they are taken through any Fast Pass line or taken to the accessible entrance (always at the front of the line) of any attraction. They are also taken to the front of any character greeting line as we soon found out. On our first day at the parks, we weren't sure exactly how this worked. So we strolled along, riding things here and there. In the early afternoon, we were strolling along through the back of Epcot and happened into "France". And there they were- Beauty and the Beast! (Fade in music) They were meeting children standing in a long line. (Fade out music) McKenzie spotted the characters and got **very** excited. So she and I headed over to get in line. A very polite Disney cast member at the end of the line who explained that the line was closed greeted us. McKenzie began the signs of a major meltdown. I quickly explained that we were on a Make-A-Wish trip, this was our first day, and these were the first characters we'd encountered. The gentleman's eyes got big and he looked down and saw McKenzie's button. I thought her lack of hair was a give away, but apparently many little Minnie Mouse "wanna-be's" sported very short hairdos. He asked us to please wait there. He went up and spoke to Beauty and the Beast's "handlers". He came back quickly and said, "Please follow me". I thought maybe we were in trouble, instead, however, he whisked us to the front of the line. I was so embarrassed. All those other children had been waiting and we were placed before them in the queue. McKenzie was a little confused at first, but then realized she was going to meet the characters. It was so sweet! They talked to her and called her by name- it was on her button. She had them sign her autograph book (the first of many) and we took pictures with them. She didn't want to leave them, but we finally wandered off with stars dancing in our eyes. That would be the first of many encounters with characters that week. We visited Mary Poppins on Main Street and the Disney Fairies including Tinker Bell in their special pavilion. And every time we were whisked to the front of the line! The funny thing was that McKenzie and I were confused the first time it happened. But by the end of the week, she was asking me, "Mommy, when are they going to come and take me to the front of the line?!" And she was never quiet! We got some funny looks. It did nothing for my attempts at discipline!

McKenzie with Beauty and the Beast- Notice the Button!

Another time, we were headed into the back lot tour at DHS with one of the cast members who had met us at the front of the very long line. We were quite a parade. Little Monroe had built himself a new light saber at one of the Star Wars shops. The cast member put the light saber up in the air like a sword and said, "Follow me, good people" in his best English accent. So all seven of us began the trek through the crowd toward the front of the line. A woman in a motorized scooter realized we were cutting in front of her and quickly zoomed in front of the last three of us in line. "You can't go in front of me!" she yelled. I took McKenzie's little hand and sidestepped around her, apologized, and explained that the Disney cast member had simply instructed us to follow him. It was an uncomfortable moment, but the show was absolutely worth it!

It was later that night when we went to see the Indiana Jones Spectacular Show. It was full of action and energy. McKenzie was enamored with Indiana Jones and asked if she could meet him. We asked the show director and after spotting the now famous button she said Indiana Jones would be right with us. What a treat- he was truly a gentleman. I guess I should make it clear that it was not Harrison Ford! It was a stunt double that looked an awful lot like a young Harrison Ford, though! He autographed her princess book, posed for numerous photos, and shook the hands of the whole family. He was so kind. I'll treasure that meeting forever.

Several of the Disney cast members who star as characters actually volunteer their time to come to Give Kids the World Village in costume and meet the children. As I've mentioned, there were many families for whom it was impossible to consider braving a Disney park for more than a few hours. McKenzie was as mobile as any other three year old and we were only limited by her stamina. It was still a blessing to get to meet Mickey and Minnie Mouse in a more intimate setting at the Village. We also got to see Belle from Beauty and the Beast again and Goofy. Some of our favorite pictures are those at the Village that included our entire family with the Disney characters. Usually in the parks, the older kids would want to ride the rides and McKenzie and I would end up in the character greetings alone. The older kids were a captive audience at the Village. Those pictures are priceless now.

We spent New Year's Eve that year (2008/2009) in the Magic Kingdom. It had been our plan to park hop between Magic Kingdom and Epcot that day, but by noon Magic Kingdom where we started the day was closed as it was at capacity. We heard from cast members that Epcot was closed, too. We didn't want to risk not getting back into the park by hopping or going back to the Village for a little rest. Courtney was determined we would make it till midnight. There would be a fat chance of that with a tired and whiny little cancer patient in our midst! Around 3pm, hats and horns were passed out to all the Disney guests. I'm not sure if that was the wisest move on Disney's part because it was really loud around there by dark! We decided to stay until the 8:45pm fireworks display and call it our New Year. That was about as late as our little Wish Kid could make it. We have some great video footage of that firework display. We were all happily saying farewell to 2008, as it had not been our year! I had so much hope at that moment. I was sure that 2009 would prove so much better. I never should have said that. Maybe it was foreshadowing because as it turned out, 2009 definitely was not our year.

Monroe

One of my favorite pictures of the trip is McKenzie hugging Monroe and Monroe hugging McKenzie while they stood and watched the red, white and blue fireworks explode above Cinderella's Castle- no fighting, no pushing, no shoving, just pure joy and love at that moment. I will forever have that image in my mind!

Jeri

We rounded out the trip with many trips to the ice cream shop at the Village. The ice cream shop was open from early in the morning until late at night. It was all you could eat and you could go as many times a day as you wanted. My son can eat a lot of ice cream and we all helped eat our share. We rode the carousel several times at the Village and made magic pillows. We ate free pizza in our villa delivered by volunteers. Finally, we put McKenzie's name on a Wishing Star and as we made our wish, put it in the Wish Box and sent it off to the Wish Fairy. Do you see a theme emerging? The Wish Fairy would place the star on the ceiling of the castle and send us a map of its location. We would be allowed to visit her star anytime we wanted. You see, once you've stayed at the Village you become an alumnae. You may come and visit, even volunteer, but never again do you come back to stay. It is quite an honor to be Village alumnae. Of course, your child has to have a life threatening illness to be invited, but an honor nonetheless. Monroe and I recently visited her star. It was humbling to know that our little angel has a place there.

Monroe

The trip was a complete success and we headed home on January 3rd, 2009. This was one year to the day after we had originally checked into the hospital with McKenzie. She had survived so much and we were excited to be moving into a new year. Jeri and I were hopeful that the worst was behind us and that we would have our precious McKenzie for a many, many more years. We hoped she was going to beat this disease and be the less then 1% that lives 5 years or longer.

Sunday, January 4, 2009 1:56 PM, CST

Happy New Year Everyone,

As many of you may be aware, we have spent the last week in the Magic Kingdom, Walt Disney World Florida. This was thanks to the Make-A-Wish organization. We stayed at the Give the Kids the World Village, which was just amazing. Everyone was so kind and generous. We had pizza at all hours of the day of night, went to the all you can eat Ice Cream Parlor daily and ate wonderful meals at the Gingerbread House. This organization and the volunteers that keep it going blow me away. What a blessing this place is to so many people.

We were able to make it to all four of the Disney Parks; Magic Kingdom, Animal Kingdom, Epcot and Disney Studios. At each park, McKenzie wore a special badge that enabled us to move to the front of most lines, so that we did not have to wait for the rides and shows. What an experience! We are truly appreciative of these organizations and the kindness of all that made this possible for our family and the many other families that we saw on the trip.

On January 3rd, 2009 we returned back to San Antonio, one year to the day that we were first admitted to the hospital that began this long journey. We do not know what lies ahead, however, we are confident we have been given a gift through McKenzie that has touched our lives and many around us. May you all have joy and prosperity in 2009. We are happy to have 2008 behind us and look forward with great joy and excitement to 2009.

May God Bless You All. -Monroe

With Mickey and Minnie Mouse at GKTWV

Life in Remission

Jeri

As I mentioned before, life in remission was pretty "normal". The older kids had their activities and Monroe and I struggled to stay involved with those.

He always tried to coach sports teams or at least be an assistant coach. The fall before we went on our Make-A-Wish trip, little Monroe played another football season with Upward through our church. Upward is a faith based league where the players play flag football, learn Bible verses, pray together, and have a weekly devotional during practice. They also have a cheerleading squad. We had become good friends with one of the pastors at church who led up the sports activities. I asked if maybe McKenzie could have a cheerleader uniform and one appeared within days. It seemed that people cared so much for McKenzie and would move a mountain if possible just to make her happy. She attended a lot of games and always wore her cheerleading uniform and carried her pom-poms even though she didn't "officially" cheer for the team.

She wore that cheerleading uniform a lot at home, too, along with all of her other costumes. As I mentioned, she had a closet full of Disney princess costumes and her aunt Kate even brought her a tub full of dance costumes she'd purchased online for McKenzie. McKenzie was always decked out in some costume or another. She would change herself about every five minutes and often I would be required to take new pictures- even if we already had pictures in that outfit! I was looking through all those pictures the other day and I'm so glad I have them. They really chronicle her personality as well as her growth.

Despite the disease in her body, she continued to grow. She was head and shoulders above the height she'd been when she was diagnosed. When she first began treatment, she had been placed on many steroids to pump up her system in preparation for chemotherapy. Her face looked even chubbier than before and she had been a chubby looking baby. Following chemo, though, she looked extremely skinny. She was just skin and bones. She never regained her chubby look. She continued growing taller and more mature looking. Some of her maturity was simply age, but much of her maturity was being forced to live in a world of doctors and hospitals. She interacted more with grownups than children for the most part and that showed. She didn't know how to relate as well to children her age. She dealt with her older brother and sisters and loved babies. She would see a baby in the doctor's office and get so excited. She would play babies with her friends only if they would let her be the "mom". What she really wanted was to boss them around! I think that was partially due to the fact that she was constantly being bossed around- in a medical sense. She grew up while we were looking like most children.

While we were on our Make-A-Wish trip, Monroe got a phone call that would change our lives again. He was offered a job as Vice President of Domestic Sales with Merit Medical, the company he had now worked for just over six years. The tricky part was that we would have to move to Salt Lake City, Utah, where the company headquarters are located. We began praying about it immediately. We'd never lived outside of Texas. With McKenzie's illness in remission, we felt like it was a possibility we could consider. We began considering all of the implications: we would need to find her an oncologist in Salt Lake with whom we could have follow up appointments; we would need to find schools for the children, we would need to find a church and find out if there was a BSF class for me. And we would need to find a home that was as wonderful as our home now. We prayed for a couple of weeks and spoke to very few trusted confidantes.

Finally, we told the children. That went over like a lead balloon. They all cried and told us we were making a huge mistake. Courtney even ran away from home one January night, barefoot. We had told them on a Monday night and Monroe had flown out Tuesday morning for business. That Tuesday evening I picked Courtney up from a basketball game and talked about it on the way home. I think her last words to me were, "I hate you. You're ruining my life." And then she got out of the car in the driveway, barefoot, and ran off. I couldn't very well go after her because I had three other children in the house to take care of. It was bedtime for the younger ones so I went on in to face them. Thank the Lord Courtney showed up about thirty minutes later, yelled some more, slammed some doors, and retreated to her bedroom. I'd never seen her act this way, but she was a fifteen-year-old girl and it was understandable after all she'd been through. Bless her heart-this would only be the beginning. Sometimes I question God's wisdom in allowing such heartbreak in the lives of our children. Every time I start to question, though, God reminds me that He is using these trying events to shape these young people into who He needs them to be. He will use every teardrop to create such extraordinary people that we will be amazed at what He is able to accomplish through them. It is difficult to watch as a mother, but necessary to fulfill His purposes.

We scheduled a trip to Salt Lake in February and took Courtney and Caroline with us. Monroe began his new job at the first of the month so while he began working in his new office, the girls and I went looking for schools. We decided it would be best to find a high school first that Courtney would like and then find a house close by that would choose the elementary and middle school. We toured three different public high schools and found two that would work just fine. The last day of our search we toured the private Christian school and the private Catholic school. While we really liked the Christian school, Courtney eliminated it as a possibility because the class size was eighteen and she'd been attending a school with a class size of 584. Going from 584 to 18 just didn't seem like the right fit for us. I'd never intended for my children to attend a Catholic school as we weren't Catholic, but we went to tour the school as a favor to one of Monroe's work associates whose children attended there. We were very impressed with the facility and the people we met there. After two hours, Courtney announced to my surprise that this was the school for her. And so we began the house search in proximity to the Skaggs Catholic Center.

Back home in San Antonio, we put the houses on the market. We had our primary residence in north San Antonio and we had our little lake house in Granite Shoals to sell. It broke our hearts to think of parting with these houses we'd loved. In these houses, we'd laughed and cried about McKenzie's diagnosis, we'd administered countless hours of chemo, and battled with the cancer dragon. I began packing things up and slimming down our personal items so the house would show well. We rented a storage unit and filled it quickly.

Monroe

In February, we prepared for a six month CT scan. Jeri and I were very anxious about what would take place and what we would find. As the days grew closer to the test, the stress of going to the hospital once again began to creep into our lives.

It seemed that, as long as McKenzie was not in the hospital, we could trick ourselves into believing that everything was all right. The problem was that every time we had to go to the doctor or the hospital, reality would crash in around Jeri and me with a vengeance.

Also on February 8th, McKenzie celebrated her fourth birthday and with (what else, but?) a Princess Party. She and ten other little girls got to play dress up and get their hair fixed just perfect. It was a sight to see and once again another milestone.

Jeri

McKenzie continued to have a great spring. We celebrated her fourth birthday in style at Sharkey's where she and ten of her closest friends tried on every costume they had. The girls had their hair and nails done. McKenzie's hair was growing back in very well. She couldn't have much of an up-do, but her hair was played with and sprayed with glitter. She couldn't have looked more beautiful to me. We had her favorite cake from H.E.B. grocery store with all the Disney princesses on it. I was so encouraged by her health and celebrated her life and birthday with gusto! We all did. Something about almost losing your daughter makes you appreciate her so much more.

Wednesday, February 11, 2009 7:10 PM, CST

Good Evening Everyone,

I wanted to give an update on McKenzie. We have had a great month and things are going well for the May Family so far in 2009.

On February 8th, last weekend, McKenzie celebrated her 4th Birthday. We are all very thankful that she was able to celebrate and is feeling so well. We praise God for this blessing.

On Friday of this week, February 13th, McKenzie will have an Abdominal CT for her six-month check up. Please pray for her to cooperate and for the test to go well.

Also, please pray for her to remain cancer free. She seems to feel well and we continue to be encouraged. However, we would appreciate all the prayers that are possible.

Thank you and may God bless you all,-Monroe

Friday, February 13, 2009 7:36 PM, CST

A very GOOD EVENING to you all! Well, I'm not sure who taught McKenzie the song "Ho-Ho-Hosanna, Ha-Ha-Hallejuia, He-He-He Saved Me, and I've got the joy of the

Lord", but that kind of sums up the sentiments at our house tonight. She has been singing that song all day and it just clicked with me a little while ago how appropriate it is! Our prayers were answered: her scans went quickly (she made it to her Valentine's party at Coker MDO) and they found nothing in the scans! Dr. Patel is out of town and his partner reviewed the scans and said they look good. We are very relieved and happy. Thank you all for your prayers. Happy Valentine's Day! With Love, Jeri

Monroe

We had made it six months! Our family celebrated this news and praised God that He had healed our little angel. For the first time in almost a year, I started to believe that we might actually beat this disease.

I started immediately making weekly trips to Salt Lake and worked in the office three to four days a week and then would journey back to San Antonio. Jeri continued to manage the kids, school and McKenzie's illness.

Jeri

McKenzie and her brother and sisters attended the annual Easter egg hunt in her grandmother's neighborhood. We'd been attending this egg hunt since Courtney was a little bitty girl and her grandfather, Grande, was still alive. We had attended faithfully every Palm Sunday. The hunt was divided into age categories up to about fourteen years old. The kids had won through the years for either most eggs found or for finding the golden egg. Courtney likes to tell that her dad would always help her scope out the golden egg visually before the hunt, but this year it would have been difficult for him to be in three places at once. This year, Caroline, Monroe Jr., and McKenzie all found the golden egg in their age categories! The prize for finding the golden egg was a huge stuffed bunny and I was never so happy to have a picture of all three of my eligible egg hunters holding that giant rabbit! McKenzie was especially proud of herself. This was unchartered territory for her- being out among other children and winning something! She had her face painted with a giant pink Easter egg and ate a chocolate cupcake chased down with orange drink. It was great seeing her get to be just a normal kid!

Sunday, March 29, 2009 9:38 AM, CDT

Good Morning Everyone,

It has been almost 6 weeks since we last posted anything. McKenzie continues to do well and is back to herself. This morning she is playing with Monroe, and they are fighting about everything. So I guess we are back to normal.

Last weekend Jeri even took her to get her first haircut post chemo and post BMT. It is great that she has enough hair to cut!

Some family news that many of you may already have heard, in June our family will be moving to Salt Lake City. I have been offered a job at the Merit home office. We are all excited and anxious about the move. We know that ALL things come from God and we will face the challenge of the move and the challenges that life provides as they come.

I hope that all of you and your families are healthy and that you can enjoy this Easter season. Life is a gift, live for the moments. -Monroe

Jeri

She also participated in the Fiesta bike parade at her school that spring. She rode up and down the cones with all the other kids wearing her helmet and with streamers flying from her two-wheeler with the training wheels. She did the Mexican hat dance with the teachers and children from her class with so much gusto! Again, I was so proud and happy for her. These were things she'd been denied while in treatment.

I began thinking and dreaming of all she could accomplish in her life. I loved the thought that she had overcome the odds and would outlive us all. I loved thinking that God had really done a miracle in defeating the cancer that had threatened her life and our happiness. I had so many plans and dreams for her- for all of us. Maybe I got a little prideful in my own part of her remission. We had scans every couple of months to check for any possible return of cancer cells. Every time we did, I held my breath and waited. I don't think I really expected a recurrence, but it was scary being back in that hospital having to subject my daughter to testing AGAIN. Every time the scans came back with no evidence of current disease, I praised God again. Then I went back to my perfect little life.

Monroe

As spring progressed, we continued to enjoy our time as a family. We had Spring Break and spring sports and enjoyed each and everyday. We were happy to have our daughter healthy and active and loved that God had brought us to this point.

We had put our house on the market and in addition to everything else, had to be prepared at a moment's notice of showings. The market was down in the spring of 2009 so we were asking less then we had originally hoped. Our attitude was that if it were meant to be, God would make it happen.

Jeri

I offered to share my testimony with a group at church and the answer the woman gave me stung. She said, "Jeri, I just can't help thinking that your story isn't complete." My reaction was anger- "what do mean, not complete?" Of course our story wasn't complete. McKenzie had so much left to accomplish. But I should still be allowed to tell of the miracle God had accomplished in our lives. I did not want to consider that we would have to endure more and have more to share. I was finished with cancer treatment in my mind and had been given my happy ending.

McKenzie and I talked a lot that spring about her room in Salt Lake City. She did a lot of dreaming of how she wanted her room decorated. As I've said, we spoiled her after having come so close to losing her so I was glad to dream with her. She wanted a pink room and a big fluffy bed. I was determined she would have it. As I house hunted, I always considered McKenzie's wishes and searched for just the right room for her. I wanted to reward her for having spent all those nights in a sterile hospital bed. I was determined to give her a big beautiful pink room.

So, life in remission was a dream come true for me. We lived with purpose and gusto. We played hard at the lake and played hard at home. We worshipped the Lord and thanked Him for returning our little girl to us. We made plans to move to Salt Lake.

Sunday, April 26, 2009 8:18 PM, CDT

Hi Everyone! I feel so out of touch! I haven't written to you in so long! Sorry! As you can guess, much is happening at the May household. With McKenzie in remission, we are going full speed ahead with our hair on fire! You know, McKenzie has hair now so she can join in. She still loves wearing her wigs; in fact, she is wearing Snow White right now! She still asks about "when her hair grows back in" and I keep trying to explain to her that she has hair now. I think what she really means is "when her hair gets long enough to put into ponytails and braids". But her hair is darling now! We can now put in a bow or wear a headband. She has been doing so many things since I wrote last. You can kind of chronicle them by the new pictures I added. We have had a birthday celebration with some friends from school, gone to the Little Heroes' Prom put on by the Leukemia and Lymphoma Society, hunted all sorts of Easter eggs, and ridden in the Fiesta Bike Parade at Coker Mother's Day Out. Check out the pictures and you can see how full of life our little girl is. She continues to do well health wise. We are visiting the doctor once a month now. We will have scans again in May. You can pray that they are easily done (she has done them twice without sedation) and that they find nothing. I can't imagine what we would feel if they found anything, so please pray that God allows them to be completely clear. As I reflect on last year and where we are today compared to where we were then, I feel so thankful not only for God healing her (although I am certainly grateful for His healing hand), but for all that He has taught me through our experiences. He has deepened my faith incredibly. I will never again take for granted the true gift of life. God's word is so much more applicable now than it was then. Ken Hicks asked the question in church today how I would leave my mark on the world. I hope that some of you have felt the mark of what we have experienced. I have tried to put down in words the amazing love of Jesus Christ through my sentiments in this journal. I am so grateful to Him for giving me McKenzie, my other children, my husband and all of you to love. I truly care about the eternal salvation of all of you. If you have any doubt where you would go if you died tonight, email me! I know where I would go and I know where McKenzie would go. Be there with us. Well, that is about it! Some fun stuff and some heavy stuff. Hope this entry finds you all well. Talk to you soon. With Love, Jeri

Monroe

In May, McKenzie had an additional test. We were very happy that we had progressed from CT scans to x-rays and an ultrasound. Both Jeri and I thought this was very positive and took it as a good sign that the medical community believed things were going well. We continued to be hopeful that everything would be all right.

By May, the family was also coming to the realization that we would be moving over the summer. Courtney, Caroline and Monroe did not like the idea, however, they did accept the fact that we would be going. They began saying their good-byes. The end of school became very emotional for the kids and for Jeri.

Friday, May 22, 2009 7:33 AM, CDT

Good Morning! All is well here at the May house. McKenzie had her latest round of scans this past Monday (the 18th). We have apparently been downgraded from ct scans. Instead, we had a chest x-ray and a pelvic/abdominal ultrasound. It was a little bit tricky because McKenzie has become adept at jumping on the table and holding still for the ct scan and this was all new. I did my best to prepare her for what was to come. I put some gel on her hand to show her what the gel would feel like on her tummy. She did okay, but it was a long day. She had to fast for the ultrasound so from Sunday night dinner, she had nothing to eat until 11:30am after the test. She cried some during the ultrasound simply because she didn't know what to expect. She was a pro for the x-ray. She stood still and grinned. After the tests, we went over to the doctor's office and Dr. Patel said we had the all clear! Praise the Lord! Today is her last day of Mother's Day Out. She has loved her school so much since we went back. Everything is hard to end this year knowing that we will probably be in Salt Lake City by mid-summer. I would love you all to pray that one of our two houses will sell quickly. We are having a very difficult time with Monroe in SLC so much of the time and the rest of us here. I question many parenting decisions I make and often

I am stressed out to the max resulting in yelling at the children and further stressing them out. We need to all live together. Please pray that the Lord unites us under one roof by July. Thank you my friends. - Jeri

Jeri

We would end up "all under one roof" by mid-July, but it was not at all how we had planned. Isn't it funny how God answers our prayers sometimes, but not in the way that we envision the answer?

Recurrence

Jeri

It was June 2009 and we had a contract on the house! We were so excited because the economy wasn't looking good and we weren't sure if the house would sell. It was a contingency contract from a couple moving with their family from California. Monroe, Courtney, and I flew up to Salt Lake and found a house for us. I had been looking for six months and was ready to finally make a choice. We chose a great home with a room for everyone and especially one for McKenzie's pink room.

Back home in San Antonio, life went on fairly normal for summer in San Antonio. It was hot as usual. We went to the neighborhood swimming pool, we went to the lake house that was on the market but not selling, we went to church, and hung out with our families and friends.

Monroe was traveling back and forth to Salt Lake every week for his job. He would usually leave on Tuesday morning and come home on Thursday evening. It was tough being apart for half the week, but it was just part of drill until we could all get to Salt Lake to live together.

Since McKenzie's surgery the year before, she had endured many stomach problems. During surgery, while scraping the disease from her internal organs, her entire G.I. system had been nicked and bruised. She ate so much that she always had a stomachache, it seemed. She ate a lot of healthy foods, but then again, she was a kid and we let her eat a lot of junk food, too. We didn't deny her much. So we were used to frequent bowel movement challenges. In June, though, it seemed to intensify. She just couldn't go to the potty and her stomach was hurting all the time. So one day while Monroe was out of town, I took her into the doctor. They sent us to x-ray. It was scary. All the implications of cancer rained down on me again. But the x-ray showed only blockage in her intestines and we were sent home with instructions for an enema. Somehow, I had escaped giving anyone an enema for the first forty-two years of my life. So let's just say it was quite an experience having to do this for my precious four year old. She had been through so much. This was just not fair to have to do this to her. But I kept telling myself that if this wasn't cancer that I could do anything. So we got through it and after two treatments, the blockage was removed. We had a second x-ray and it showed clear.

So we went back to the business of packing and planning for our upcoming move. The rest of June passed without event.

Thursday, June 25, 2009 2:55 PM, CDT

Hello everyone! I was on here updating some pictures, so I thought I would drop you all a little note. We are doing fine. McKenzie is doing great. She seems to feel well. We are busy with summertime activities- swimming, movies, and fighting with her siblings. Right this moment, she is sitting here playing play dough. She got to play a few minutes with a friend this morning. These are all things she wasn't doing last year at this time and I am so thankful she is doing them now- even fighting with her siblings. That is one area where we could use some prayer. I feel guilty asking for this because I think we all have children that argue. I know I did with my siblings as a child. But, I think with all she went through, she doesn't understand why everything is not all about her. Monroe thinks that because she wasn't disciplined for a year that she is emotionally behind. I buy that, too. But, none of it changes the fact that she is a constant challenge to the family balance. I know of at least one of her siblings who really just doesn't like her and I know she irritates the other two. Things are so much easier when she is not around because she ALWAYS demands her own way. Now understand that she doesn't always get it, but she does always demand it. So as you are praying for patience and creative parenting skills for yourself, please pray for us, too. I'll lift you up as well... With Love, Jeri

Monroe

By the end of June, Jeri and I had agreed upon a house in Draper, Utah that is a suburb of Salt Lake. We had made an offer and had closing date scheduled for August. We had a contract on our house on Manhattan Way and planned on moving as soon as it sold. We were excited about the adventure ahead.

We still had our lake house and hoped that it would sell soon, however, since it was still ours we planned one last July 4th celebration at the lake. It was a bittersweet weekend; it would be the last weekend we had our boat and that the house was put together. We had arranged to have an estate sale to get rid of everything in the house, the weekend after the 4th of July holiday. In addition, I had arranged to sell the boat on July 7th.

Jeri

July 4th- Independence Day- found us back at our beloved lake house, all together. We knew this would be a hard weekend because it would be our last at the lake with the boat and all the family. Monroe's aunt and uncle were having everyone up. There would be food and family and fun- for us the last time before our move. The lake house had not sold, but Monroe was taking the boat on Monday morning and selling it back to the wholesaler we'd bought it from. We did our best not to think about it and just have a good time. It was always a blast to sit around at the lake with the May family telling stories and laughing. The kids could swim, launch water balloons at each other, and go inside if they got too hot. The boat was just a few feet away and we would take turns with Monroe's cousins taking the kids out to ski or knee board. Everyone treated McKenzie with special care and love after all she'd endured. Her whims and requests were almost always granted. Her sisters made sure she swam with them if she wanted to swim. If McKenzie wanted to be pulled in the inner tube, someone was almost always willing to oblige. The grand finale that weekend was that we planned on taking all the boats out after dark, tying together, and watching the fireworks from the water. The kids swam following a twilight ski session. There was much laughter except from McKenzie. She was fussier than I'd seen her in a while. Monroe and I took turns trying to deal with her. Usually, she would hang out with the other kids, but this night, she clung to Monroe and me. She whined and complained about everything. Even Monroe's jokes weren't enough to calm her down. She was miserable and we were, too. We didn't understand it at the time, but we would eventually. We managed to get back to the house and get everyone to bed. We sold the boat the next day and began saying goodbye to all that we loved- the boat, the lake house, and the family. We just didn't know whom else we would have to say goodbye to yet.

Monroe

The weekend after the July 4th celebration, things would once again change in our household! Our worst fears would once again become a reality.

Jeri

A week later on Saturday, Monroe and I drove up to the lake house to pick up a few things we planned on moving to Utah with us. I had a lady coming to do an estate sale with the majority of the furniture and decorations. McKenzie stayed with my parents while we drove up. The other children were spread out at friends' houses. McKenzie always had so much fun with my folks. We could usually count on her being in a good mood when we got back. But this day, July 11th, when we got back, my parents brought her over to our house and she was obviously not feeling well. She complained that her stomach hurt. She lay on the sofa and cried. After a while, Monroe and I didn't know how to coax her out of it. Our coping mechanisms all failed. I started thinking that maybe her blockage had returned. She hadn't been to the bathroom in a couple days. Maybe that was it. Finally, I called the doctor's office.

Our regular doctor, Dr. Patel, was unavailable, but his partner told us to bring her on in- to the emergency room. We avoided the emergency room at all costs. The doctors and nurses there did not know or understand McKenzie. The nurses on the 4th floor Hem/Onc unit did. If Dr. Patel was available, he always called and had her admitted sending us directly to the 4th floor unit. The other doctor, however, did not have Dr. Patel's clout at the hospital or his finesse with patients like McKenzie or parents like us. This would become a pattern and problem for us over the next few weeks.

We went to the emergency room, explained our situation, and we were placed in a room. As usual, the nurses had a difficult time accessing McKenzie's port. We'd had a concern since the previous August during stem cell transplant that her port would stop working altogether. Already, only one of the two accesses was working. They finally got it and we were sent down to get a C/T scan. I felt totally on display as we walked through the unusually "quiet for a Saturday night" Children's ER. I remember thinking, "These people think we're here because McKenzie has cancer, but really we're only here because she is having stomach problems." We had the scans done easily because by now McKenzie was an old pro at following scan instructions. We headed back to our ER room. Finally, the doctor came in. I still think I heard him wrong. He said, "We have recurrence." I was shocked. Literally, I was in shock. I don't remember much after that except the ringing in my ears. Okay, I remember tears. I remember trying to hold it together for McKenzie who was so much more aware of what was going on than at her original diagnosis. I remember looking at Monroe. He says now that he knew. He knew when we went in that day what they would find. I, ever the optimist, never suspected. I think I was more blown away at recurrence than I was at first diagnosis. My mind started clicking on what needed to be done- call the grandparents, update the website, circle the wagons. There was no doubt in my mind that we would fight this again and that, again, God would heal my baby girl. There was just no other alternative in my mind.

Sunday, July 12, 2009 12:17 AM, CDT

> *Hello everyone. I'm just going to come out and say it. We have recurrence. We took McKenzie into the hospital this evening because she has been having abdominal pain for almost forty-eight hours. They did a C/T scan and found a mass. She is there tonight and will have a bone marrow biopsy in the morning. We'll see after that. So we need your prayers. Please pray for clear information from the doctor. Please pray for wisdom as Monroe and I make decisions. We will need to make decisions about her treatment as well as decisions about our pending move. On a practical level, her port is not working and we need prayer for resolution to that problem. I will keep you posted as we go. Good night, Jeri*

Sunday, July 12, 2009 1:09 PM, CDT

Hello again, it is Sunday afternoon now. McKenzie had the biopsy this morning, but we don't have the results yet. I did want to let you all know that the oncology nurses were able to get her port working. That is a big answer to prayer. So thank you. Right now she is just sleeping. It would probably be best for us not to have visitors right now. She is really hurting. Thank you for your continued prayers. With Love, Jeri

Jeri

Finally, McKenzie was admitted onto the 4th floor unit. My mind was working on the here and now. What did we need to do to make her comfortable? How could we stop the pain? Monroe, ever the visionary, was working on much farther-reaching questions. How could we move to Salt Lake with this going on? Should he go ahead and quit his job today or next week? Somehow, we told the family. Somehow, we formed the words to post it on her website. I know the prayers began immediately. God's people immediately began storming the gates of heaven on our behalf. I felt none of it. McKenzie was all that mattered- taking care of her immediate needs. I have no recollection of who stayed with her that Saturday night although I'm sure it was Monroe. I think it was Sunday afternoon when I came to stay for my night that I found the doctor there wanting to talk to me. Sometime during the diagnosis and admittance, we found that Dr. Patel was out of the country and would be for two weeks. This was devastating news for us because we really disliked dealing with anyone else. We couldn't believe this would happen when Dr. Patel, who had been such a strong supporter for us, was unavailable. This doctor was suggesting we begin treating again right away. We were not ready for this. We wanted to wait until Dr. Patel came back. This doctor wanted us to take McKenzie, by ambulance, to the Cancer Therapy and Research Center for a PET scan. I was not about to subject McKenzie to the frightening experience of an ambulance. Somehow, in our year and a half of treatment we had avoided that. She was scared enough as it was. I refused to do that. I did offer to drive her there myself. But, hospital protocol would not allow that. So I refused. I also reasoned the fact that we had not had a PET scan at original diagnosis and I didn't really see that it was completely necessary now. We knew she had cancer and that was enough for now. The humor of this situation now occurs to me, but it was anything but humorous at the time. Part of the problem was that McKenzie would not deal with this doctor. She refused him to be in her room. When he came in to examine her daily, she yelled at him. So he would be in the hallway or across the hall in the family room and I would have to go out and across to visit with him. I would have to wait to visit with him when McKenzie didn't need me. If she was asleep or busy visiting with one of the nurses or child life specialists, I could sneak out. That was rare. And then I would have to consult with Monroe on the telephone as he was with the other children. It made it a challenge to gather information on our options and to make decisions reasonably. We finally decided to allow the doctor to administer one round of chemo. This would buy us the time we needed to wait until Dr. Patel returned. It would also address McKenzie's pain issues.

Monday, July 13, 2009 7:24 PM, CDT

Hello Everyone,

Thank you all for the prayers, notes and help with our other 3 children over the last 48 hours. Jeri and I appreciate all the continued support from each of you.

This afternoon the doctor confirmed that the cancer has spread to the bones once again (stage IV). Not the news we wanted, however, we were not surprised either. She is back to where she was 20 months ago when we originally began this journey.

Tomorrow, McKenzie will receive an injection that will remain in her body for 24 hours enabling them to do one additional test on Wednesday. Then on Wednesday, we will also begin 3 days of chemo. We are trying to prepare for all the side effects that will accompany the chemo. She is comfortable at the moment; however, it is obvious that she is not feeling her best.

Please pray for wisdom for Jeri and me as we make decisions about McKenzie's treatment, as well about our upcoming move. There is ALOT going on and we want to make the best decisions for ALL of our children.

Thank you all-Monroe

Jeri

Our next issue of decision was what to do about the move to Salt Lake. Monroe decided it would be best for the company if he quit his job. He felt there was no way we could make the move right away and that would be unfair to Merit as they had already waited seven months for us to get our house sold. Our contingency contract had, by then, firmed up and we had movers scheduled at the end of the month. Merit had chosen the moving company and the packers were to come in a few weeks so I had packed very little. Monroe spoke to his boss who talked him out of quitting. This was good because I knew we would need our health insurance. It was also good because it reassured Monroe that he was the man for the job. We talked and prayed about it and felt that we had come to a good compromise by Tuesday, July 14th. We would rent a house for six months and stay in San Antonio to see what would happen next. Monroe came up with this option and I thought it was an excellent one. I got online and started searching for houses for rent in our same school area. The Lord knew I couldn't handle this one on my own so he sent me our good friend, Phil Essex, who had sold our house for us. I called Phil from the hospital and told him what we needed. He sent me some choices and on Tuesday evening Monroe, Phil and I toured three different properties. Only one would really work for us and Phil helped us get the lease contract going. We met the owner of the home and were thrilled that she was a member of our church. It was reassuring to me that she might be a Christian and this would go smoothly. We really needed something to go smoothly-anything. It worked out in the short term, but in the long term, this rental would be another difficult part of our journey.

The other part of the moving puzzle was packing. Previously, the moving company was supposed to pack our things over a three-day period. Now we were responsible for the packing and the moving to the rental. I was a little panicked trying to figure out how we would get packed and moved over a two-week period while caring for McKenzie in the hospital and the other children as well. But, as usual, God knew this and He provided the plan. You see, Monroe has a group of high school friends who still see each other regularly even after twenty-five years. The wives of these friends have formed a tight network. Some I know pretty well, others I've only met once or twice. But, that week, every evening that I was home from the hospital, a group of those women (whether I knew them well or not) showed up to pack our household goods. They showed up with boxes and packing tape. They showed up with and without husbands. Husbands worked to take down our trampoline. Wives packed boxes and called in others. Some of those dear women had organizational skills that I will never possess. Others showed up with wine and added to the fun factor. Either way, they were all such a blessing to me that I'll never be able to thank them with words. My heart beats faster when I think of the overwhelming love with which they worked. They were the hands and feet of Christ to me.

Tuesday, July 14, 2009 10:32 PM, CDT

Well, it is late, but I wanted to let you guys know the latest. McKenzie had a good day. She has been awake most of the day and received little medicine. She did get some morphine about 9:30pm. Right now she is eating a Popsicle. I made her promise that after the Popsicle she would try to get some sleep. I know I'm ready. We are figuring she might not want to eat again for a while since chemo starts tomorrow. We'll see. Y'all pray that she doesn't get too sick.

We made another important decision today. We will rent a house for 6 months and Monroe will continue traveling to do his job while we figure out how McKenzie's treatment will go.

So for all our San Antonio friends, we'll still be here a while... For all our Salt Lake friends, we still hope to be there soon!

Well, I'm going to try to get her to sleep. Good night all! Jeri

Wednesday, July 15, 2009 9:07 PM, CDT

Hello Everyone,

Day 4 in the hospital and it did not go quite the way we had thought. The doctor decided to push off the chemo treatment one more day. So it was really a rather quiet day. Jeri and McKenzie had the MIBG test around lunchtime and then she rested much of the afternoon. McKenzie did have a couple of visitors. Courtney, Caroline and Monroe all came to see her for a few minutes as well as Dee Dee. Tonight we are currently watching, GiGi, my favorite, and we just finished Enchanted. I am hopeful she can get some rest soon, because tomorrow will be a big day. Tomorrow we will have another MIBG scan and then the doctor assures us we will begin 72 hours of chemo. Please pray that the side effects are kept to a minimum. We are anxious about what it will do to her. Also, please pray for the pain to go away. Today we have given McKenzie morphine more and more frequently. I hate to see her in pain, but I hate that she is on morphine as well. That is it for today; we will update everyone tomorrow as we begin chemo treatments.-Monroe

Thursday, July 16, 2009 8:11 PM, CDT

Hello everyone! Jeri here. Just a short update: we did begin chemo today at 5:30pm. There was a technical delay with the hospital policy- a conflict with them not allowing the doctor to attempt a combination of drugs for which there is no documented proof of success. The frustration came again in lack of communication between the doctor and us. We began a five-day treatment instead of a three-day one. I don't truly believe there is documented proof of "success" with any combination, but we must try something to fight this freight train of disease that is bearing down on our daughter. In addition, she is now on a morphine drip to help control the pain. The doctor believes that the chemo will begin to help with the pain within two to three days and we will be able to wean her off the morphine within that same time period. I hope so. I want to believe it. We will see. We will know quickly if the disease will react to this treatment. On the home front, we continue to make decisions that will affect our housing situation. Please pray for a smooth transition into our chosen rental home. Our children need some semblance of order in their home life. Everything has been so up in the air. I just keep telling the girls that they are blessed because they will have a place to live and they know with whom they will live. These things they can know for sure unlike so many children in the world. God knows the exact place we will live and I pray that He will reveal it soon to us! Hug your babies! Thank God for your home! Kiss your spouse and tell them you love them! Have a restful night. I'll check in tomorrow. With Love, Jeri

Monroe

To say the week of July 11th was stressful for the family is an understatement. All of the children were concerned about the move and about their sister. Then to have to make quick decisions about where we would live, where they would go to school, and when we would move to Utah was almost more than they could stand. The tension was high and the only choice we all had was to keep moving ahead. McKenzie was in the hospital, our closing date was approaching, and we had to prepare to move.

In addition, since we decided to stay in San Antonio, we moved ahead with letting our oldest daughter, Courtney, begin Driver's Ed. Originally, we had planned on letting her wait and get in when we got to Utah, however, with the delay, we thought it would be best to move ahead and help her to get her license. We signed her up and she was driving within a couple of days with a parent in the car. At age fifteen, this was a rite of passage and something we had to let her do. It was one more thing to keep up with, however, it was a great distraction for her and gave her a great deal of confidence.

Also, during this time, we wanted desperately to wait for Dr. Patel to return from his trip in order to make plans for future treatment. His partner refused to listen to our wishes and our desires for McKenzie. All he could discuss was that we would begin chemo and go down the same course as before-chemo, surgery, and then stem cell transplant. Statistics said she had less then a 10% chance of survival. Jeri and I began to have our doubts.

I tried several times to have a discussion with him, however, each time I came away feeling that he just was not listening.

The only thing he wanted to do was treat this little four year old girl with everything he could throw at her. I refused to believe that this was best course of action.

Jeri and I decided we would follow his suggestions until Dr. Patel returned. Dr. Patel knew Jeri and me very well at this point and we believed he would give us honest answers to our very direct questions.

Throughout McKenzie's fight and hospitalizations, Jeri and I often found ourselves comforting those around us. Other people have told me that they too have shared similar experiences. It seems that people show up with the best of intentions and then tend to tell you how difficult all of this is for them. They feel so bad and they just don't know what to do or to say. This happened over and over again, in and out of the hospital. Emotions are an interesting thing and are very difficult to control. Jeri and I were often called to check ours so that we would not offend others, and yet it seemed that we got to listen to really thoughtless comments and suggestions. I finally reached the point where I would not let people into the hospital room and would even ask people to leave.

Monday, July 20, 2009 9:38 PM, CDT

Well, we have a small cause to celebrate tonight. McKenzie is home! Maybe just for tonight, but I am hoping and praying that we get to keep her here much longer. She got her last day of chemo today and started trying to get her ready to go. She said she didn't want to go and refused to take the oral medication for a while. But she finally agreed. We were so glad we did! Once she got home, she agreed to eat and drink and go to the bathroom. She went to sleep easily at bedtime and is quiet now. It is a great thing. She always heals better at home. Have a good night. Jeri

Monroe

LETTER TO MCKENZIE, FROM DAD-Personal Journal:

July 21, 2009

Dear McKenzie,

McKenzie, here we go again. Last Saturday night, you began complaining about pain in your legs and stomach. We were concerned as always but not worried. As a family we were in the process of selling two houses and buying a house in Salt Lake City, so we had a lot going on. We had been at the lake for July 4th and that was our last weekend at the lake. We had just put money down on a house in Salt Lake and we were all getting excited about the move. Life was moving fast....

On Saturday night, July 11th, you lay on the couch and cried. You yelled that your legs hurt and your stomach hurt. We searched our brains about possible explanations besides the obvious. After a short period of time, we called the doctor and went to the ER at Methodist Children's Hospital. Within a couple of hours, it was confirmed that the cancer was back. On Sunday morning, you had a double bone biopsy and, once again, we were told it had spread to the bone marrow. On Thursday afternoon, we began five days of chemo. On Monday, July 20th, after five days, we went home against the recommendations of the doctor. Now, we wait to see how the tumor responds to the chemo. The statistics are not good and your mother and I are at very different places as to how we should proceed. Your diagnosis is recurrent neuroblastoma with at least two bone lesions.

In the meantime, we have gotten out of the contract for the house in Utah and we have rented a house in San Antonio and will remain here for the next six months. I will continue to travel to SLC and your wonderful mother will hold down the fort in SA. We are blessed with many wonderful friends and family to help us all through this. God will do the rest, as He always does! May He bless your soul and your life. -Love, Dad

Friday, July 24, 2009 9:05 AM, CDT

Good Friday morning, everyone. Yesterday was our doctor visit. She received a dose of chemo and some other drugs to keep her comfortable. She also had a neupogen shot in her leg. These neupogen shots daily are what she most fears. She cries each day until she gets it and then rebounds in her emotions a little. So, once we got that yesterday and then were on our way home she was in a much better mood. She was in a pretty good mood the rest of the afternoon and was very pleased when her daddy got home from Salt Lake. We were shocked that she did not get blood or platelets yesterday, but today is another day. Monroe is taking her for her appointment now. The only good thing I can say about her health right now is that at least she hasn't spiked a fever! Keep praying for us as we "just keep swimming". Go watch Finding Nemo if you haven't seen it in a while. We need prayers for strength, wisdom, patience and abundant love for each other. -Jeri

Friday, July 24, 2009 5:21 PM, CDT

Update on the day....

Courtney, our oldest daughter, passed her driving test today so we have an official student driver. Caroline is heading to a swim party tonight for church and then a sleepover. Little Monroe is heading for the beach with a friend for the weekend and McKenzie is headed back to the hospital. It was almost a typical summer day in South Texas. As they say in the movie Get Smart, "Missed it, by that much..."

McKenzie had been to the doctor earlier today for four hours and received platelets to help her blood recover from chemo. She took a three-hour nap and woke up with a 100.9-degree temperature. Anything over 100.5 and we are supposed to go straight to the hospital, do not pass go.

Jeri and McKenzie are heading for Methodist and I will join them later.

We will keep you posted. "Just keep swimming". -Monroe

Sunday, July 26, 2009 8:56 AM, CDT

Good Sunday Morning,

McKenzie is doing a little better this morning and is actually eating a little. She slept well last night and had a special guest, Meemaw, spend the night with her in the hospital. It was a nice break for Jeri and me; we went to church and dinner.

Courtney and Monroe are at the beach with friends and we hear there is an abundance of sand dollars to be found. Caroline is still with friends and we saw her briefly at church and she seemed happy and to be doing well.

There are whispers that McKenzie may come home tonight or tomorrow, which would be great because we are supposed to close on the house on Monday and then move on Wednesday. We will keep you all posted.

A friend via email sent this to us and we wanted to share it with everyone. Thank you, Lisa.

I Asked God

I asked God to take away my pain.
God said, No.
It is not for me to take away, but for you to give up.
I asked God to make my handicapped child whole.
God said, No.
Her spirit was whole, her body was only temporary.
I asked God to grant me patience.
God said, No.
Patience is a by-product of tribulations;
It isn't granted, it is earned.
I asked God to give me happiness.
God said, No.
I give you blessings. Happiness is up to you.
I asked God to spare me pain.
God said, No.
Suffering draws you apart from worldly cares
And brings you closer to me.
I asked God to make my spirit grow.
God said, No.
You must grow on your own, but I will prune you to make you fruitful.
I asked God for all things that I might enjoy life.
God said, No.

I will give you life so that you may enjoy all things.
I asked God to help me LOVE others, as much as he loves me.
God said...Ahhh, finally you have the idea.
Enjoy your day and hug your kids. -Monroe

Jeri

So much of the time during recurrence, God carried us in the palm of His hand. Okay, even as I write that I know the truth is all of the time during recurrence, God carried us. Many people question their own faith during a time of tragedy. But, rather than make me question my faith, somehow McKenzie's recurrence made it possible for me to really work out my faith in my own heart and mind. What did I really believe about God? Soon, I would feel justified and solid in my faith in Jesus Christ despite the tentative ground on which I stood. That, my friend, is unshakeable faith.

The day before moving day, we busted McKenzie out of the hospital. We had permission, actually, but it was not without coaxing that we brought her home so that all six of us could spend the night together one last time in our beloved home. I took some great pictures of the girls horsing around together. They dressed up in anything they could find. They were so cute! They were so loving toward McKenzie. These memories are so precious to me.

Also, the day before the move, we had an appointment with Dr. Patel. He was back in town. Monroe and I went to meet with him at the end of his day. We sat down in his office where we'd been so many times. He came in joking and smiling as he always did. The conversation began lightly, but moved into the serious zone quickly. He told us that once recurrence happened in a stage IV Neuroblastoma patient, there was a 100% chance that it would always return. Our treatment plan, if we chose to fight this disease again, would be exactly as it had been before. We would do multiple rounds of chemo; attempt again to surgically remove the mass, and then the stem cell transplant. He said that usually the disease reappeared during or shortly after the stem cell transplant. There were no long-term survivors of stage IV recurrence. So Monroe's next question was the same as it had been on the day of her original diagnosis, "What if we do nothing?" The answer was remarkably unchanged, "You will have her for only four to six more weeks." It hit me like a ton of bricks in the face, **again**. Monroe and I had been quietly talking about this for the previous two weeks. But, to hear it spoken out loud was very difficult. Monroe was clear that he did not want to fight this again. He felt that McKenzie had been through too much. She had suffered greatly from the chemo, surgery, and transplant. He didn't want to do it all again, especially if there simply was not a chance that she would beat it this time. At least the first time we fought, we'd had a 50% chance she would beat the cancer. There were tears all over the office. I was on the fence. Throughout McKenzie's fight, I'd been so sure that God would use the treatment to cure our little girl. I'd been so sure that He **had** cured our little girl. It came down to faith for me. This was the key. For me, I thought we should fight again because McKenzie could turn out to be THE ONE that beat the odds. If we repeated the treatment all over again, she would be the one to whom the cancer did NOT return- if I just had enough faith. But then again, I was tired of fighting, too. I was tired of all that time in the hospital. I was tired of the constant risk of infection, administering drugs to my baby, and trying to balance her treatment with the lives of our other children. But, just because I was tired, was that a reason to withhold treatment from my daughter? It was a moment of decision. As the conversation progressed, we turned to asking Dr. Patel his opinion. He had never been less than honest with us and this time he was painfully honest. I appreciated that more than I can tell you. It was this moment when he endeared himself to me completely. His story that day will forever be engraved on my heart. He told of losing a sister to cancer as a young lad. He told us how he felt during her treatment. He told us how he felt at the time of her death. Finally, he told us how her death had affected him all his life. It affected every decision he made. I began to see the greater picture of what ELSE God could be doing here. Instead of simply giving him the glory because He healed her, it may be that He wanted us to give Him the glory despite the fact that He chose not to heal her. The conversation with our good friends a year and a half earlier flashed in my mind, "Even if He does not, I will yet praise Him." (From Daniel 3:18, implied) God had chosen not to save McKenzie. God had allowed this disease to return. Maybe it was His choice to take her home to heaven, to allow her to die. And what would I do? Would I praise Him anyway? This might be my test. Would I pass the test? And what if God wanted to work a miracle? Did He have to have chemo going on in order to work His miracle? Couldn't He, if He chose to, simply have the disease disappear? He could. I had to admit that He was able. He is still able today. He has ALWAYS been able. He had been able since the day McKenzie had been diagnosed. I had to trust Him. I had to trust that He would work this out in all of our lives just the way it was supposed to. I was laying McKenzie at His feet and stepping away. I was not her God. He was. He loved her more than I did- that was hard to believe, but it was true. I had to trust that He knew best for McKenzie. I was placing **my** life in His hands to do with as He pleased. I was placing my marriage in His hands. Not many marriages survive the death of a child. By the grace of God, mine would survive. I was placing in His hands the lives of my 3 other children. How would they survive the death of their sister if in fact that were what we chose? I had to trust that, like Dr. Patel, God would use all circumstances in their lives for their good because they loved Him. Maybe one of them would be the one who found the cure for cancer. I hated to think we'd have to wait as long as it would take for them to grow up and do this, but you never know. This was, without a doubt, the toughest decision I'd ever had to make. It was the toughest decision Monroe had ever made. It was literally a life and death decision. Or was it? If I believed that God was completely in control, wasn't it just a decision of trust? Did I trust Him enough with either outcome- life or death for McKenzie?

We asked Dr. Patel one final question that day. "What would you do if this were your daughter? Would you treat her a second time or would you just enjoy the time you had left with her?" Dr. Patel had become a friend to us. We trusted him not only because of his medical experience, but also because of three other reasons. First, he had grown close to McKenzie, as he seemed to grow close to most of his patients. He put his heart and soul into those children and he had a vested interest in their health. Most doctors we know (including Dr. Patel's partner) seem to have a motto of "treat the disease no matter what". They seem to see themselves as some kind of god who can truly alter the outcome of this person's life for the better if they just keep trying another drug and another and another, despite the effect of that drug on the quality of life of that person. Dr. Patel had never operated that way with McKenzie. He had always listened to our concerns and made decisions based on the whole person, not just the protocol or policy. This made us value him and his decisions all the more. Second, his experience with the death of a sister gave him credibility to answer the questions we asked. And finally, the fact that he has a daughter made him capable to empathize with us. He spoke often of his children and his love for them shone through whenever he did. His answer was, "It is very difficult for me to imagine placing myself in your position, but I don't think I would treat." We appreciate his honesty every time we consider it.

This was a monumental decision, but we decided that day not to treat McKenzie a second time for this disease. Instead, we discussed how to keep her comfortable so that she could live life to the fullest for whatever time she had left. We discussed palliative chemo treatments, ministrations of chemo drugs that would not touch the disease, but rather address the pain. The one thing we can all agree on is that we never wanted McKenzie to experience any unnecessary pain. We discussed drugs we could administer at home to lessen her pain. We discussed hospice care. It's a weird thing to discuss hospice care for your four-year-old daughter. But that's what we did.

We were in Dr. Patel's office for at least two hours that day. It was a turning point, a hinge, in my life. It was obviously a turning point in McKenzie's life. As we left, we received hugs from the staff members to which we'd grown close. They had waited for us to finish our discussion. There were tears in every eye. They knew the decision we had made. They offered us the first round of love and support we would receive.

Monroe

During that discussion with Dr. Patel, we laughed, we cried, and we came away with a decision that Jeri and I will have to live with forever and ever.

Dr. Patel gave us answers about the palliative treatment ahead and realistic outcome potential. We talked for over two hours and at the end of the discussion, Jeri and I came away with a very real understanding of what was ahead. We both came to the same decision. McKenzie deserved to have quality of life over quantity. I believe that this conclusion is one of the most Christ-like decisions we could have made for our daughter. It was also the most difficult decision I believe I will ever have to make.

Personal Journal:

July 27th, 2009

After two weeks, it looks like we have our answers. Dr. Patel returned from his trip to England and we were able to sit down and talk to him. The prognosis is not good! With recurrent Neuroblastoma, she has less then 1% chance of survival. He presented us with the options of fighting hard- surgery, BMT, heavy chemo in which the outcome would eventually be death, or we can go to palliative care and begin down the road of trying to make her comfortable. Jeri and I agree that palliative care is the best way to go. On Wednesday of this week we must move the family to a rental house and then by this Friday we will need to have a quiet spot for her to rest and play. I will stop traveling for the near future and we will try to keep the family CLOSE to us. We love our daughter and only want what is best for her. No more pain, no more hospitals and no more tears! As a parent, this is the hardest decision we will ever have to make, as a human this is without a doubt one of the greatest act of humanitarianism that we may ever be called upon to do.

Dr. Patel tells us four to six weeks. We will do our best to make these the best days of her life.

May God bless her little soul and may He agree with the path we choose.

Monday, July 27, 2009 10:01 PM, CDT

Hello Everyone,

Well we got to take McKenzie home today for a while. She was happy to break out and as always was cheerful and excited to be away from the hospital.

This afternoon Jeri and I were able to meet with Dr. Patel and have some candid and honest conversation. We appreciated his time and honesty.

We will be continuing to work with Dr. Patel closely in the days and weeks ahead.

Thank you all for your prayers and kind words. We cherish your support.

Monroe

Jeri

Next, we had to tell our parents and our other children. That was hard, too, but not as hard as actually making the decision. There was eventually understanding and acceptance, though initially it was difficult. We all wanted what was best for McKenzie, whatever God's plan was for her. We were united in seeing her through this. We would love her and care for her, no matter what- and "no matter what" was coming, it seemed.

So we spent one last night together and then began to move our things to the rental house the next morning. We did have the moving company move our heavy furniture and we took the boxes in a rented truck. When I say "we" took the boxes, I am talking about Monroe, me, and our army of friends. Again, our friends showed up in droves to help. Again, we were so grateful. We could not have done it on our own. Our parents helped, as always, also. They have walked every step of our journey with us as well. I feel so blessed to have such loving parents and such an incredible mother in law. They kept McKenzie or Monroe Jr. whenever we needed them to. Courtney and Caroline were old enough to help and help they did.

Tuesday, July 28, 2009 7:24 AM, CDT

Good Morning everyone. Just a short update- McKenzie is at home today. She slept through the night. She is lying here on the sofa watching her favorite show- Little Bill. She is eating a Ring Pop. We spent the evening last night watching video from her Disney World trip last December. She is so precious. We are loving every moment of having her home...

Jeri

In light of the decisions we'd made, every moment with McKenzie seemed to move in slow motion. I grew to appreciate more watching TV with her, I became a little more patient when she wanted to change costumes *again,* and a little more forgiving when she fought with the other children. You would have thought that her first diagnosis would have changed me completely, leaving nothing else to learn from. But you know if we were changed completely, God would be finished with us and we would be seeing Him face to face. He's still not finished with me!

Monroe

After much prayer and discussing our decision with our children, Courtney, Caroline, Monroe, and then both of Jeri's parents and my mother, the time came to let others know what we had decided.

Tuesday, July 28, 2009 10:16 AM, CDT

Ecclesiastes 3:1-8

"For everything there is a season,

a time for every activity under heaven.

A time to be born and a time to die.

A time to plant and a time to harvest.

A time to kill and a time to heal.

A time to tear down and a time to build up.

A time to cry and a time to laugh.

A time to grieve and a time to dance.

A time to embrace and a time to turn a way.

A time to search and a time to quit searching.

A time to keep and a time to throw away.

A time to tear and a time to mend.

A time to be quiet and a time to speak.

A time to love and a time to hate.
A time for war and a time for peace."

I am drawn to these verses this morning for many different reasons and wanted to share them with you.

After our discussion with the doctor yesterday, we feel that it is time for peace. McKenzie has waged war against the enemy for the last twenty months and the time has come for her to have peace. We have made the decision to stop the aggressive battle against the disease and instead turn to COMFORT and quiet. Dr. Patel is going to help us get set up with hospice and we will turn our efforts toward making McKenzie happy on the good days and comfortable on the bad days.

I know that many of you will be shocked with this decision and I would like to ask you all to remember this was not made without guidance from our Father above. And although you may not agree with it, I would ask that you respect our wishes and continue to support our family over the next several weeks. We will continue to keep you updated.

I know that many of you would like to help, however, for now please wait for us to ask. We will need help in the future and will request it when we feel it is appropriate. Our love for our child and our family is never ending. We want only what is best for all of our children and must place them first on this journey.

Thank you for your continued prayers and support. We will keep you all posted. -Monroe

Monroe

Dr. Patel had provided us with the information and the statistics we needed to make our decision. We would stop the fight and make McKenzie as comfortable as possible for as long as possible. The doctor seemed to think that our precious baby daughter had about four to six weeks of life left. We were determined to make them the best we possibly could.

As a father, there is no harder decision I will ever have to make. Without treatment, McKenzie would die. The cancer had taken over her little body and had invaded all of her major organs once again. The tumor had grown rapidly and was not stopping! Words are not enough to describe the weight of this decision. We knew that only through death could she be free of pain and cured from this terrible disease.

I know other parents have had to face a similar decision. But when it comes to your own family and own daughter, there is no way to describe the feelings. Even as I sit and write this passage and as you sit and read it, I know that I will never be able to move ahead. This is a decision that I will have to face for the rest of my life. I believe as parents we made the correct decision, however, as parents, we face an empty bed and empty room that will forever be a reminder of a missing member of our family.

From the time of decision to the end, EVERYTHING took on new meaning! Every moment was valued and cherished. Every outing was celebrated and every occasion was special. Shouldn't we all strive to face every day like this?

Jeri

From that point on, we didn't really tell McKenzie much. Beyond the initial explanation that her "boo-boo was back in her tummy" when we went to the hospital, we didn't really tell her much except when we got to leave the hospital or when we had to go see Dr. Patel or when we were moving or when we were trying a new medicine. It seemed that from that point forward, McKenzie would begin to do the telling to us.

Life in Recurrence

Jeri

We moved that week. It was quite a chore as moving six people's worth of stuff is bound to be. But, we had so much help! People showed up out of the woodwork to help move us that day. We were so grateful. And then as we began the task of settling in to our new home, the help didn't stop. I had women who helped unpack the dishes in my kitchen, women who helped me decorate and hang pictures, and women who listened to me talk and cry as we completed each task. I loved spending time with those precious people who counseled me as we worked. Mostly, they just listened and that was counsel enough, but often we prayed and read scripture together.

It seems the moving and McKenzie's final days were synonymous. I'll never be able to picture living in that rental home without seeing her in every room.

Thursday, July 30, 2009 6:59 AM, CDT

McKenzie has spent the last two days and nights with her grandparents, Meemaw and Grandpa, and is doing well. Sounds like she has had very little pain, but she also does not have a lot of energy. We are anxious to get her back and miss her very much.

Over the last two days we have been moving. We moved out of our house on Manhattan Way yesterday and today our furniture will be delivered to our new rental house on Winding View. Last night we "camped out" at the new house. Little Monroe and Jeri slept on Monroe's bunk beds and Courtney, Caroline and I spent the night on air mattresses and mattresses on the floor. It was very restful!

Thank you to our friends Phil, May, and Stuart who helped move "stuff", and unpack boxes yesterday. We appreciate your friendship and help.

We will keep you all posted, but I wanted to make sure everyone realized we are no longer at our Manhattan Way address.

Thank you, Monroe

Saturday, August 1, 2009 7:05 AM, CDT

Good Saturday morning everyone, we just spent night number three in the new house and I think we are getting settled. We have beds, coffee, and a refrigerator with food, telephone and Internet. I think we will survive. On Friday, McKenzie and I ventured back to see Dr. Patel. She did not need blood or platelets, which was a blessing, and Dr. Patel even decided not to put her through the pain of accessing her port. So after a brief exam we were out of there and on our way to get a Chicken Nugget Happy Meal. The rest of the day was spent trying to find some order in the house and put things in their place at the house.

At one point during the day McKenzie discovered a walk way on the side of the house that she had named "The Secret Garden". We spent some time picking a few flowers and drawing in the dirt with sticks- normal four-year old stuff. The only down side to yesterday was that McKenzie's hair started coming out. On our way home from the doctor, she reached up and pulled a big handful out and said "Hey Dad, look!" I was not expecting it and my reaction upset her. I felt bad. Well, today is the first Saturday morning in 4 weeks we have not been in the hospital, so we are going to try to enjoy a quiet day. Thank you all for your continued prayers and support. Hug your kids. -Monroe

Sunday, August 2, 2009 8:43 PM, CDT

Hi everyone. Sunday night, Jeri here... McKenzie had a pretty good day today. She started out in a pretty crumby mood. But she improved throughout the morning with her daddy. The girls and I went to 11am church service. Robert, your point was well taken about your dad's continued service during his battle with cancer, but you lost me when you retold his taking his last breath here and his first in heaven. I've heard you say it before, but it takes on new meaning when you believe your baby is about to walk through that threshold.

Sorry, guys, on a happier note back to McKenzie's day. We took her to a swimming pool birthday party this afternoon. She swam a little, ate a Popsicle, and hit a "Nemo" piñata. She actually hit the piñata off the rope! Then she was ready to go.

We have some friends who have been graciously working to redecorate McKenzie's room. When we got home from the party, she worked with them for a while even helping create some custom princess and crown pictures on canvas with her handprints. She loves paint...

We ate dinner as a family- all six of us at the table! She is eating pretty well. We made s'mores after dinner and now she has fallen asleep watching Gigi, God's Little Princess.

Also, for those of you who haven't seen McKenzie in a couple days- her hair is almost all gone now. Many of you know this is a sore point with me. My vanity gets in the way. Her curls are so beautiful and we've waited so long to get them back. I cried when I unpacked her hats in her room on Friday. We had a friend come by on Saturday and take some pictures just before the majority fell out. She kept saying she didn't want to take the pictures, but she cooperated wonderfully. In fact, she was a total ham! The results are breathtaking. Her big brown eyes show so much love. She is so precious.

Well, that is the weekend in a nutshell. We thank you for honoring our wishes for protected family time. We are enjoying every moment with her. We need your constant prayers and that's about it. With much love, Jeri

Monroe

<u>Monroe's Personal Journal Entry:</u>

August 3rd, 2009- Monday

It has been one week since we met with Dr. Patel and McKenzie has done well. We have only had to give her morphine twice and she has been relatively happy and active over the last week. The chemo, no doubt, helped to boost energy and slow the tumor. I sit with her this morning and cannot help but wonder, "Have we made the most of the past week?" Are we now down to three to five weeks left in her little life? As a man, I mark much of my life by the marching of time and the use of numbers. Time and numbers are used for my company sales, Merit stock, hours of vacation, and meeting times. The clock controls my life. I feel much like Tom Hanks in Castaway- tick tock, tick tock....

And yet there are times when I look at McKenzie and all of my children and I can almost swear that time stands still. We have had many visitors the last week and people that mean well and want to help, but often, I feel that they are only here to get a small look at a dying child. All of this is very complex and I know that in order to get to the end of this chapter of my life, time must move forward, however, if possible I would stop the clocks and enjoy only the good with my four children for a few more minutes. That which does not kill us makes us stronger. I guess we are all growing by the second, the minute, the hour, the day and the week.

Jeri

One of McKenzie's dreams was to have a "pink" room in Salt Lake City. Since it became apparent that dream might not be fulfilled, we decided to make her room at the rental house fit her dream. A group of women, one who is a professional artist, offered to decorate McKenzie's room. Knowing it was not our house and that we would have to repaint when we moved in six months, I asked them to go ahead. They worked for days, even letting McKenzie help paint. She was thrilled. Everything in our lives became about her at this point. The room she would be living in was actually a small office, but we chose it because it was right next to the master bedroom. We still spent our nights with her in her room, so we wanted it to be convenient. I found her a day bed with a mattress underneath where Monroe or I could sleep. When the great unveiling of the room was complete, we were amazed. The walls were pink with flowers. The ceiling was sky blue with clouds in the shape of Mickey Mouse, a heart, and a butterfly. It was so cute! “Ms. Shawn”, as McKenzie called my artistic friend, even had incorporated McKenzie’s handprints into two canvasses that she turned into a golden crown and a pink and purple princess with dark curly hair that was amazingly like McKenzie’s hair!

Since we were told only to expect four to six weeks with her, we began quickly making plans to do everything fun with McKenzie that we thought we could cram in. If she mentioned offhand that she wanted to go bowling, we hurried everyone into the car and rushed down to the bowling alley. We thought that, perhaps, tomorrow she would not be strong enough to go. We have a dear friend who works with Shamu at SeaWorld. He got us tickets and led us personally on a back stage tour. We all got to pet a giant killer whale and stroke the back of a beluga whale. It was amazing! Another friend gave us tickets to Six Flags Fiesta Texas. Again, it was so much fun! We rode every ride twice I think! We saw the shows and the characters. Toward the end of the day, we ended up in the carnival games. One of the other children won a Supergirl cape for McKenzie. It was pink with a giant “S” on the back of it. I thought, “how appropriate” for our little super girl.

Wednesday, August 5, 2009 8:30 AM, CDT

Good morning. It's Wednesday morning now. We continue to have great family time this week. Monday was a busy day for McKenzie. We took her to SeaWorld; we were blessed with a behind the scenes tour where we got to actually touch Shamu and a beluga whale! Thank you so much to our dear friend who made that possible! She got to see the afternoon feeding in the aquarium and also to feed the dolphins. She had stamina enough to last five hours! But we decided it was time to go when she curled up in the bottom of the stroller. Also, Monday evening, McKenzie's new princess room was completed! She loves it and feels so pampered! The bedding and the artwork are incredible! We are so grateful to those sweet friends that did this for our baby girl.

Tuesday was spent at the house fairly quietly. We did some unpacking and playing. Today should be about the same.

McKenzie is doing fine during the day, but at night, she is not doing as well. She cries out in her sleep. She needs someone sleeping in her room. It's so hard to tell if she is hurting because she is the strongest person I know. She has a very high tolerance for pain. She refuses to admit she hurts, but as days go by, we are not convinced that she is not. Time will tell. Only God knows the body of His baby girl, McKenzie.

On that note, let me point something out to all of you. Many of you have commented on how strong Monroe and I are, what good parents we are. We claim no amazing power except that of Jesus Christ. By His power alone do we make our way through this maze. By His power alone can you make it through your personal maze and come out on the side of eternal life. Don't look to us and be impressed. It is only by His power and authority that we walk daily. I give Him all the glory. You are seeing the Holy Spirit at work if you see anything out of the ordinary.

Okay, with that, I leave you to walk your walk.

With much Love, Jeri

Saturday, August 8, 2009 8:43 PM, CDT

Good Saturday Evening Everyone,

Wanted to provide an update on the end of the week activities. Friday, McKenzie went to see Dr. Patel and all is about the same. He did not access her port, which made her very happy. He did, however, recommend doing palliative chemo next week on Wednesday, Thursday, and Friday. He believes that it would help slow the growth of the cancer and keep her pain free. We are planning on doing this beginning Wednesday. This week on Friday, McKenzie got to go and play with a friend for the afternoon and today, she spent some time at Dee Dee's house and her cousins, Rusty and Billy, came over to play. The rest of us went to do some back to school shopping during the day for the other kids. Tonight, we made it to CBC for church and even let McKenzie go to Sunday School. She seemed to enjoy being there. She wore her new wig she got from the American Cancer Society yesterday.

Tonight we are allowing Courtney and Caroline each to have friends over to spend the night. Monroe has decided to go to his grandmother's for the night. Smart boy! McKenzie, however, is in the big middle of all the girls!

We are cherishing each day and love the time we get to enjoy McKenzie and all of the kids. We are happy that we have almost made it through another week. Thank you Lord.

Well that is it from the May Family household for the day. I wish you all the best and don't forget to hug your kids and grandchildren. -Monroe

Wednesday, August 12, 2009 4:50 PM, CDT

Hello everyone! Well, we are finally home from our first day of palliative chemo treatment. I wasn't sure quite what to expect, but it turned out to be a long day for McKenzie and me. We arrived at the doctor's office around 10:15am. She was accessed about 10:45am. She started fluids around noon and then chemo about 2pm. We got home around 4pm after stopping by McDonald's for her current favorite, a vanilla cone. So far, no nausea, but we are giving her Zofran every four hours around the clock to keep that at bay. She is happily watching PBS kids TV on my bed and eating a ring pop (another favorite). She ate a great lunch and we'll see about dinner. Monroe will take her tomorrow and then Friday will be her third and final day for this round. Dr. Patel expects her to be tired and irritable this weekend, so we will plan to just hang around the house. Y'all enjoy the rest of your day and we will keep you posted on all the latest with McKenzie as it happens. With Love, Jeri

Thursday, August 13, 2009 9:39 PM, CDT

Good Thursday Evening Everyone,

McKenzie made it through chemo in just over three hours today. This was much quicker then Wednesday. She is still feeling fairly well and does not seem to have any nausea. We will continue to give her the Zofran every four to six hours and will return on Friday to the doctor for the last round of chemo.

This afternoon, we began the task of meeting with the hospice organization from Christus Santa Rosa. The lady that came to the house was very pleasant and seems to really care about the children and the families that she works with. On Friday, they will return and officially enroll us in their program.

Often times, this journey of ours seems like a dream. We often question if all of this can be happening to our darling little McKenzie, as well as our family. Then we step back and take a breath and realize that it indeed is happening and we are living this experience.

People say to me "I can't imagine what I would do". Well we cannot imagine it either. We live it one minute at a time, one hour at a time, one day at a time. It is all anyone can do! God continues to carry this family and McKenzie. We cannot look too much into the future, so we focus on today.

Well, I have rambled on enough, it is time to give McKenzie her next round of Zofran and then off to bed for a few hours of sleep.

Thank you to all our friends and family who so faithfully watch over us and help take care of us. Don't forget to hug your kids. -Monroe

Monroe

At some point around this time, McKenzie's Caringbridge website reached over 100,000 hits. We continued to be amazed by the outpouring of support and care we received via the web. We had people we had never met following her story and posting positive comments. It was truly humbling to be a part of the process. We gained strength and support from the wonderful comments people would share.

At the same time, we waited for things to change. Every day we watched carefully and expectantly for the smallest change in attitude or appetite- anything that would signal what was ahead.

Jeri

By this time, McKenzie had completely lost her hair again from the palliative chemo. We continued to administer the palliative chemo through most of the fall. It allowed us to control the pain much better than with morphine only. We had pain medications to administer at home, but, amazingly, with the palliative chemo in place, we initially used very little of them. We asked McKenzie often about her pain level, remembering that this time that had been our indicator that the disease had returned. But, she always claimed to have no pain. I wonder if she really knew the meaning of pain the way you and I do as pain was most likely all she'd ever known. Sometimes it was just worse than others.

During her first bout with cancer, she had plenty of wigs. She had two pink ones, a Snow White one, a Hannah Montana one, and a whole slew of hats. This time, I decided, that maybe she should have a real nice one. The American Cancer Society offers a wonderful service for cancer patients in which they provide a free wig. So, she and I went one day and tried on every wig they had! The first one she tried on was a cute, but straight, dark bob. McKenzie had curly hair and I wanted her to get something that resembled her own hair. But, every time we tried on another one, she said, "I like the first one." So, the first one she would have! It was very cute on her, but it gave her a whole new look. I always tried to have her wear it or a hat when we left the house. I loved her "baby head" as she called it. But, I didn't want people to treat her differently than other children. She would usually succumb to my wishes, at least at first, but was often seen pulling off "her hair" in public, always shocking others and bringing laughter to the rest of her family. Eventually, I got used to it and just let her do whatever she wanted; that was the way it usually went for us!

When McKenzie was first released from her July stay in the hospital, a close friend of ours offered to take some pictures of her. We were just settling into our new home and I wasn't sure the time was right. But then again, I really wanted some pictures of her before her hair fell out again. So, I agreed. I am so glad I did. Those are some of the most treasured pictures I have of McKenzie. Becky dressed her up in multiple outfits and posed her in the most precious settings. Our new home was ideal and we took everything outdoors. The whole family watched and McKenzie totally hammed it up! She loved the attention. Okay, she always loved the attention. But, she was perfect as a little model this day, really cooperating in an unusual way for her. The most ideal thing about this picture shoot was that her hair began falling out in earnest the next day. God knew, I believe, that I needed one more set of pictures with my daughter's beautiful curls in the starring role. What a blessing!

Wednesday, August 19, 2009 11:23 AM, CDT

Hello Everyone,

We just got back from Dr. Patel's and everything is about the same. No big changes in either direction. McKenzie is mostly happy and seems comfortable. We will go back and see him next Monday.

It is interesting to me sitting in a Pediatric Hematology/ Oncology Office and watching people around us stare at McKenzie. It is humbling to know that she is the sickest child in the room with a room filled with sick children. And yet she continues to shine and offer other children the toys she is playing with. She even comments on "Oh, how cute" the baby is across the room. She is special and I enjoy every moment we spend together.

Our hospice nurse, Becky, came by for the second time yesterday and McKenzie seems to have taken a liking to her. Becky will come by on Tuesdays unless we need her before.

Overall McKenzie is doing well. I made the comment that her appearance is very deceiving and as only Dr. Patel can put it he said, "Yes, my friend, it is."

So we will focus on Today and This Week and enjoy the time we have been given. I enjoy the touch of her hand in mine and the sweet sound of her voice when she says "Daddy", and the question,"Can you give me a piggyback ride," for the hundredth time today. Those are the most important parts of the day.

We appreciate your guestbook postings with so many comforting and encouraging words.

Have a good rest of the week and we will keep you posted on what is going on. -Monroe

Sunday, August 23, 2009 9:24 PM, CDT

Happy "Back to School Eve" everyone. Our McKenzie has been a busy, busy girl. On Friday when she got home from the doctor, we asked her, "What do you want to do today?" "Go swimming!" she answered. So we did! We went to see our cousin at her house and swam until McKenzie was worn out! I posted some pictures for your enjoyment! Friday evening after making a gingerbread house with her grandmother Dee Dee, McKenzie discovered some bath products from Lush that my sweet friend gave us. We had a bath with Berry Pink bath bar and the "Pinkalicious" bath was born! We've been having one or two every day since. Saturday, she spent a bunch of fun time at Grandpa and Meemaw's house while the rest of us went to church and out to dinner. Today was a very fun day for McKenzie! She got to go to Chuck E. Cheese for her friend, Haley's fourth birthday party. She had SO MUCH FUN! She didn't care that she didn't get many tickets; she only cared that for two and a half hours she got to run, climb, and play with her friends. She even showed one of her grown up friends, Mrs. Shawn, the view from the top of the tunnels! She was worn out tonight and we got her to sleep before 9pm for the first time in ages! Tomorrow is another doctor visit. I'll let you know what happens after that. Y'all have a great first day of school! With Love, Jeri

McKenzie Goes for a Swim

Monroe

The first day of school was very difficult. The children had to go back and face all of the kids that they had already said good-bye too. We were supposed to be in Salt Lake City beginning a new school year. But instead, they were all going back to the same schools. It was really hard, too, for them to share McKenzie's prognosis with people they knew. Jeri sent emails to their new teachers explaining our situation so that someone would understand if they fell apart. We had no idea what would happen in the weeks ahead or how long we would have until McKenzie would take a turn for the worse. This is a lot of stress for two parents, however, for a fifteen-year old, twelve-year old and eight-year old, it is almost more than you can imagine.

However, none of us had a choice. McKenzie had to face her illness on a day-to-day basis and deal with the increasing pain. The rest of us had to face our day-to-day lives and move ahead. We had to change and life changed around us.

Tuesday, August 25, 2009 7:38 AM, CDT

Monday was a busy day as Courtney, Caroline and Monroe all started back to school. It was with mixed emotion for us all as we had hoped to begin this school year in Utah, however as you know God had other plans.

As we prepared for school Sunday night and Monday morning the stress was obvious with the Courtney and Caroline. They were each very concerned about the weeks ahead and what is going to happen with McKenzie. We all know that things can change quickly and they needed the reassurance that they will be allowed to be with us and with McKenzie when things begin going downhill. They were also concerned facing their friends and teachers and trying to explain why we are still in San Antonio.

I have thought a lot about conversations I have had with both the older girls and my heart goes out to each, I know they will be stronger as they live through the next phase, but at the same time I cannot imagine being 12 and 15 and having to go through what we are facing.

Cancer affects everyone around it! McKenzie is obviously a huge concern on a day-to-day basis; however, we love all of our children and only want what is best for each. Please pray for continued strength that surpasses all understanding for all of our children.

We will keep you posted.-Monroe

Thursday, August 27, 2009 7:14 AM, CDT

Recently, a friend of ours, Alice, posted this clip on her Facebook page. Jeri sent it to me and we feel that this is a great clip that we can all learn from. Our attitudes play a constant part in our lives and how we face the challenges of the day.

This week, Jeri and I are making some plans and decisions that are once again challenging and very emotional. This film clip from Facing the Giants was a great reminder that we can ALL do more than we think we can.

Thank you, Alice.

http://www.youtube.com/watch?v=-vB59PkB0eQ
I hope this works for you on your computer. -Monroe

Monroe

The video clip above came from the movie **Facing the Giants**. This is a movie about a high school football coach that turns his life around as well as his season when he turns everything over to God. This clip is a scene where he challenges one of his players to give everything he can to complete a very physical task. The player is encouraged to keep going. The coach keeps telling him "don't quit, don't quit". And in the end he accomplishes far more then he ever thought he could.

Our lives are filled with these moments. Our family did not quit; we kept supporting McKenzie and each other throughout the tough times. Sometimes, all you can do is put your head down and keep moving forward. You are never beaten until you stop. With God's help, we can all do much more than we think we can.

Jeri

That video clip really described our lives just as Monroe said. We were ready to give up so many times at this point. But, how do you give up being a parent to a terminally ill child? You don't. You can't quit. And we felt that, not only could we not quit, but also that God was carrying us on His back all the way down the football field. It wasn't us crawling every step of the way, but Him.

Saturday, August 29, 2009 7:40 AM, CDT

Good morning everyone! It's Saturday morning. I feel like I haven't been doing updates much lately. I feel a little guilty about it because I want you guys to know what is happening with McKenzie, but I have been keeping awfully busy having fun with her throughout the day and meeting the needs of the other children. Monroe, too, is my partner in all these activities. However, he is better at spending a few moments with his computer. When I get online, I tend to spend way too much time here! Now about McKenzie: she is having some very fun days. Friday, we went for a play date/coffee for the Mom's with some of my friends. Some of her friends were there, too. On the way home, we stopped and bought her some ballet shoes because she is going to take a dance class on Monday. I am both excited and worried about it. She wants to do it and seems to have the energy, so we will go as long as nothing changes. Then in the afternoon, we had a visit from one of McKenzie's youngest cousins. She had a great time playing with this cute little man and his mama and grandma. Last night, we decided to venture out to Olive Garden for dinner and picked up some ice cream from Coldstone Creamery for dessert. She was too tired to eat her ice cream by the time we got home, but we saved it for her! Now about the nights: McKenzie is not sleeping well. She cries in her sleep all night long. She often wakes up and cries for one of us. Usually, her daddy is the chosen one to sleep on the mattress on her floor, but one of us is there 90% of the time by morning. We are starting to believe that this crying in her sleep is pain manifesting itself. Because she is adamant that she is not hurting during the day, we really haven't used the morphine on hand in any regular pattern. But, I think we are about to start. She hates taking it so much. We hate to force her, but I think we need to. Please pray that we will have wisdom in this matter.

Thank you all for your continued love, prayers, and support.
With Love, Jeri

Tuesday, September 1, 2009 5:13 PM, CDT

Hello to all! Hope you are doing well today. Well, McKenzie continues to do pretty well. We had a good weekend with family and friends. Monday morning rolled around and we decided we would rather go to dance class than go to the doctor's office. So we did. McKenzie was in a creative movement class with eight other little four-year olds-all dressed in pink! It was so cute! She was able to keep up; in fact, she did great. She had so much fun that I think we'll go back again next week if she feels up to it. We stayed home today. She got to feeling a little bad this afternoon, but she bounced back. Whether that was from the medication I gave her or simply because it was a stomachache, I don't know. All I know is that she is back to arguing with her brother and sisters.

We head back to Dr. Patel tomorrow morning and hope to play with a friend after that. I will let you know soon how that all works out.

Have a great day and don't forget to make some Labor Day plans for the weekend. With Love, Jeri

Thursday, September 3, 2009 9:21 AM, CDT

Well Hello! I meant to do an update yesterday, but didn't get around to it. It's funny; I don't think that you guys are really wondering how we are doing throughout your day. But, at least 3 times yesterday I ran into people who either knew exactly where we were or knew where we'd been and wondered how it had gone! It was kind of nice, kind of weird to think that everyone knew my day's schedule- of course, they knew because I had posted it on the Internet! Anyway, we did go see Dr. Patel yesterday. It was not quite as fun as dance class, but it's always good to see him nonetheless. He said she is doing surprisingly well. Her blood counts are looking good. He wants to do another round of palliative chemo next week. He wants us to be sure we are giving her medication when we suspect she is hurting. He said that if we think she is hurting, she probably is. Dee Dee said a friend who is a pharmacist recommended a little Hershey's syrup with the oral morphine to cut the bitterness. We tried that last night and she still hated the morphine, but loved the chocolate syrup. She slept pretty well. We heard her crying in her sleep a little this morning between 6 and 7 (of course, we were up with the other children), but she slept until close to 8. She seems to feel bad between 5:30 and 7am. Right now she is fine. We are watching The Game Plan, one of her new favorite movies. First she ate Dee Dee's spicy pretzels for breakfast and then she switched to Cap'n Crunch Peanut Butter cereal. Just now, she said she wanted some of both cereal and pretzels on her plate at the same time. "The Plate" is her new princess plate Aunt Kate and Uncle Russell got her. Speaking of gifts, we are thinking we are going to cut her off. She has received so many nice things from everyone that she is getting truly spoiled. I know it seems cruel to discipline a terminally ill child, but as Dr. Patel says, "she needs boundaries". As her life seems to stretch out before us (a true miracle gift from God), we are finding that we are called to continue to be the parents that God intended us to be. That means we GET to decide when enough is enough. We will continue to enjoy life with her like there is no tomorrow. However, we are going to begin withholding any new things that arrive at our home until we need to use them as incentives. Please don't take offense at this, we just need to be able to truly enjoy these last days with her and we can't enjoy a selfish spoiled little "brat" (I really hesitated to use that word, but that is how she acts when every day brings a new toy, wouldn't you?). "Ungrateful" is another word that comes to mind and I believe the Lord calls us to be thankful, not assuming of our blessings. So, in summary, please, no more gifts for the time being for our little angel...

Today is a quiet day. Tomorrow is a little busier and we have some fun plans for the weekend.

Please pray for restful night sleep for McKenzie, Monroe, and the whole family. Please pray for health for the family. Please pray for wisdom as we make daily decisions for her.

We'll keep you posted...

Monday, September 7, 2009 7:00 AM, CDT

Happy Labor Day! Hope you are having a fun one. We are except for having to get up early to take Courtney to Cross Country this morning! Tee Hee. On Saturday, we took it easy and went to 5pm church. McKenzie went to Grandpa and Meemaw's house instead. We don't really like to take her and have to explain to the teachers there about McK. Sunday morning, we found several of our friends at the Country Lanes Bowling alley for $10 all you can bowl. What fun! McKenzie has been asking for some time to go bowling, so that was fun for all. Then we had a lunch out at Wendy's and went furniture dream shopping at Lack's. We spent the rest of the day (mostly) at home and had Grandpa and Meemaw over for barbecue ribs and sunset basketball in the front yard. McKenzie continues to do pretty well. She has a sniffly nose. We are giving her Benadryl on top of the occasional morphine. She hates taking it all. That's about it. We'll talk to you soon. With Love, Jeri

Jeri

We also took a set of pictures with the entire family that weekend. I had scheduled the session with Becky on the evening of Labor Day. That happened to be the day we spent at Fiesta Texas and on the way home my husband kept saying, "Call her and cancel. Everyone is exhausted." But we talked about the fact that there were no other days anytime soon when we would all be able to get together. Monroe was traveling between San Antonio and Salt Lake most weeks for three days to do his job. We were now well past the four-week mark following McKenzie's diagnosis. They had told us four to six weeks, so now we knew we were living on borrowed time. We knew if we wanted another set of family pictures, we better work quickly. So Becky came over and we suffered through our exhaustion. We got some fabulous pictures of not only the entire family, but of the individual children as well. I am so glad we stretched ourselves that day. Those are some of the most treasured pictures I own.

Shortly after McKenzie's July release, we also met with a hospice nurse at the house. She was a very sweet person. She worked well with McKenzie. But we really didn't have much use for her. McKenzie was feeling pretty well. She was up and about. She wore out easily, but she always had. We had pain medication from the doctor. But she wasn't experiencing any pain. The lack of pain was attributed to the palliative chemo we'd done. So we saw the hospice nurse every couple weeks for a regular visit, but never had to call her to the house.

Since the palliative chemo worked so well in controlling the pain, we went ahead and administered a second and a third round. McKenzie hated it, but at least we were being treated by Dr. Patel as outpatient instead of being hospital bound. We were surprised when the six-week mark came and went and our little girl showed little sign of slowing down. We weren't sure what to expect. Would she just crumple one day? Would she die in her sleep? Would it be slow and painful? How would we know? We took a lot of these questions to Jesus and Dr. Patel. Jesus gave me the comfort I needed through Scripture and friends. Dr. Patel gave us some idea of what to expect, but even he didn't know for sure. He said McKenzie would play up until the very end. He said we would do everything possible to keep her free from pain. So we pressed on.

Monday, September 7, 2009 9:41 PM, CDT

Well, the cape says it all. "Supergirl" was at Fiesta Texas today. We had a great time (thank you, Michelle, and the Dairy Queen family) and she had plenty of energy. In fact, tonight when I put her to bed, I was asleep on her floor long before she gave up and drifted off. Monroe had to come wake me up and finish the job. I think my snoring was keeping her awake. My parents went, too (Dee Dee was in Las Vegas celebrating her birthday). The kids took friends. Caroline's friend convinced her to try a roller coaster and now there is no stopping her! She has been converted to life upside down. Not me! I did the log ride and screamed the entire way! That is it for me.

On another note, thank you to the Johnson High School Cross Country Team for dedicating their season to Miss McKenzie. "Miles for McKenzie" is what their t-shirts read on the arms, with a pink crown to go along with the theme of her life. Thank you to them for being so kind! They will have their first true meet this coming weekend. Last Saturday's meet actually got rained out if you can believe it! Again, thank you all; especially the guys who are wearing pink crowns on their "game day" shirts!

Well, Monroe has gone to brush his teeth so I better finish up. Y'all have a good "short week". They are always the longest, aren't they?

Prayer requests: Chemo this Wed, Thurs, Fri. Quick, relatively painless treatments... And also I would love to have you pray for my sweet friend Bethany who is having a difficult knee surgery on Wednesday. She needs the doctors to be wise and for her to heal quickly.

Good night. With Love, Jeri

McKenzie as Supergirl on Labor Day 2009

Wednesday, September 9, 2009 1:18 PM, CDT

Definition of Palliative= To Palliate= To Cloak

That's what we are beginning to do: to cloak the pain. McKenzie woke up Monday night in extreme pain. We had given her morphine before bed, but we quickly gave her some more. This is the beginning of the disease causing her so much pain that she is actually willing to admit it and remember it. We will begin with morphine and will eventually move to other stronger drugs to keep our baby from hurting. We also are having three days of chemotherapy this week. Monroe took her this morning for the first session and we will also go on Thursday and Friday. This chemotherapy, again, is for cloaking the pain and not intended for healing or fighting the disease at all. I have spoken to many of you who are praying for a miracle healing. Thank you. I pray for healing either here or in Heaven. I believe God loves this little girl so much that He died for her enabling her to be healed for all eternity with Him! That is FOREVER! We feel like we've been fighting this disease forever, but it is nothing compared to the eternal healing she will experience. So, please keep lifting her up. And keep lifting us up asking for wisdom and strength for each decision. We keep asking ourselves, "Do we really need to do this round of chemo?" We are moving forward in hopes of alleviating the pain in our baby.

On a lighter note, McKenzie did get to attend dance class yesterday afternoon. It was a make up class for her since Monday was Labor Day. She did great and had lots of fun.

Please pray God's protection for our entire family as swine flu has reared its ugly head at our son's elementary school. That is not what we need!

All right, go and enjoy the much-needed rain (if you are in the San Antonio area).

With Love, Jeri

P.S. Oh, I attached the picture of the cross-country t-shirt sleeve with McKenzie's dedication...

Jeri

To administer chemo with the intention of cloaking the pain rather than with the intent of healing was a complete dynamic shift for me. I voiced some of these thoughts to our reading audience as confirmation of what I was learning as much as education for them. I had given up the dream of McKenzie outliving me at this time. My hopes would rally once more, but I believe God used that hope as a glimpse of how she would truly be healed eternally.

Saturday, September 12, 2009 7:21 AM, CDT

Good Saturday Morning Everyone from a very wet San Antonio, Texas.

We finished chemo yesterday and McKenzie was once again very happy to have all the needles and tubes removed and to be free. She went directly to Meemaw and Grandpa's yesterday afternoon to celebrate, play dolls and watch movies. She then returned home for a nice long bath and we had a small celebration with Dee Dee and some close friends at our house for dinner. McKenzie made it until 10 PM and then crashed. She is still asleep this morning and seems to be very comfortable.

This week marked several benchmarks for McKenzie and our family. On Monday, my mom celebrated her seventieth birthday, on Thursday, McKenzie's website went over 100,000 hits, on Friday, our nation marked the eighth anniversary of Sept. 11th and it was also the two month mark of McKenzie's recurrent cancer.

Today, we are celebrating the day and counting the days that we have together. Everyday is a gift with her, with each other, and with our other children.

This week, I have struggled with the ups and downs of McKenzie's day-to-day illness. We know we are in God's will for our child, however, the waiting, and **WATCHING** *is difficult. We always are watching and wondering what is next for our little angel. So, Jeri and I try to remind each other to enjoy today, enjoy the moments. Life is filled with moments for us* **ALL**!

Well, I have rambled enough, we are off to a Johnson Jaguar Cross Country meet this morning and I think it is the only outdoor sporting event in San Antonio not cancelled due to weather.

Have a good weekend and God bless you all and don't forget to hug your kids. And for Stephanie- coffee and shorts. -Monroe

Jeri

Life was stressful during those days of watching and waiting for something to change for McKenzie. That often showed up in our website postings. But, also, we had a lot of humor and private jokes that made their way into our postings. For instance, I had a conversation with Stephanie one day about how weird it was that everyone knew what we were doing all the time. Of course, they knew. We published our every move for the world to read on the Internet. It gave me a very small glimpse of how it must feel for famous people like movie stars to have no privacy. Now, I'm not claiming we were movie stars or famous, but I felt like I was given a small glimpse of their lack of privacy. Stephanie made a joke about she just always wondered what we were wearing when we were posting on the Internet and if we were eating or drinking anything at the time. I conveyed this humor to Monroe and the end of the above post was his response. Stephanie and I got a good laugh out of it anyway.

<u>Monroe's Personal Journal Entry:</u>

Sept. 17th, 2009

Things are rather quiet right now. McKenzie is feeling fairly well during the day and not so good at night. I have been gone for four nights to Salt Lake for a Sales Meeting and I am returning home today. I am looking forward to being at home with the family and holding McKenzie in my arms. I missed her this week as well as the all of the children. It is very difficult; when I am home, I want to be in SLC and when I am in SLC, I want to be at home. Thank you Lord for the week and for taking me home. Please let me arrive safely.

Wednesday, September 23, 2009 9:24 PM, CDT

Hello Everyone,

It is Wednesday mid-week and McKenzie continues to be active. Today she had her visit from hospice and they seemed pleased with the way she is holding up.

We also made a visit to McDonald's today and she seemed to have a good time. The highlight for me was after she had played with ALL the kids at McDonald's for a half hour she decided she was hot, so while everyone was watching she pulls her wig off and says "here you go, Dad". The look on the parents and children's faces around us was priceless. I had a hard time not laughing, because it was great watching the reaction of everyone around her. It just goes with the territory.

Jeri and I continue to battle with a couple of questions, is this real and what is ahead? It is hard not to be totally honest about our lives and what is going on around our house. We are all anxious and we are all tired of not knowing what will happen next. Please pray for ALL of our children and for strength for Jeri and me as we deal with the day-to-day routine of our lives.

I thought today of a poem I had memorized for one of my classes at Southwest Texas State and thought I would share it with you. It is by Robert Frost and many of you I am sure will know it. It just goes with our lives. We all feel like we are traveling the road less traveled, and in my heart I know it will make a difference in the future, but for right now it is difficult to continue down a road that you cannot clearly see.

Two roads diverged in a yellow wood,
and sorry I could not travel both
and be one traveler, long I stood
and looked down one as far as I could
to where it bent in the undergrowth.

Then took the other, as just as fair,
and having perhaps the better claim,
because it was grassy and wanted wear;
though as for that the passing there
had worn them really about the same.

And both that morning equally lay
in leaves no step had trodden black.
Oh, I kept the first for another day!
Yet knowing how way leads on to way,
I doubted if I should ever come back.

I shall be telling this with a sigh
somewhere ages and ages hence:
Two roads diverged in a wood, and I--
I took the one less traveled by,
and that has made all the difference.

Have a good evening everyone and hug your kids and spouse.-Monroe

Hi everyone! Jeri here. Monroe is so eloquent, but I feel like I haven't written in so long that I wanted to throw my two cents worth in here, too.

He is right- we watch our fairly energetic four year old and I wonder how the doctor can be right. I believe he is right, but it is hard not knowing when or how. One of my friends told me today that she would be glad to check on eBay to see if they were offering a special on crystal balls. Tee Hee! No, we don't have one, but I know A Guy who knows how many hairs on my head (a lot more than on McKenzie's!) and how and when this will all end. She does seem to be a little more tired some days than others. We believe that is a sign. She is very irritable some days especially with her siblings. It's hard to know if that is because she is hurting or because she is just so used to everything being about her. We believe that God is able to heal her; we just don't believe that is His plan in McKenzie's case. We just continue to pray for His will to be done.

Well, I won't ramble on any longer. Hope to see you all out and about...With Love, Jeri

Thursday, September 24, 2009 8:44 PM, CDT

Well, we think we've seen a change. Yesterday, the hospice nurse suggested we give her a small dose of morphine in the afternoon to cut down on the extreme moodiness we usually see in the afternoon (which we interpret as pain personified). So today we did give her a small dose about 3pm. Then about 6:30pm, she began complaining that her "heart" hurt. We asked her to show us where and she started with her heart and pointed all the way down in her abdomen. We spoke to the hospice nurse again and she said it would be safe to offer another dose of morphine. The pain seemed to ease and then came again a little bit later. Once we gave the next dose of morphine and put her to bed, she relaxed. We'll see how the night goes.

She and I had some candid conversations tonight, too. She asked me about when her boo-boo in her tummy was going to come out. It was hard to answer, but I said that they were not going to be able to take it out. She asked if it would get better in heaven. Of course, that I can answer yes. Then in the next breath she asked me about what she could be when she grew up. Those are also the hard questions.

It was a more difficult evening for me than others recently. Please pray for God's perfect will to be done in our lives. Pray for Monroe to get a good night's sleep. Pray for the other children with all they walk through daily and what they will go through soon.

With Love, Jeri

Jeri

Bible Study Fellowship begins their new study each fall in mid September. Not expecting to be living in San Antonio still, I had not registered either McKenzie or myself. I had already called to enroll myself in the San Antonio class, but as this time period was in the four to six-week-mark Dr. Patel had given us in expectation, I had not enrolled McKenzie. My dad was more than willing to stay with her on the Wednesday mornings that Monroe was traveling. I went the first week and it was very emotional for me. These people had been on their knees for me for twenty-one months now. Their support meant so much to me. I had said my goodbye's in the spring at the end of class and never expected the blessing of getting to see them again, let alone study God's word with them.

As the days wore on and we were entering the second week of the study, I began feeling a little silly leaving McKenzie at home when she felt so good and when she was begging to go with me. I called or emailed Jan Dunlap, the Children's Supervisor for my class- probably emailed her as she and I had a great online friendship- and asked if she had a spot for McKenzie. She had exactly one spot open and felt God had held it for my little girl and no other child. So I began taking her each week and I'm so glad I did. The children who attend BSF don't simply get "babysat". They attend a children's class faithfully taught by a group of women (or men in the Evening Men's Class) complete with hymn time and a miniature version of the lesson learned by the adults. This is no watered down Bible story. This is God's truth taught powerfully to children. God's very Word and truth is tucked deep into their hearts. McKenzie had learned this truth for two years now and she hungered and thirsted for it just as I did and still do. She loved going.

As the weeks turned into months, we were all amazed at McKenzie's fortitude and endurance. We still believed that God was calling her home to heaven, but were surprised at the fact that we were given the gift of extra time and fun with her. We weren't just living with her; we were living abundantly.

Sunday, September 27, 2009 10:30 AM, CDT

Hi everyone! Just a quick note to let you know that we are having a pretty good weekend: McKenzie does not complain of any blatant pain. However, her temperament continues to deteriorate. She can often be described as "just plain mean". This meanness can be directed at her siblings or just as easily her parents. She walked up yesterday and out of the blue, whacked her father on the little toe. And she is strong! We believe this ugliness stems partially from the pain she claims she is not feeling. Please pray for us to make the best decisions for her as we discuss the true nature of her temperament.

We had one really fun thing happen on Friday evening. The doorbell rang and UPS had delivered a box full of clothing from Chez Ami, one of McKenzie's favorite clothing lines. The owners of the line had been told of McKenzie's challenges and were moved to send her several fun outfits complete with monogramming. She looks darling. She wore one next door to wish her friend a Happy fifth birthday and then another on Saturday to go to church. We are very grateful to the Aiken's and to our sweet friend who told them about McKenzie. I will attach some pictures.

Y'all have a great weekend.

McKenzie's New Outfit

Thursday, October 1, 2009 9:54 PM, CDT

Good Evening Everyone,

Looking at the website tonight I noticed we had not put an update in since Sunday. Oh how time flies!

The week has been fairly quiet and uneventful. We have had a couple of times with pain; however, with medication we seem to be able to control it fairly well. She has been sleeping through the nights and seems to feel fairly well most days. McKenzie went to Dance on Monday, and has spent a lot of time with Mommy and Daddy this week.

We have not been to see Dr. Patel in almost two weeks so it has been a nice break from doctors. The hospice nurse, Becky, came today and paid McKenzie a visit and seemed content with her condition.

We will keep you posted, but for now things are stable.

Thank you all-Monroe

Monday, October 5, 2009 4:54 PM, CDT

Hello Everyone,

Well, where do we start? Last week, Jeri, Little Monroe, and Caroline all went for a flu shot. The week before, I had one while in Salt Lake and as our luck would have it- the shots worked. We ALL got the flu. Courtney, who did not have a shot has felt fine and continues to go strong. So on Saturday morning, we shipped McKenzie to Jeri's folks' house and she spent the weekend with Meemaw and Grandpa. This morning after everyone being on Tamiflu for the weekend, we thought the worst was behind us. At 8:30 AM right after school started, I received a phone call from Monroe's school and he had just thrown up in his class, and for some reason they wanted me to come and pick him up!

So he went back to the doctor today and we found out that he was also having an asthma attack that was causing him to feel even worse. This afternoon, everyone "seems" to be doing better. We have all been on Tamiflu for three days and the doctors tell us we are safe to be back in society.

Once again our lives have not gone quite the way we were planning, and yet we are all still here and seem to be all right.

Over the weekend, I thought of a book that my mother and father used to give as a college graduation gift. It is titled "Oh, The Places You'll Go" by Dr. Seuss. It is really a book about life!

Here are few lines that seem to apply to where we are currently:

"You will come to a place where the streets are not marked. Some windows are lighted. But mostly they're dark."

Our streets are not marked and I cannot seem to Google "Current Location", but we keep moving at a break-necking pace and grind on for miles...

Not sure what is next for us, but God is! As my high school football coach used to say, "If in doubt, fire out." We keep firing out and we hope to be going in the right direction.

Thank you all for continued prayers. McKenzie is going to see Dr. Patel on Wednesday. We will keep you updated. -Monroe

Monday, October 12, 2009 7:19 PM, CDT

Hello everyone! Happy Columbus Day! The kids had off today so everything was a little off. Poor Monroe had the ruckus in the background in all his business calls today. Courtney had a cross-country team picture and a violin lesson. Caroline and I squeezed in a trip to the mall. McKenzie had dance class. She is doing very well. Last week on Wednesday morning she woke up with a fever. I cancelled going to BSF and took her on in to the doctor. We figured it was the flu, but weren't sure what the doctor might do if her fever continued to rise. Well, we didn't have to worry because by the time we arrived at Dr. Patel's office, she had NO fever. He examined her and again was amazed at how well she was doing. In regards to the fever, he put her on an antibiotic to help her system fight off infection. While she was busy playing at the office, Dr.

Patel and I talked and decided we were both curious as to what was going on inside McKenzie. After all, eleven weeks ago, he guessed we wouldn't have her for more than four to six weeks! We are all amazed that God has not chosen to take her home to heaven yet! So he and I agreed to do a c/t scan. That was the easy part. We were home by 1pm or so from the hospital and began waiting to hear from the doctor about the results. I called twice a day until Friday morning when Monroe was able to finally catch him available to discuss results. He said that amazingly, there has been very little change or growth in the size of her tumors since July. He is surprised, as are we. We are uncertain of how to proceed. Our lives are in limbo. We still plan to move to Salt Lake City at the end of the year. For now, we just plan on keeping our plans the same. We can't believe she would still be here at Christmastime, but we simply wait on God's timing. It's kind of an oxymoron: we move forward, but we wait. We pray for His will to be done. We feel the stress in every member of our family. McKenzie is certain that everything revolves around her- you've heard us talk about this on previous posts. The other children are stressed to the max wondering when this will happen. Monroe and I watch her constantly and also work to make plans not knowing whether we will be taking her with us in the move or not. It's all very taxing!

So, please pray for us to be patient while waiting on God's timing in McKenzie's life. Please pray for us to learn the lessons He has for us. Please pray for our other children and for McKenzie that they would be shaped by His hand and not distressed by our circumstance. Please pray for Monroe and me to be the parents that we need to be.

I've added some new pictures- McKenzie had some special moments last week with the Johnson Cross Country Team and with some beautiful dancers at a dress rehearsal at P.A.C.T., her dance studio. Thank you, everyone!

Well, it's almost time to begin the bedtime regime. Y'all have a great week! McKenzie and I will be at the Silpada party tomorrow at my friend, Stephanie's, if anyone wants to join us! Good night!

Jeri

As the weeks turned into months, I also began to question her future. I began to question her future after death. I am assured of my future. I believe, without a shadow of a doubt, that, because of my profession of faith in Jesus Christ as my Savior, the moment I die I will be with Him in Paradise just like the dying thief on the cross. But what about McKenzie? She was just a little girl. She was only four years old. Even though she had an "old soul", so wise and mature for her age, she was still a child. She had never made a public profession of her faith. We talked about Jesus at home, in the car, at church, and at BSF. I knew she knew Him, at least Who He was (and is and is yet to be). But I began questioning if that was enough. Was her knowledge enough to ensure her a place in heaven eternally? I knew that my merciful God would not turn away a child younger than the age of accountability. But I struggled with exactly what was that age of accountability. My other three children accepted Christ and made a public profession of faith through baptism at ages five and six. McKenzie was awfully close to that and, as I've said, she was very mature. I didn't want to force baptism upon her, although she would probably have enjoyed swimming through a big baptismal pool and I knew any minister in our church might have been willing to help. I went to a close friend of mine to share my concerns. My dear friend, Jennifer Gonzales, is a woman of God upon whom I knew I could depend. When I posed my questions to her, she did not answer. Instead, she did what she should have- she told me to go to God's Word and find my answers. "Jeri, you know God's Word. He will give you what you seek if you will go there and look." I knew she was right however hard it was to hear.

I began searching for answers during my daily Bible study. One section of Scripture I found particularly comforting was in 2 Samuel 12. David sinned with Bathsheba and she conceived a child. David had her husband killed and made Bathsheba one of his several wives. Nathan was directed by God to confront David with his sin, Nathan did, and David repented. David was told, however, that his child would not live. Now I knew that McKenzie's expected death was by no means a punishment for any sin committed in my life or my husband's, but the correlation remained. While the child (my McKenzie and David's) lived, we (David and I) begged God to let that child live. But after the child died (David's), he made a statement in verse 23 that he would go to that child one day. This was a good reminder for me that even though McKenzie may not live, that I would see her again someday. I had also to prepare myself for that time in between the day McKenzie died and the day I saw her again. David asked in the same verse, "Why should I fast when he is dead? Can I bring him back again?" I would not be able to bring McKenzie back. I could not change the events (at the time still in my future) in my past, but I could begin to formulate a plan for how I would react to her death. Would I be inconsolable in my grief or would I pick back up the assignment of making disciples of all men? I had a choice to make and I began making that choice before McKenzie even left me. It was as if God began preparing me for the future before it even happened. And I could be assured, as David was, that I would see her again. My God, a merciful God would take my precious daughter to heaven where she would praise Him until I arrived someday to join in the heavenly song.

Something else happened around this same time that ended my questions. As I've mentioned before, McKenzie was not always forthcoming in answering my questions to her. We would go to BSF and I would question her on the way home as to what her story was about. I knew because it correlated with mine, but I always asked just to see if she would answer. Rarely would she just come out and tell me. She was willing to answer the question when my mother asked on the telephone, but not for Mommy. She was sly that way. But, we would often have conversations in the car- conversations that counted. It was almost as though, once she was strapped in her car seat behind me, she could sift through the thoughts and events in her head. Then she might, just might, privy her mother with her thoughts. Maybe it has to do with not having to look me in the eye- she could just say whatever came to mind. I don't know. We spent a lot of time in the car. As the youngest of four children, she often went with me to run errands. I loved the times when she decided to open up. One day, we had a particularly important conversation. It went something like this, "Mommy, the other day in BSF, we talked about Jesus dying on the cross." I simply replied, "Oh?" She went on, "Yes, Mommy, did you know that Jesus died on the cross for me so that I could live forever in heaven with Him?" My response as I uttered a silent prayer of thanks for the answer I'd been seeking was, "Yes, Baby, I knew that." She completed the conversation with, "And, Mommy, Jesus died for you, too, so that you and I can live there together forever." Wow! I thought, I just heard my dying four-year-old make a public profession of faith. Those were the words I had longed to hear. If I'd try to coax them out of McKenzie, they wouldn't have been so pure, so spontaneous. But, she'd evidently heard this truth, thought it through, and then shared it willingly with me. Again, wow! God gave me exactly what I needed to prepare myself for the future. I knew, without a doubt, that when McKenzie died she would go straight to heaven. She would be waiting for me when I got there.

Besides BSF, that fall, McKenzie asked to take ballet. I'm sure you get the picture, by now, that McKenzie was such a girlie girl. She had always wanted to take dance, but the past two years had been challenging enough physically for her without trying to learn to dance. My other two daughters had taken dance when they were about the same age, so I was excited by the prospect. McKenzie loved to shop and shopping for pink leotards and tights were no exception. We found some beautiful dancewear and for days, she wouldn't take it off! Daughters of two of my friends agreed to put their girls in dance class with McKenzie if we could find a place. There was a new studio close to our house and another friend of mine said her son, a wonderful dancer we knew from church, was studying there currently. Next came the tricky part: I had to call the studio and explain McKenzie's situation. Since it was now September and we were well past the four to six week window the doctor expected her to live, we didn't know from day to day what to expect ourselves. But McKenzie still seemed strong and ready to live! So I called and spoke to a very kind man named Jeff and told him all about McKenzie. He said they would be happy to have McKenzie for whatever amount of time she was with us. He even agreed to let me pay weekly instead of month to month. This class turned out to be such a joy to McKenzie and to me. She went every week excited to dance. And dance she did! She and Haley and Alex had a wonderful teacher who was so sweet and patient with them. McKenzie loved to prance in and do all the moves as Ms. Ashley taught them. Only a couple times did she feel bad and have to come out of class to me. On those days, it was a sad reminder that this class, along with this life, was temporary for McKenzie. The studio was preparing for a competition later in the fall and even allowed McKenzie to come watch their final rehearsal. They dedicated that competition performance to her. All the dancers showed up at the rehearsal with gifts for her. She loved every minute of it. It was just another example of the kindness of people toward our precious girl.

This fall, the fall of 2009, Courtney, our oldest daughter, was running Cross Country for the second year. We didn't go to many of her meets either year, but we attended more the second year she ran. If you've never been to a Cross Country meet, you won't know that the students have to be on the bus at like 5am. The meets start between 6 and 7am especially in South Texas where the heat after 8am is stifling. So the meets start early and run into the late morning and the larger meets into the early afternoon when it's really hot. During the two years of McKenzie's illness, we had not attended many outdoor events. It was just too hot for McKenzie. Courtney usually caught a ride to practice with some neighbors. I felt like a terrible parent. I think the one 2008 meet I attended just to see Courtney run, I missed the start and may have missed her running altogether. We attended almost every single Basketball game because they were indoors and McKenzie could do indoors and enjoyed cheering for her sister. To this day, I attend every sporting event for all of my children that I can possibly be at, in part to make up for all that we missed those two years. When I attended the parent meeting at the beginning of the Cross Country season, Marcia Nelson approached me. Marcia's daughter was Dannielle, or Dani, one of Courtney's best friends and a Cross Country runner. Marcia said the coach was considering dedicating their season to McKenzie if we would be okay with that. Wow! Of course, we would be okay with that. It was such a kind thing for them to do. So "Miles for McKenzie" was printed on the t-shirt sleeves of the runners that season along with a pink crown to represent our little princess. Our whole family got t-shirts. We had a picture taking opportunity with the entire team one day at the high school and McKenzie felt like quite the little star. Everyone wanted to sit by her. It made her feel so special. And yes, we attended some Cross Country meets that fall.

We had another close friend whose daughter was the head cheerleader at Johnson High School. Kathy called one day and said that the cheerleading squad had heard about our special girl and wanted to do something. They offered her to come down to visit the cheerleaders during a football game. She was able to meet the official mascot, the Jaguar, and do a cheer with the girls. They posed for pictures with her and made a huge deal of how cute she was. And, of course, they were right! She also got to go down at halftime and meet the dance team and the band majors. She again felt special!

It was times like these when she was having so much fun that we could forget about the countless hours spent at the doctor's office and connected to chemo. We could forget, for a little while, her cute little baldhead. We could ignore, although not forget, the awful prognosis that her little life would not go on for much longer. You know, it may not seem like much that a cross country team would dedicate a season to her or that a group of dancers would dedicate a performance or that some cheerleaders would invite her down to the field level during a football game, but these things meant and still do mean so much to us. Sometimes, it was difficult for Monroe to accept these things. He kept saying how he didn't want charity or to feel an object of pity. But, I kept reminding him that these were simple things that people could offer to McKenzie that made them feel that somehow, they were participating in her life. People need to feel needed. People want to do things for people who are going through a difficult time like losing a child. Just like the little boy who offered Jesus his fish and loaves, no matter how little they appeared when five thousand men needed to be fed, these friends offered their gifts in love. They offered what they had and the Savior turned these things into something miraculous. He loved us through them. We felt as though Jesus had taken on flesh and was personally serving us. He had. In addition to making our little girl feel important, with every event she attended, we created some incredible memories. We cherish each picture of McKenzie doing all of these incredible things. I have pictures of her with Monroe and me and with each of her siblings. We often pore over these pictures just to catch a glimpse of our little princess.

Monroe

As we moved to the end of October, we began to think about the holidays. Halloween was right around the corner and that would be followed by Thanksgiving and Christmas. Once again, we were all determined to make everyday special. As we neared these dates, I began to pray that nothing would happen on Thanksgiving or Christmas. Once again, I did not want our other three children to live with that sorrow for the rest of their lives.

<u>Thursday, October 22, 2009 9:23 PM, CDT</u>

Good Thursday Evening! It seems as though our days get busier and busier and our journal entries get farther and farther apart. McKenzie has been busy along with the rest of us. She has been to Bible Study Fellowship twice since I did an update- she is really enjoying it. I know this because she sings the songs and does the finger plays all the time. She told me all about Jesus turning the water into wine, but was unwilling to discuss being born again. She is a difficult little thing!

This week, she went with her daddy to get his teeth cleaned. She told everyone she was going to get her teeth cleaned and sure enough, climbed up into the chair and let the dentist clean her teeth. Just like her brother and sisters, she has very advanced teeth. At four years old, she has her six-year molars and may even have a couple of loose teeth. She only asks me a few times each day if they have come out.

She's been playing at the park a lot lately. Her daddy has taken her and her siblings a couple of times to do some normal kid playing. She likes to swing and ride her bike.

We've seen some different symptoms like pain during the day and some nausea/vomiting this week. It's nothing too serious to make us worry, but a small change all the same. We see the doctor again tomorrow. We'll let you know if he says anything interesting, but don't count on it.

Have a great evening. Enjoy the great fall weather or go enjoy the great indoors at Shop Ole'. Either one, I pray health and safety for you and yours. Please pray those for us, too.

Thursday, November 5, 2009 11:10 AM, CST

Hello Everyone! So much is going on at our house that I forget that you guys start to worry when you don't hear anything. I have been reminded by several friends recently with emails or when I have seen them out and about that I have not updated the website lately and is everything okay? The answer is "yes" everything is okay. There has really been very little change with McKenzie. That is actually a huge praise because Monroe and I received from God a great blessing last week because McKenzie has experienced very little change. Monroe had a business trip to Galway, Ireland. We had known about it for quite some time, but were not sure that we should plan to go because we were worried about either something happening with McKenzie while we were gone or worried that if we planned to go and then she passed away right before we left, we would have to cancel our plans. We would not leave the other children grieving. After much prayer and asking God if we should go, His answer was, "I have placed nothing in your way, go." The grandparents were all on board. McKenzie stayed with my parents while Monroe's mother did the balancing act with the other 3 children here at our house. Both sets of parents had huge challenges and met them exceedingly well with God's help. Also, my sweet friend, Stephanie helped immensely by having little Monroe stay at her house on school nights. **Thank you so much to all of them for being the hands and feet of Christ in order for us to go.** *We had a great trip (minus some awful travel hiccups) and Monroe and his colleagues accomplished some important tasks while there. I got to sightsee and shop with some of the other spouses and we had a great time together. If you'd like to see photos of the trip, check out my Facebook page. I have seen very little change in McKenzie since my return. She is very, very, very, (okay, you get the point) very emotionally needy. She constantly needs my attention. This is detrimental to accomplishing anything around the house and also detrimental to giving the other children what they need from me- my undivided attention.* **This is an area where I need much prayer- I lose my patience with her and need Jesus to help me in this.** *Right now, I have her stationed watching a new Barbie Christmas movie I ordered her from Netflix so that I can do this update without distraction. We'll see how long it lasts.*

This past week in my Bible study, I came across a verse that God pulled off the page and used to smack me in the head. In John chapter 4, a royal official approaches Jesus. Verse 47 says, "The royal official begged Jesus to heal his son, who was close to death." It struck me that although many of you have told me verbally or via email or via guestbook entries that you are praying for the miracle of healing for McKenzie, I have not prayed that, much less begged Jesus for it. When she was first diagnosed in January 2008, I did beg Jesus for that. I yelled at Him and literally begged Him to heal my daughter, who was close to death. I believe He did heal her then. He used the hands of the doctors, but He did the healing work all the same. However, since July of this year, I have taken it for granted that she would not be healed on this earth. I have taken it for granted that the doctor knows what he is talking about and that she won't be healed this side of heaven. Maybe I've been wrong- at least in not asking. I know that my faith in Jesus is strengthened when I put my trust back where it belongs- in Him alone. I don't claim to know that He is going to heal McKenzie here on earth, but I do know that God is commanding me to begin **begging Jesus to heal my daughter, who is close to death.** *He may not heal her here, but I know that He will heal her in Heaven if not here. And the close to death part? Well, she is doing well right now. She seems to be experiencing pain now and then and we continue to give her nightly morphine to help ease her pain in sleep. We try to live a normal life. Her prognosis may not change with my begging, but my faith in Jesus as the only source of healing and life is being strengthened. I pray that yours is, too.*

Many of you have also asked the question, "Are you still moving?" The answer is "yes". We don't know exactly why, but we feel like we have totally been within the will of God to stay in San Antonio these extra 6 months. (We've been here only 3 so far) But, we do still feel within God's will to move to Salt Lake City as soon as possible. Monroe is looking at houses when he is there and **we would love you to pray for him to find just the home where God would have us live. (Acts 17:26)** *I feel as though part of the emotional healing that our family needs will only be found when we all live under the same roof.*

Well, thanks for reading the "diary of a madwoman- Jeri's link to the outside world" and thanks for praying for us. We continue to covet your prayers. In the hope of Jesus Christ, Jeri

Jeri

This was the point at which I began to hope a little again that she might be healed. The fall seemed to stretch out before and behind us. Every time we thought we saw changes in McKenzie's stamina, she would rally again. So, I began to think that, perhaps, God had answered the prayers of those who prayed for miraculous healing. It would have been an amazing thing for Him to do. I didn't expect it because I had wrestled with the possibility of her leaving us and was at peace with that expected outcome, but it felt good to hope again.

One day late in the fall, McKenzie had a special Visitor. As I've told you, she knew Who Jesus was. She knew what He'd done for her. One morning when she woke up, she told us a pretty incredible story. She told us Jesus had visited her. She said He stood at the foot of her bed and told her that soon she would be coming to live with Him. She didn't say it was a dream; she said He was standing at the foot of her bed. She said He also told her that she would be getting a white dress and wings. Now, I don't know if humans are supposed to have wings in heaven, but I do know that McKenzie was strongly convinced that Jesus had visited her and that she'd been promised these special gifts. The interesting part to me is that we had never talked much about her leaving us. We had discussed her boo-boo being back and the medicine we gave her to keep her from hurting. But, we had never told her that she was leaving us or going to heaven. We had never told her, I don't think, how sick she was. Maybe she instinctively knew because of all the emphasis put on keeping her comfortable or because of all the fuss being made over her. But, I seriously doubt that since she'd been fighting this disease for almost two years now and we'd always fussed over her and spoiled her, especially since original diagnosis. I believe that she actually saw Jesus and that He told her that she would soon come to live with Him and that she would be given a white dress and wings. I have no reason not to believe completely what she told me. She and I would talk, sometimes, about what the white dress and wings would look like. She told me how beautiful and sparkly they would be. I also asked her what Jesus looked like and all she would say was, "Oh Mommy, you know what Jesus looks like!" I guess I do!

Friday, November 13, 2009 4:40 PM, CST

Good Friday Afternoon Everyone,

Well, it has been an interesting week. On Monday, we went to the doctor and we all believe we are starting to see some changes. She is sleeping more, having more pain, and her color is not good. Dr. Patel said he would guess we would continue to see things change. The family waits and waits. All of this is taking its toll on us all. We worry about Courtney, Caroline, and Monroe. They are feeling the pressure....

Since I was in town this week, we decided it would be a good week for Jeri to fly to Salt Lake to look at houses. So she and her mom left on Wednesday afternoon and will return home tonight. The good news is that they found a couple of houses and we have made an offer on one. Hopefully, we will be able to work out the details over the weekend.

We will keep you all posted. Please continue to pray for peace and comfort for McKenzie and all of our children.

Hug your kids and have a great weekend. -Monroe

Saturday, November 21, 2009 8:22 AM, CST

Good morning everyone! I pray this finds you healthy and thankful for all that God has given you! We'll be celebrating Thanksgiving here at home with family- some we see most every day and some we haven't seen in a while. All are blessings and I am thankful for each one.

This morning's entry will be long, so get a cup of coffee and make time for it if you can. If not, put us aside for another time...

Now about McKenzie: the best I can tell you is that she is doing okay. "Okay" seems to be such a generic word, but it's the best I can decide on. In one respect, she is doing amazingly well. In another respect, she seems very fragile and imminently about to leave us. So, "okay" seems to fit the bill the best. I was sharing her story with someone new this week. They were shocked when, after telling her history and the doctor's prognosis, they asked if she was in a coma and I said "no". She was at Bible Study with me in the Children's Program that very morning. They were amazed. And yes, if an adult were told that they were in the state McKenzie is in, they would simply lie down and die. But if you ask McKenzie if she is sick, she would look at you like you're crazy and say, "No". She lives each day full speed. But every once in a while, she has to slow down the race. Rather than a race, I am seeing her little life more like a vase of fresh cut flowers- especially gladiolas. When fresh cut, they are tall and the stems are extremely strong. The flowers are multiple on each stem and the ones at the tip aren't completely open. That frustrates me because I want the whole thing open so that I can enjoy its' beauty. McKenzie has been tall and strong. Her beauty is obvious, with so much unfolded because she has only lived such a short four-year-old life. Sometimes the blooms on the bottom of the stem begin to shrivel and die even before the blooms at the top can open. You begin to see shriveled spots on the blooms and it saddens you. That is definitely how I see McKenzie because we are starting to see some change in her. She tires easily. She more frequently asks for pain medication. She used to never ask. She clings to us like she doesn't want to waste one moment she has with us. But then her stem is still tall and strong. She still plays full force. She has a new friend a couple doors down and she is relentless about asking to play with her. We know fresh cut flowers don't last forever. We know they will eventually shrivel completely and die. We know she will, too. But even knowing they will die; we do everything to nurture them into lasting. It's the same with her. It's the same with all our children. None of us will last forever physically. But spiritually, we go on forever. The question is where? Do we accept Jesus as Savior and live eternally with Him or do we reject Him and risk being separated from Him? To prepare for that physical death, we nurture the flower in the here and now. We speak of living in

Heaven with McKenzie. She understands. She knows there is more than this life. When she is in pain or extremely frustrated, she has even been known to say, "I wish I already lived in Heaven." She is a vase of fresh cut flowers, cut at the stem, but sharing her beauty with all of us.

So how do we respond? We search for answers in God's Word, we look to each other for comfort, and we do what we can out of love for each other while here on earth. Our daughter, Courtney, is being an example of doing what she can out of love for others. Courtney turned sweet sixteen this week. She has two good friends who have birthdays close to hers. Instead of being selfish, these two girls asked for money to visit Courtney in Utah at Spring Break. In return, we decided to honor all three girls with a birthday party at our home this weekend. The girls invited only friends who knew all three of them. They had a dilemma. They didn't want to ask these people to bring 3 gifts and how do you share a gift? The answer- you give it away. In lieu of gifts, these girls have asked their friends to bring money to be donated to the American Cancer Society. Pretty selfless, huh? It's not how I pictured Courtney's sweet sixteen party. I pictured dancing under the stars- something grown up and beautiful. But, with us moving in a month and things always so crazy at home, we didn't get that done. Things aren't always the way that we picture them. But God knew. He knows how this would look. He knows how McKenzie's life will end. He knows how mine will end and He knows how yours will end. He will make something beautiful and grown up out of it- if you let Him. Give it all to Him.

I give thanks to God for all of you and ask that He give you His peace. Happy Thanksgiving! Jeri

Monroe

Just before Thanksgiving, we celebrated Courtney's sixteenth birthday. She had originally wanted a "Sweet Sixteen Party", however because our lives were still upside down, Courtney, and two of her friends Emily and Danni decided to do a group party at our house. Instead of gifts, they requested that anyone who attended bring a donation for the American Cancer Society. These "Sweet Sixteen" girls managed to raise just over five hundred dollars. We were very proud of all of them.

Jeri

As the fall progressed, we watched her every day for changes. When someone tells you in July that your daughter has four to six weeks to live, you are definitely pleasantly surprised when you still have her with you close to Thanksgiving. Finally, in mid November, McKenzie began requesting pain medicine. This was shocking to us because, with the exception of diagnosis of recurrence, McKenzie had never complained of pain. I know I shouldn't have questioned it, but I did anyway because the medicine we gave her was an oral liquid. She complained of the bitter taste so my mother in law came up with a great idea. She suggested that whenever we dispensed the liquid that we have a teaspoon full of chocolate syrup ready to follow. This worked like a charm. McKenzie would tentatively take her "chocolate syrup medicine". So we began down the road of pain. I was never sure if she just wanted a spoonful of chocolate syrup or if she was really in pain. Again, I should never have questioned it, but I did. From that time on, she began requesting pain medication more frequently until the day finally came when we could no longer control it.

Monroe and I had several times throughout our marriage hosted the Thanksgiving holiday meal at our house. Knowing that we wouldn't live in Texas forever close to our families and that, as far as we knew, this would be McKenzie's last Thanksgiving with us, we asked the family if we could host again. It turned out to be a great day! We had my parents, my brother and sister and their spouses, Monroe's mom and aunt, and, of course, all of our children. This would be the last holiday we would celebrate complete as a family. We had everyone at one long table. McKenzie was really very fussy, but with the help of her friend, chocolate syrup medicine, we made it through the day.

Also, that weekend, we went and toured the Living Heritage Museum at the LBJ Ranch. We had been there so many times and always enjoyed it. There is an old farmhouse decorated in the fashion of the early Texas settlers and a working kitchen. They strained milk and made cheese and butter there. Occasionally, they had peach cobbler made from the peaches their trees produced. There were chickens and roosters and the kids had an opportunity to collect fresh eggs. There were pigs and cows and sometimes the kids would get to help with those animals. Monroe and I enjoyed watching the kids chase the chickens and search very carefully under those hens sitting on their eggs. We even drove over to the "Texas White House" where Lyndon and Ladybird Johnson lived. We toured it and eventually headed home, tired and happy. It was great to spend a day whole and happy even if a little morphine was involved. This was our last family outing.

We decorated our Christmas tree together that weekend. We didn't hesitate to get it up and completely decorated. We knew that we must do everything while she was still up and moving. We turned on the Christmas carols and had the annual bickering of whose ornaments were whose and whose turn it was to stand on the kitchen stool to reach the top of the tree. It makes me cry so hard today to watch the video of that day. I was singing to McKenzie "Merry Christmas Darling" by the Carpenters. You know the one that goes,

"Merry Christmas darling
we're apart that's true
but I can dream and in my dreams
I'm Christmas-ing with you"

I knew that, in the future, any "Christmas-ing" I did with McKenzie would be only in my dreams.

<u>***Thursday, November 26, 2009 7:19 AM, CST***</u>

Happy Thanksgiving Everyone,

We are up and watching TV and McKenzie is ready for the day. We are looking forward to seeing the Parades and Family today and hopefully some good football. (If the Cowboys show up for the game)

I wanted to give you a quick update, we went to the doctor on Monday and all of her blood counts are low. He wants to see us again on Monday and possibly give McKenzie blood and platelets. We are seeing her pain increase and occur **MUCH MORE REGULARLY**. *We have had to give her morphine up to three times a day and she woke up this morning hurting already. So we wait to see what the day will bring.*

Yesterday we took all the kids and drove up to Marble Falls to have lunch. Then we drove over Johnson City to go to the LBJ Ranch. We did the tour and had a great time. McKenzie and Monroe got to pick eggs from a chicken coop, they thought that was great! We also got to visit the house that LBJ lived in and used while he was in office. Jeri and I thought it was interesting; the older kids just tolerated the trip. The good news was we all got to spend the day together. As long as we have morphine, we can go most places.

This Thanksgiving, I am extra thankful for many things. Below are a few:
I am thankful for the parents that raised me.
I am thankful for the family I grew up with.
I am thankful for my wife and her family.
I am thankful for my job and the people I work with.
I am thankful for the country I live in.

I am thankful for the God in Heaven who watches over us daily.
I am thankful for ALL my children.
I am thankful for all of you that support us through prayers and actions.
I am thankful for one more Thanksgiving with McKenzie.
I am thankful for the doctors that watch over McKenzie.

One final note, Courtney's birthday went well Sunday night. For her Sweet 16 Party she, Emily and Dani raised $500 to donate to the American Cancer Society. Wow!! I was proud of the girls for having this idea and for all of the teenagers that attended the party. Nice job everyone. You can contact us by email by Sunday if you would like to add to this Birthday Donation.

Have a Happy Thanksgiving, and don't forget to hug your kids and even the rest of your family around the table today. -Monroe

Monroe

On November 28th, we pulled out all of the Christmas decorations and began getting ready for the holidays. As a family, we decorated the house and the tree. We even went so far and paid to have lights hung on the outside of the house. We wanted to make sure that McKenzie got to experience as much as possible. We had no idea that the next week would bring much drama. We also had no idea of know how little time we had left.

Leaving Us

Friday, December 4, 2009 6:42 AM, CST

Good Snowday Morning Everyone! It's supposed to snow in Texas today! Wow! Little Monroe just said he doesn't want to wear his big coat until we get to Utah. We'll see about that! The kids have school today and he is really bummed out. He was sure that it would be cancelled. I'm not surprised they didn't cancel, but I also am a little worried about how they will get the 65,000 kids in our district home safely if the weather does get bad in the middle of the day. McKenzie went to bed very excited last night because of two things: 1) her daddy came home last night while she was sleeping and 2) it is going to snow today and she has never seen snow! Well, her daddy did get home; I hope the snow doesn't disappoint her.

We went to see Dr. Patel on Monday. After last Monday's visit when her counts were so low, I really expected to have to go for blood. But, nope! Super girl's counts have rebounded! It is amazing to me. It is also very confusing. Just when we think we are seeing the change in her that we believe is inevitable, she rebounds. She truly is living on God's time, not ours.

Okay, the next paragraph will be a little graphic- of the bathroom kind. Just warning you... She had some additional constipation problems last week. It's kind of a vicious circle. She hurts, we give her morphine, the morphine constipates her, and her belly hurts. So then her belly hurts, she asks for morphine, and it constipates her. She finally had a breakthrough last Friday. Unfortunately, the breakthrough came at a friend's house. Her friend's mother described it as "impressive". Only a mother of four can say that with a smile on her face! Again on Monday, she had a b.m. at another friend's house. This time, she came home wearing someone else's panties. Her friend's mother said she just threw away McK's panties, they couldn't be salvaged! Only a mother of three could say that with confidence! I tell you all this to help you understand that the pain was then relieved for several days. She went from asking for morphine two or three times a day to not asking at all. Then yesterday, she began complaining early in the morning about pain, but this time it was in her legs, not her belly. Please understand that she has lesions in her legs from the cancer. She had morphine four times yesterday. We'll see how today goes.

So maybe this is the "change" we watch for. Only God knows. Seriously, can you imagine being told that your child only has four to six weeks left to live and then getting to keep that child for another eighteen weeks and counting? That is where we are. We are amazed, confused, glad we have been given this gift of time with her, and yet know we won't get to keep her forever. None of us are here forever. We must contend with the choice of accepting or rejecting eternal life through Christ and then choose each day to live hand in hand with

Him. These days, well, and for a long time now, I have felt more like He is carrying me. Today will be no different. I need your prayers. Please pray for wisdom and stamina as we live through this crazy time. We need wisdom as we make decisions for McKenzie and for the other children. We need stamina for dealing with the emotional issues of McKenzie and the move.

Well, that is about it. I'll let you know how the snow turns out. If it actually sticks, I'll send you some pictures. Have a great weekend. With Love, Jeri

Jeri

As the fall had progressed and we had been continually amazed at McKenzie's resilience, I began asking Dr. Patel what we should expect. Was this a miraculous healing? Should we expect her to die in her sleep? Should we expect to move McKenzie to Salt Lake City with us in January? He didn't have the answers. He was as surprised as we were that McKenzie was going strong and fairly energetic. The only prediction he made was that she would be strong until the very last minute. It didn't help me know what was coming any better, but it did turn out to be very true.

Saturday, December 5th found McKenzie playing with the little girl who lived a couple doors down. As I've told you, McKenzie was very strong willed, even bossy, with other children. This little girl she was playing with was also strong willed so they were evenly matched. However, this day was different. I kind of followed the girls around if they were outside and they decided to jump on the trampoline, so I followed them out there. McKenzie became verbally aggressive with her friend and downright rude, insisting that they do things her way. I had already corrected her a couple times and finally called an end to the play date. I walked her friend home and apologized for McKenzie's behavior both to her and her mom. When I returned home, I found McKenzie hurting- bad. We gave her more pain medicine. She rebounded slightly, just enough to hang out with the family comfortably around the house. I don't remember a lot about that day, but I do recall that it wasn't a good day for McKenzie.

Monroe

On Saturday morning, McKenzie got up and immediately needed morphine. The night had been long and under normal circumstances we would have taken her to the hospital. However, we knew Dr. Patel was not available and we did not want to submit McKenzie to another doctor's care. We had decided we would do all we could do and make the best of things.

Saturday night was another long night and she was in pain through out the night. I once again slept on the floor in her room and watched, as she was very restless. By 7:00 on Sunday morning, McKenzie agreed to go to the hospital. This never had happened before.

Something inside of me told me to wake the other children and have them come sit with their little sister as we prepared to go. This would be the last time that everyone would be together. And even though McKenzie was in pain, Courtney and Caroline were able to get a smile. Monroe watched TV and talked to us and for just a moment it was life as normal.

Shortly after that, we departed for the hospital to admit her, once again to the fourth floor at the Methodist Hospital.

Jeri

I know that going into the night, Monroe and I just hoped for the best. He insisted on staying with her just as he had since her original diagnosis. I went to bed and slept. I think he woke me up some time that night and said he was giving her more medication, but for me to go back to sleep.

I do remember clearly what happened the next morning. Monroe woke me at 5am and said he'd been up with her all night and asked for me to relieve him. I gladly did so. I figured McKenzie was just restless and was refusing to sleep. I went in to the family room and found her watching television. Only she wasn't really watching- she was just lying on the sofa, writhing in pain. She was rolling back and forth, back and forth. She groaned, "Mama, need more medicine-y. Need more medicine-y." I hated to wake Monroe, but he hadn't told me when her last dose had been. So I went in the bedroom and said quietly, "Honey, when did McKenzie have pain meds last? She is asking for some." He bolted upright and said, "Jeri, I gave her a full dose right before I woke you up." Our eyes met in the early morning light and we both knew the time had come. It was time to take our little baby back to the hospital.

We'd spent so much time in the hospital over the previous two years and we knew McKenzie always did so much better at home. However, this time was different. We had discussed with Dr. Patel that, since we were not living in our own home (it was a rental) that we did not want McKenzie to die in this house if we could help it. We were prepared to accept that if she died in her sleep, but if we knew the end was coming, we had planned to take her to the hospital. Now, it seemed, that end was coming.

We packed her things (McKenzie always liked a lot of her own things to comfort her) and got ourselves ready. We had spoken to the children previously and the girls had asked if they could accompany us to the hospital whenever we went. So we woke them and loaded up. McKenzie tried to be brave, but she was hurting so badly. It was a long drive to the hospital.

When we got there, Monroe dropped her and me off and I carried her up to the fourth floor. The nurses said that we would have to go through the Emergency Department for admission. Oh, how I dreaded that. But we went back downstairs and went through the formality of triage, ER nurses trying to access McKenzie without success, and then another strange doctor examining her before agreeing to admit her. All this time, McKenzie was writhing in pain. It was one of the toughest times as a mother. Couldn't they see I just needed them to access her and give her something more for the pain?!

Finally, we were admitted to the fourth floor Hem/Onc unit. Once there, it was much better. They were able to get McKenzie on a morphine drip. It took a little while to strike the right balance (a couple hours), but once they did, she was herself again. I still thought at this time that she would just drift off to sleep. But she didn't. She rebounded again. She became almost energetic. And definitely demanding- yes, she was herself again and that was reassuring.

One of our favorite nurses, Dallas, was on the floor that morning. She knew McKenzie well and our situation. She was both kind and efficient. She knew we needed to know our options. She and I spoke privately and she told me something

I didn't know before. The hospital actually has a room designed specifically for children who are expected to die. Wow, that is still a hard one for me to get my head around. They called it the "cloud room." It was larger than the usual hospital room. It had extra amenities like a refrigerator and visiting hours did not apply here. It was currently available (I feel like I'm describing an opulent hotel suite or high rise penthouse apartment, but let me assure you nothing in the hospital is that glamorous). We could choose to move McKenzie there right away and stay as long as we needed. The down side was that it was down the hall and around the corner from the Hem/Onc unit nurses station. It was always comforting to be able to stick my head out of our room and get someone's attention most of the time. This would be a "more on our own" type situation. We would have regular visits from staff, but not as regular as on the unit floor where we were comfortable. We decided to think about it for a little while. Our other option was to remain in a regular room on the unit floor where we were comfortable. In the end, Miss McKenzie would have the final say on this decision.

Sunday, December 6, 2009 10:24 AM, CST

Hello everyone. It's Sunday morning in the Methodist Children's Hospital. We decided early this morning that we were unable to manage her pain effectively at home any longer and brought her in. The pain in her left leg has been increasing since Thursday. Already, after waiting a couple of hours, we are accessed and she has received a dose of morphine which has decreased the pain much better than anything we've given her at home the last few days. She is coloring and has worked a puzzle.

I'll **beg** *for your prayers at this point. Please pray that Monroe and I have wisdom in every decision made and stamina for what is next. Please pray for our children- that God would not allow them to be stretched* **beyond their ability to cope**. *I know He will provide the means of escape. He will use all of this to shape them into whom He needs them to be. He will use it to shape Monroe and me, too.*

She has relaxed enough to eat my bean and cheese taco that Monroe brought for me. I'm glad to sacrifice it!

Please don't take this the wrong way, but I'm going to ask that for now the only action you take be on your knees. We are not up to visitors. We'll see you soon enough and keep you posted here. With much love, Jeri

Jeri

You will notice, I hope, a change in my tone. I truly began to panic a bit. Even after four months of considering what was ahead, I wasn't sure I could endure McKenzie departing. The only way I could calm myself was to beg for the prayers of others.

This was Sunday, December 6th. This was the day when Dr. Patel sponsored an annual Christmas party for all of his patients. Back in July when McKenzie had been diagnosed with recurrence, we had gone to the clinic one day for an appointment. As we were being shown into the examination room, one of our favorite nurses, Aurora, brought me a piece of paper and asked me to fill it out with what McKenzie would want from Santa Claus at the Christmas party. I felt this was kind of cruel considering we had already decided at that point to discontinue treatment and didn't expect to have McKenzie with us any more than another few weeks. But McKenzie had already heard what was going on and started dictating her Christmas wish list. So with tears in my eyes, I filled out the form and handed it back to Aurora. Only God could have known that McKenzie would make it until the Christmas party day! So the day had finally arrived only we were in the hospital now expecting our daughter's imminent death. Since we had RSVP'd and Santa was expecting us at the party, I passed the word to someone in the office that we would be unable to make it after all. I never expected the surprise visit we received later that afternoon. McKenzie's pain was under control and she was resting well. All of a sudden, one of the nurses said we had a visitor. Visitors were not usually announced so I was really curious. All at once, Santa Claus was in our room! He had brought McKenzie's Christmas presents! Several members of Dr. Patel's staff accompanied him! What a great surprise! McKenzie had a blast opening her new Barbie's- all of the Disney Princesses! Wow! I got some great pictures of her with Santa- what a sweet time! It was so touching that Santa made deliveries to the hospital for my sick little girl. It remains one of my favorite memories of her last days.

McKenzie's Visit from Santa Claus

Sunday, December 6, 2009 5:20 PM, CST

Just a short update: McKenzie is receiving hourly doses of morphine as she is complaining that often of the pain (with the exception of the three hour nap she took). The doctor is trying to evaluate her dosage needs prior to putting her on a morphine drip. She is extremely irritable, but wouldn't you or I be under the same circumstances?

She had a surprise visit from Santa Claus earlier. He brought her the presents she would have received from him at the Christmas party (for Dr. Patel's patients) we didn't make it to today. She got a huge box of all the Disney Princess Barbie's, a Barbie Pet Vet, and a puppy in a purse. All so cute! She enjoyed the diversion, as did I. Thank you to those sweet elves who organized that!

All right, we'll keep you posted. Please stay on your knees...

Monroe

Once at the hospital, she rebounded a little. The doctors were able to manage McKenzie's pain and keep her comfortable. We thought that we would have some time to adjust and that perhaps we would even still be able to take her home if we got the pain under control.

An additional concern on this trip was to make sure the hospital understood our desire for McKenzie. Several months prior to his hospitalization, we had signed a "DNR", a "do not resuscitate" order. We did not want the hospital to further perform any extraordinary measures. We presented this to the hospital and made sure that everyone understood clearly why we were there and what we wanted to happen. We only wanted our daughter to be pain free and have her last hours be peaceful.

It was an extremely difficult decision and discussion to have. Our four year old lay facing life and death and we as parents had decided for her that this would be her final stand. One question came into my mind: was this for her or for me? I believe she had fought gallantly and that this was the most humane action we could provide for her. It was just another in a long line of decisions that we will have to live with the rest of our lives.

Jeri

As always when we were admitted to the hospital, Monroe insisted on staying with McKenzie that night. Despite the fact that he'd had no sleep Saturday night, he took a Sunday afternoon nap and was ready to take up sentry by her side for the night. There was never any arguing with him on this. He did it out of love for her and for me. He is such a great father to our children and a loving husband to me. Sunday night passed without anything else special happening- no more surprise visits from either Jesus or Santa (although we know Jesus was there!).

Monday morning the other kids were in school and I was at the hospital as early as possible. Dr. Patel visited and decided that McKenzie was rallying. His plan was to apply a Fentanyl patch for pain, which would be stronger than the morphine we'd been trying. He would watch her for a couple days to see how she reacted to the patch and try sending her home on Wednesday. We were amazed by this news. We never expected to bring her home again once we brought her in to the hospital this time. We were grateful to Dr. Patel for his understanding of our desire always to be at home with our little angel. So we had a plan. But you know what they say, "the best laid plans of mice and men often go astray"...

Monday, December 7, 2009 3:33 PM, CST

Good Monday afternoon everyone. Well, "good" for us is kind of questionable. It is "good" in that McKenzie is finally resting comfortably. They finally got her on the morphine drip close to midnight last night from what her daddy tells me. She has been extremely irritable even up until I got here around ten this morning. Then, finally, after our lunchtime (McKenzie is eating nothing), she began to relax a bit. She hasn't snapped at anyone too bad. She finally got out of bed and used the restroom this afternoon for the first time since yesterday morning. She has asked for additional morphine for pain control once since I got here. Mostly, she is sleeping with the occasional rousing to scratch. The morphine makes her itch. She has had one dose of Benadryl and I'm sure more will come.

I can't tell you how comforting it is to constantly hear both on this guestbook and on my Facebook page of all the prayers being offered on our behalf. I knew I would simply have to ask and God's people would storm the throne room of heaven. So thank you! Please don't stop. Right now prayers are all we need. It is good to have her hospital room quiet. It is conducive to her sleeping and my praying.

I'll update soon. With Love, Jeri

Jeri

Monday afternoon found us almost all at the hospital for a family visit. Courtney was not there as she had an orchestra rehearsal. Otherwise we were all there- Monroe, Caroline, little Monroe, Meemaw, and me. Now this should have been my night in the hospital. But on that day, McKenzie was insistent, "I want Meemaw to stay with me." And what McKenzie wanted, McKenzie got! So Meemaw had packed her bag and come to the hospital. I still wonder today if McKenzie wanted it that way because she knew what was coming. Did she know she couldn't separate herself if I was there? Did she know I wouldn't let her go if I was there? We'll never know. As the rest of us left her room that night it was a sweet scene. She hugged and kissed each one of us for a long time- even Caroline and little Monroe seemed to get special attention. I will always remember the feeling of her arm around my neck that night. I'll always remember her smile. I'll always remember her "goodnight's" and "I love you's" to each one of us. That would be the last time I would see her smile or hear her voice. It would be the last time for almost all of us.

Monroe

On Monday, Dr. Patel came in to see McKenzie and talk with the family. She was comfortable; however, he explained that this was the change we had been waiting for. Caroline, Monroe, Jeri and I were there with McKenzie and she was in a great mood. She gave hugs when it was time for us to go and showed her sister and brother love that I had not seen in a long while.

Jeri

We headed home Monday evening probably after collecting Courtney from her evening activity. Courtney realized that everyone else had gotten to see McKenzie at the hospital that night and asked if she could go in to school late so she could squeeze in her own visit. I was glad to let Courtney, a straight A student even through the toughest times, have this time with her baby sister. I had been missing time with Courtney myself so we took our time getting out of the house that morning and even stopped at Starbuck's on the way to the hospital. The coffee house was busy and it added more time to our commute. Oh, how I regret those decisions. In my mind, there was no hurry to get there. I expected to be at the hospital from the time I arrived until the following morning. I couldn't have known the true urgency; no one did until I got there.

Monroe

Earlier that morning I could not sleep and had gotten up to journal my thoughts on the website. As always, I continued to be concerned about all of the children and the pressure they were under.

Tuesday, December 8, 2009 6:43 AM, CST

This is going to be more of a family update than a McKenzie update. I am sure for the next few days we will be doing a couple of updates a day, so this is number one of Tuesday.

Last night, Jeri's mom was asked by McKenzie to stay with her at the hospital. So, Meemaw agreed to the sleep over and we have not heard a word from anyone. So we are hopeful that all is going well. The funny part was Jeri made sure her mother had her cell phone with her so we could stay in touch. And yes she has the phone, but NO it is not turned on. She promised to call if anything happened.

We are letting the other children sleep in this morning after a rather emotional afternoon and evening yesterday. Dr. Patel came in late yesterday afternoon and spoke to Jeri, Caroline, Monroe, me, and of course McKenzie. I am so touched by this man and the job he does. The word "job" is not close describing what he does for his patients and their families. It is a calling for him!

He stood in the room and explained what he believes will be the path for the next week or two. We are going to try a "pain patch" that will last for seventy two hours and start taking her off of the morphine drip. The patch is a drug called "Fentanyl" which is stronger than morphine and should help her to relax. If this works, there is a small window of hope that we may get to bring her home for a day or two. If it does not work, we will remain in the hospital and be moving to a hospice room. With tears in his eyes, Dr. Patel said, "I am sorry." Can you imagine a doctor apologizing?! He is truly a special physician; I know many people that read this have him treating their children. We are all blessed to have this man and his staff in our lives.

So once again, we are at the crossroads. It appears that McKenzie is nearing the end of her fight. A week, maybe two, he believes is the path we are on. I would like to ask that you all pray two prayers for our family:

1. If death is coming, that it does not occur on Caroline's birthday which is December 17th.

2. That it does not occur on December 25th.

These two dates would be even more of a challenge for Caroline, Courtney and Monroe.

Jeri and I knew we would get to this point and we knew the end would eventually arrive for McKenzie. In this difficult time, I would ask that you respect our privacy at home and in the hospital and give our family the time we need to spend with McKenzie. If you are wondering what you can do, please wait to be asked. We will contact you when we need you. We appreciate your thoughts, words, and notes. Your postings lift us up when we are down and your emails are comforting to us all.

We will keep you all posted on McKenzie's story as it continues.

So, for now, hug your kids and be thankful for all that God has given you and your family this Christmas Season. We are all blessed, even the May family. Sometimes we need to just be reminded.

Hug your kids. -Monroe

Jeri

My mom met Courtney and me in the port-a-cochere said, "She hasn't woken up yet this morning." When Courtney and I walked into McKenzie's room, I immediately noticed a change in her. I realized right away the reason Mother had said McKenzie had not yet woken. McKenzie was dying, NOW. Her breathing was labored, that sickeningly slow intake and barely there exhale that I had heard at the bedside of her grandfather the day he died. I yelled for the nurse and asked her how long this had been going on. She hadn't realized it either. She had checked on the medication levels just minutes earlier, but hadn't heard the change in McKenzie's breathing. She thought, like my mother, that McK was just sleeping late. But it was 10am and my mother said she'd been sleeping since late last night. She'd never woken up after my mom tucked her in. I next called Monroe; he was already in the parking garage and was there within a couple of minutes. I called my mom, she hurried on to her house, picked up my dad, and came right back. Monroe called his mom and she went to Caroline's school to pick her up and bring her as quickly as possible. We had discussed with the girls their wishes and they both wanted to be there when McKenzie passed away if at all possible. I regret that decision a little because of the images now burned into their memories, but I truly believe that I would have regretted more not allowing them the privilege of being present when that little angel drifted out of our lives. They most likely would not have forgiven me if it was within my power to have them there and I had chosen not to.

After the flurry of activity and phone calls, the world slowed down. I curled up beside McKenzie in the bed and sang and talked to her. Courtney sat beside her, held her hand, and talked so sweetly to her baby sister. The rest of the family came as quickly as they could and everyone had their turn to talk to her. Dr. Patel came and checked her and confirmed that, indeed, these were McKenzie's last moments on earth in this sick little body. I believe that she was on her way to heaven then. I almost believed I could see her as she crossed a bridge to the open arms of Jesus on the other side. It felt like she was looking back at us, unsure of whether she should complete her journey. I urged her to run to Jesus! Run, don't walk! I promised I would see her again. I know I will. As her breaths came slower and longer in between, Caroline and Jane, McKenzie's sweet Dee Dee, came in. I know she took at least one last breath just as they arrived. It was as if she was waiting until everyone was in his or her place before she could completely let go. It was one of the sweetest experiences of my life. It was one of the most agonizing experiences of my life. I had been there when that precious being drifted into our lives and I had the privilege of being there when she drifted out.

Monroe

We had decided to leave Monroe at school because, after many discussions with our little boy, he had decided he did not want to be at the hospital at the end.

As God had it planned, we were all exactly where we needed to be. For the next hour and a half, we sat and held McKenzie's hand, lay next to her in bed, and stroked her hair. She was peaceful, but obviously fought for breath.

If you have ever been with someone when they passed away or worked to take their final breath, it is a sound that you will never forget. It is somewhere between a snore and a gasp. It is labored and difficult and as you sit and listen, you think every one is going to be the last one.

Dr. Patel came in to see her and talk to her and tell her goodbye. With tears in his eyes, he told her she had fought a good battle and they would meet again one day in heaven. He hugged each of us and then apologized for not being able to do more. His words, his actions, and his emotions mean so much to me as I sit and write this that I am still very touched by this man and what he did for our child.

He left the room and then it was Jeri, Courtney, Meemaw, Grandpa, McKenzie and I. We sat and watched and waited. We told McKenzie we loved her and would miss her very much. She never woke and never cried; she lay in the bed and fought for every last breath.

At around 11:30, she took her final breath and the fight was over. The cancer monster had won. We all cried and waited for the arrival of my mother and Caroline. They walked in the door just a few moments later and Caroline swears that she saw McKenzie take one more small breath.

I had no idea what to do with myself. I had my youngest daughter who had just died from a two-year battle with cancer. I had my wife who had just lost her baby. I had my two oldest daughters to take care of who had just lost their sister and all of McKenzie's grandparents there with their granddaughter. I was not sure who to hug or hold. I remember just walking from one to the other.

Jeri

Dr. Patel returned and pronounced her death. With his typical compassion, he hugged me and said, with tears in his eyes, "I am so sorry." I would hear that over and over from many people, but it meant so much and still does to hear it from him. I felt like I should say the same back to him after all he had done for her and for us.

The scene at that point became surreal. I still feel like I can only remember glimpses of the rest of that day- crying for a while with the girls, crying with Monroe, Monroe deciding that he would go and tell little Monroe and get the girls home. Little Monroe was still at school and needed to be picked up. All the scenes of that day were filled with tears. I still feel the wetness of tears streaming down my cheeks, most quiet, some accompanied by louder moans and wails. Sometimes I was surprised to find it was I crying out loud.

I'd like to not write about what happened between Monroe taking the girls and heading to get Monroe from school and the time I left the hospital, but these are some of my strongest memories. Michelle, one of the nurses, stayed with McKenzie and me. Michelle and I undressed my precious angel and gave her a sponge bath. Together, we talked to her and about her.

It was much like she was still in the room and I think maybe part of her was. I mean, I firmly believe her spirit resided immediately in heaven. But I also believe she could see and hear us. I still do. The smell that permeates my memory is of baby lotion. We rubbed baby lotion on her and dressed her in the clean pair of pajamas I had brought to the hospital. I still have those pajamas and they still carry the scent of that day. The hardest part was when the gentlemen from the mortuary came into the room to take her away. I didn't want to leave there. I didn't want them to take her. It was so final. As long as we were at the hospital, there seemed to my mind a chance of healing her. My mind could not conceive of the fact that she was already healed and living gloriously in heaven. My mind still does not believe me when I tell it she's gone. Even today, I find myself trying to figure out a way to get her back- as if she is at my mom's house and they'll drive up any minute. I have to convince myself that she is truly unreachable for the time being. I didn't want those men to take my baby. I wanted to accompany her at least down the elevator and to their vehicle. Michelle, having been in this position before, knew it was best for me to say goodbye there. But she promised that she would accompany McKenzie down the elevator and safely on her way. That is an ironic statement- safely on her way- because McKenzie was already safely tucked away where nothing else could hurt her. This was truly "goodbye" for quite a while. They wheeled her away with Michelle as her escort and I left with my mom and dad to head home.

That was a long ride home. I finally gave myself permission to fall apart. I had been strong for so long, but now was my time to weep and mourn. Throughout the next few months, I did my best not to fall apart when the kids were around, but they weren't with me on that drive. The grief threatens to overwhelm me even as I write this. I ache for her now as strongly as I did on that first day of separation. It's a physical pain of longing. If you've ever grieved someone you love, you know what I mean.

My mother told me something interesting on the car ride home. We were reviewing the events of the last sixteen hours. I wanted to know every detail of the moments I'd been away from McKenzie. Mom said that she and McKenzie had watched TV until late. Mom said that she had gotten tired and lay down on the other bed without even washing her face. She said McKenzie had been asleep, too, when she lay down. She said that somewhere in the middle of the night she had heard voices. She assumed one of the nurses had come in as they always did. She heard McKenzie having an animated discussion with someone. She decided to get up and see what was going on. But when she did, no one was there. McKenzie was sleeping peacefully. She believes she heard McKenzie having a conversation with Jesus. He had come to take her home. I'm sure she is right. I really think McKenzie knew Jesus was on His way to take her to heaven and that is why she refused to let Monroe or me stay with her that night. We had a Do Not Resuscitate order on file with the hospital, but if I'd been there that night, I'm not really sure what I would have done. As it was, by the time I arrived in the morning, it was too late to do anything except say our goodbyes. I also believe she hung on until we got there to be with us one last time. She needed us there urging her spirit to cross the bridge to the other side.

Tuesday, December 8, 2009 2:29 PM, CST

I just want to let you know that McKenzie went home to live with Jesus today. No more pain, no more cancer. She is running around with her Grande and so many others who were waiting for her.

We will post service information as soon as we have that finalized.

With Love, Jeri

Jeri

We met that afternoon with Robert and Julie Emmitt, our pastor (from Community Bible Church- CBC) and his wife. Julie had been such a good friend to me during McKenzie's illness. She had come to the hospital to visit. She had prayed for all of us and visited with me when I needed her to. I was already regretting the decision to have let Courtney and Caroline be there at the time of McKenzie's death and yet questioned the decision to exclude little Monroe. I was regretting deeply my decision to let my mom spend the night. I should have been there. I should have heard McKenzie's last words. Julie simply stated, "Everyone was right where God wanted them to be." She was right and this brought me great comfort. We discussed the details of what we wanted at her memorial service. Monroe and I had since July to think about and discuss these details. Our plans were firm in our minds; we just needed to communicate them to Robert. He, Julie, and Betsy Buhler became our best friends during these days. They seemed able to move mountains to accomplish any little thing we desired to celebrate the life of our McKenzie.

Tuesday, December 8, 2009 8:15 PM, CST

Good Evening Everyone,

We have been overwhelmed with the outpouring of Guestbook entries today. You have all been very kind to our family during this difficult time.

We will finalize the arrangements on Wednesday afternoon and get the information out to everyone.

Thank you to all the family that came by today to shed a tear and a hug. Also, thank you to Pastor Sean, Pastor Robert, and Julie for your visit today and helping to shape the plans for the service on Friday.

We appreciate all of the support and kind words during this time.-Monroe

Monroe

The outpouring of support was once again overwhelming as word spread about the death of McKenzie. Below are some of the entries from our friends.

Tuesday, December 8, 2009 3:05 PM, CST

Dear May Family,

We love you and are praying for sweet memories of McKenzie to bring you smiles through the tears...

The P. Family

Kris P.

Tuesday, December 8, 2009 3:03 PM, CST

I don't even know what to say, but I am SO sorry for the loss of precious McKenzie. Part of me is SO sad. But part of me is so grateful that her suffering is done and that she is truly home. The people that she and her story have touched are all changed by what she went through. As a family, you have touched so many by selflessly sharing yourselves, your stories, and your emotions with us, sharing your ups and downs, but never never losing the faith. We love you and will pray for you as you come to grips with the "new normal." We are praying for God's comfort and peace for all of you.

Amy B.

Tuesday, December 8, 2009 3:06 PM, CST

Jeri, Monroe and family,

We are relieved for the release from earthy troubles and saddened for the loss left behind. Our hearts are always with you. Whatever you need, we're here when you need us.

Amy and Chad N.

Amy N.

Tuesday, December 8, 2009 3:15 PM, CST

Rick, Jeri, and kids,

Please know that not only my family but also Dad and Matt and Cindy are thinking of all of you. Your strength and courage have been a lesson to us all! May Family you are in our hearts and prayers! God Bless You! Love Always, Kris, John, Brianna, and Kyle

Kris May S.
San Antonio, TX

Tuesday, December 8, 2009 3:20 PM, CST

We cannot understand.......but one day we will. Jesus could wait no longer. He needed McKenzie to be with him. She will be watching over all of us now. God bless you, sweet McKenzie, we will miss you.

Robin H.

Tuesday, December 8, 2009 3:28 PM, CST

May Family,

My heart aches for all of you today, thank you so much for letting us be part of this journey with you all. I think each and everyone of us walked away learning something from this. May Mckenzie rest in peace and be free from her pain and may you all have the strength to get through this difficult time. We are all thinking of you and praying for you...

Tiffany T.
Merit Medical

Tuesday, December 8, 2009 3:42 PM, CST

Jeri and Monroe - I don't think you will ever know the number of people you and McKenzie touched through this journey. I am so sorry for your sadness but I know God's faithfulness and grace will sustain you. I rejoice at the thought of McKenzie being cancer free and pain free and sitting in God's loving arms. Your family is so, so loved. I pray that you feel that love surrounding you right now.

Susan H.

Tuesday, December 8, 2009 3:52 PM, CST

My thoughts and prayers are with you all today and in all days to come. McKenzie touched my life in ways I never thought possible. She is an inspiration and I am blessed to have had her as a Butterfly. Heaven gained a beautiful, precious Angel today and I know she is dancing. Thank you for sharing this journey with me, and know how loved you all are.

Love,

Miss Michele

Michele C.

Tuesday, December 8, 2009 3:53 PM, CST

I am so sorry to learn the news today of McKenzie. I am a friend of Kris P.'s--she gave me the news. I have prayed for McKenzie (she has been on our church prayer list since her diagnosis). I ache for your loss. I also rejoice for McKenzie! This is her "Victory Day" --that is what we call it--there is story behind that--but that is for another time. We also lost a daughter to neuroblastoma (diagnosed with stage 4 at 5years old, died at age 9). McKenzie reminds me of M.E. (our daughter) ---God builds in them that resilient spirit---keeps them fighting and feisty! Sweet Dr. Patel also treated M.E.

He is amazing---it is indeed a calling for him. I wanted to share a prayer with you that we found very meaningful:

"We seem to give her back to Thee, dear God, who gavest her to us. Yet, as Thou didst not lose her in giving, so we have not lost her by return. Not as the world giveth, givest Thou, O Lover of Souls! What Thou givest, Thou takest not away. For what is Thine is ours always, if we are Thine. And life is eternal; and love is immortal; and Death is only a horizon; and a horizon is nothing save the limit of our sight. Lift us up, O strong Son of God that we may see farther; cleanse our eyes that we may see more clearly; draw us closer to Thyself that we may ourselves be nearer to our Beloved who are with Thee. And while Thou dost prepare a place for us, prepare us for that happy place, that where they art and Thou art, we too may be; through Jesus Christ our Lord. Amen." (Written by Bishop Brent---the emphasis is mine).

One more thing I would like to share---a definition of dying that gives me strength and gives a wonderful visual image. It is called "Gone From My Sight" by Henry Van Dyke.

"I am standing upon the seashore. A ship, at my side, spreads her white sails to the moving breeze and starts for the blue ocean. She is an object of beauty and strength. I stand and watch her until; at length, she hangs like a speck of white cloud just where the sea and sky come to mingle with each other.

Then someone at my side says, "There, she is gone."

"Gone where?"

Gone from my sight. That is all. She is just as large in mast, hull and spar as she was when she left my side. And, she is just as able to bear the load of living freight to her destined port.

Her diminished size is in me--not in her. And, just at the moment when someone at my side says, "There, she is gone," there are other eyes watching her coming, and other voices ready to take up the glad shout, "Here she comes!"

And that is dying......"

I believe M.E. was one of those standing on the shore--shouting jubilantly along with Jesus---"Here she comes!!" Today there was a victorious celebration in heaven for McKenzie!

Your family will continue in our prayers that God would hold you and comfort you in His warm embrace and give you strength.

Susan H.

Tuesday, December 8, 2009 4:37 PM, CST

The thought that McKenzie is now without cancer, without pain, without medicine and with our dear Savior brings comfort and peace. i pray that you will each, moment by moment, be enveloped in that peace and comfort and that you will rest in knowing that her short life was filled with love...more than many will know in 80+ years. You are an amazing family, parents, siblings...you brought such joy to such a precious little baby girl. May sweet memories flood your minds and hearts and may her life be a gift that you will forever treasure. We love you all.

Kathy H.

Tuesday, December 8, 2009 5:36 PM, CST

Jeri and Monroe,

We hate to hear of your loss of your beautiful child. We have been following your journey ever since our meeting with you two when our son was diagnosed early this summer. We can't even begin to imagine the emotions you and your family are enduring. Hold on to all the memories. Also know that your faith and spirit have been very inspirational to so many people. We will now pray for healing in your family . . .

~In His name, Dion, Amy, and C.T.

Dion and Amy T.
San Antonio, TX

Tuesday, December 8, 2009 5:38 PM, CST

Richard and Jeri, I can't begin to grasp the depth of your battle for McKenzie, but I want you to know how much you have inspired me to be a better husband and father to my family. The Holy Spirit pressed this scripture on my heart for you both, Mathew 25:14-30. It's when Jesus is discussing what the Kingdom of Heaven will be like with the Parable of the Talents. I believe that the Lord has given you McKenzie for this brief time and you have done much with her. He says in verse 19 that **19***"After a long time the master of those servants returned and settled accounts with them.* **20***The man who had received the five talents brought the other five. 'Master,' he said, 'you entrusted me with five talents. See, I have gained five more.'* **21***"His master replied, 'Well done, good and faithful servant! You have been faithful with a few* *things; I will put you in charge of many things. Come and share your master's happiness!'*

You have been faithful to the Lord and it is now time for you to hear, 'Well done, good and faithful servant!'

We will be praying for you all.

In Christ,
Pat and Amy F.

Tuesday, December 8, 2009 8:33 PM, CST

You know how hard I struggle with words regarding McKenzie. Thank you for the time you let me spend with her. I will treasure it! I can't think of any situation larger than this with which to trust Jesus! How grateful I am that He is indeed trustworthy!! I thank Him for answering your specific prayers. I thank Him for giving you such a wonderful and caring doctor. I thank Him for taking McKenzie safely unto Himself and caring for her perfectly! I'm so sorry for your pain. I pray you will lean on Him to ease the pain and you will hold on to each other tightly. I love you! Angelia

Angelia T.

Tuesday, December 8, 2009 9:12 PM, CST

From the Johnson Cheerleaders to you:

We are SO SO SO unbelievably fortunate to have gotten to spend one of our football games with your beautiful little girl. She is precious, and has touched the lives of so many people with her story. We'll never forget the way she waved that little spirit stick around, and got so "into" that game! She's an inspiration to many and it's amazing how somebody so young and fragile can have such an enthusiastic and positive aura about her. She's courageous, compassionate, and we are SO blessed to have gotten to know her. We are praying for you and your family, to find peace and comfort during the Christmas season. We have total confidence that she's dancing around up there in Heaven!

Johnson Cheerleaders

Tuesday, December 8, 2009 9:00 PM, CST

I kept thinking I would find words to express. Your faith and testimony through all of this sadness and pain has taught so many of us how to return to our knees and put HIS will ahead of ours. God's plan is for the greater good and glory. Rest in His ultimate comfort. Find rest in His unfailing love. Know we are all praying on your behalf and when you can't the Holy Spirit actually cries and mourns for you.

I was led to 1 Corinthians 15:50 tonight. God will transform us all and I loved my study Bible's interpretation... we will be more capable in Heaven... we will not be weak, will never get sick, and will never die. Never!

I just keep imagining McKenzie's smile and free spirit asking an angel or two to play with her. We all loved her so much. Thank you for sharing her with us. You have an amazing family and have become parents we all aspire to be.

We love you~ May, Phil, Bailee, Avery, and Camryn

May E.

Tuesday, December 8, 2009 10:48 PM, CST

Our hearts are deeply broken with yours; but, we also rejoice in our faith that McKenzie is dancing and playing with our Lord in heaven with no more pain, no more illness, no more crying. I can only imagine that twinkle in her eye as she enthusiastically asks Jesus to play.

We continue to pray for each of you, for endurance and strength, wisdom and clarity, assurance and your deepening faith, as you continue this journey; and that you feel God carrying you as He makes Himself more real to you throughout these first hazy days of decisions, plans, and saying goodbye to your precious McKenzie; releasing her to Him to hold for you until you can hold her again yourselves. The reunion will be sweet in Heaven, won't it?

He has used little McK in big ways to change lives and draw many of us nearer to Him and know him a little better through you. Your transparency in sharing your struggles, your joys, your musings, and your steadfast faith, and walk with Him, is a gift we humbly receive. May you receive the blessings back ten-fold. We love you.

With His Love & Light,
Your Prayer Warriors at Casa M.

<><

Victoria M.

Wednesday, December 9, 2009 11:17 AM, CST

Jeri & Monroe, and Kids,

We are so sorry and so very saddened to hear about McKenzie. Our hearts are hurting for you all, even though we know she is in a much better place. It just doesn't seem right; we want to make it all go away. You all have taught us so many lessons on this journey you have been on, even little McKenzie herself, about love, family, relationships, prayer, devotion, commitment, and unwavering faith in God. I can't tell you how much that is evident in who you are as parents. God is proud of you! God is welcoming His precious angel, McKenzie; you have done a great job with her. We love you and are continuing to pray for all of you. All our love!!!!!! Joan, Javier, & Analisa

Monroe

On Wednesday morning after a sleepless night, Jeri and I ventured out to make the final arrangements for McKenzie's service. It is very difficult to go to a funeral home and know that you are making plans for your youngest daughter's burial. Parents are not supposed to bury their children.

When you make funeral arrangements, you have to make hundreds of decisions. The obituary must be written, viewing times decided, flowers chosen, music, pall bearers, locations, transportation and many more. But one of the hardest parts is walking into the display room to choose the casket. Everything in the room reminds you that you have just lost a child. It is almost overwhelming, only with God were we able to make these decisions.

One of the decisions we made was that we would have private burial. Only Jeri and kids and grandparents and I would do the graveside. We wanted to keep it very quiet and peaceful and it was.

The other decision we had to make was where to have the viewing, as luck would have it McKenzie died on a busy day and the mortuary did not have any room for an additional viewing on Thursday night. We turned to our church and they came through for us once again. In no time at all it was decided we would do a two-hour viewing at the church. They arranged for us to have a room with screen to run an endless roll of pictures and music that we requested.

Jeri

We had pre-planned the funeral service with the mortuary- a crazy thing to have to do for your four-year-old daughter. But when we contacted them the next day about the visitation and the service, amazingly, there was not an area available large enough for our visitation on Thursday evening at the mortuary. So we called the church and scheduled it there. In hindsight, this was the best situation possible. We were comfortable at church and felt so loved by the friends and staff there. They gave us a feeling that they would do anything for us. This was exactly what the body of Christ was instructed to do by Jesus- love their own. And they loved us so well.

Between Tuesday and Thursday, not much happened. The kids went to school on Wednesday because they would miss the rest of the week. I met with two of my best friends on Wednesday morning, Trish and Stephanie. They had amazingly never met. It was a sweet time with the three of us. Trish knew so much of my history and Stephanie knew so much of my present. I will always cherish the strengthening effect of our time together. Their love enabled me to press on with the coming events.

Even though Monroe and I had planned the service with only the two of us speaking, his sister had prepared some things she wanted to share at the memorial service. We thought it was sweet and decided to post it on the website.

Wednesday, December 9, 2009 4:08 PM, CST

Below are some very kind words I would like to share with you from my sister, Kate (Aunt Kate). They are from the heart and I deeply appreciate how much McKenzie has touched Kate.

Thank you all for the outpouring of sympathy during this time.-Monroe

Celebrating the life of McKenzie Jo May
By Kate Wilson

One of my favorite Bible verses has always been Isaiah 40 that states:

...But those who hope in the LORD
will renew their strength.
They will soar on wings like eagles;
they will run and not grow weary,
they will walk and not be faint.

These words are comforting because we know that, once in heaven, her earthly body no longer shackles McKenzie and she is no longer in pain or suffering from illness.

As I look to each of you, I see my own sorrow in your eyes. Behind the tears that fall for McKenzie I see great love and admiration. We are humbled that you took time from your busy schedule to join in celebration of McKenzie's life and on behalf of our family, thank you for the prayers and support that you've offered.

I still remember the day my brother, Monroe, called me to tell me that he and Jeri were going to be parents once again. Their happiness was evident and when McKenzie was born, just one day away from my own birthday, she proved to be another child of their dreams.

She was filled with energy, zest for life, and was amazingly feisty. I admired her spunk and will tell you that although sometimes her behavior left something to be desired (just as most young children do) she truly was an angel on earth.

McKenzie loved to play dress up and always dressed as a Disney princess. Her dreams came true when Make-A-Wish was able to send the family to Disney World where she had a special costume to meet each Princess in.

She possessed an impish grin, curly brown hair and was wise beyond her years as demonstrated when she told our uncle, who lost his hair due to chemotherapy, that it was okay, he shouldn't worry – that his hair would grow back just like hers did!

McKenzie and my own son are six months apart in age. When McKenzie lost her hair my own son became fascinated with her baldhead. One of my favorite pictures is of the two of them sitting together where he is rubbing her head. She thought it was funny and the picture is a constant reminder of just how short life really is.

As a precocious child, McKenzie was always up for the action! I remember her having a black eye and a bump on the head after running and playing with her three older siblings, but she still insisted on "driving" the boat at the lake the next day. She loved spending time with the family at the lake.

Just as she had a zest for life, McKenzie had a temper to match. My mom would call her "McDougal" when she was in a "mood" and one day Mom must have been in a mood herself because McKenzie turned the tables and told her she was being McDougal! Needless to say – that turned the mood right around!

It will be odd to move into the future without McKenzie in our midst. I loved her dearly and am sorry that she suffered so much during her short life. If we find comfort, it's to believe that she's bravely moved on into the heavens above and as she walks through the hallways of heaven, she does so with my Dad, and all those who have gone on before, by her side.

In her memory, I would like to read this short poem. It is entitled "Why God Takes Children" and the author is unknown.

> *When God calls little children*
> *To dwell with Him above,*
> *We mortals sometimes question*
> *The wisdom of His love.*
> *For no heartache compares with,*

The death of one small child,
Who does so much to make our world,
Seem so wonderful and mild.
Perhaps God tires of calling
The aged to His fold,
So He picks a rosebud
Before it can grow old.
God knows how much we need them,
And so He takes but few,
To make the land of heaven
More beautiful to view.
Believing this is difficult
Still somehow we must try,
The saddest word mankind
knows will always be Good-by.
So when a little child departs,
We who are left behind
Must realize God loves children,
Angels are hard to find.

Jeri

The day of the visitation arrived and it was surreal. Monroe and I had taken McKenzie's clothes to the mortuary on the previous day and seen McKenzie briefly. Nothing could have prepared me for the gut wrenching feeling of leaving my daughter there alone. I constantly had to remind myself that she wasn't really there or I might have swiped her. But, on the day of the visitation, we met as a family at the mortuary to see her one more time before we would allow others to see her at the church. My parents, my sister and her husband, Monroe's sister and husband, Monroe's mother, and the five of us were all there. We saw her briefly and again it was shocking. We read through the flowers and cards that had been sent. And then it was time to head over to the church.

We had a very large room in the back of the church building. McKenzie's casket was there. She didn't look like herself, but rather a shadow of herself. The spark that we had come to know was missing. She was dressed in a dress, matching tights, and matching headband that the girls and I agreed upon. When we were first told of her diagnosis in July and began making arrangements, I had chosen a beautiful pink summer dress. But that definitely didn't work in December and I really like the one we chose. McKenzie liked this one better, too. She hated the dress I originally chose- she refused to wear it every time I pulled it out for her. So, this was better. We had a few minutes alone with her before we saw others. The church media staff had put together a video of her pictures set to music and we played it on a continuous loop in the room at both ends. You couldn't hear the music once the room filled up because of all the conversation, but that was fine with me. We also had a table with photo albums laid out and I enjoyed hearing laughter around the table as the evening progressed. We saw friends and family we hadn't seen in forever. I met people who either knew Monroe through work or were family friends with whom we'd never crossed paths. The number of people who had flown in to see us was really overwhelming. We were there for just over three hours, but it felt like twelve hours. I thought I was ready for the outpouring of love from people, but I was in no way prepared for the mass of humanity who showed up to see McKenzie one more time and to see all of us. So many people had prayed for her and for us. It was truly overwhelming and humbling.

Monroe

On December 10th, we had people from all over the country and from all over the city visit. Jeri and I stood and greeted people for over three hours. Almost five hundred showed up to pay their respects. People we had not seen in years came to tell McKenzie goodbye. People that had never met McKenzie but knew our family showed up. It was an incredible outpouring by many.

Finally that night, it came time to close the casket and for Jeri and I to say goodbye for the final time. Monroe Jr. had left with friends and it was Courtney, Caroline, Jeri and I left. We placed a necklace on McKenzie with an angel on it and her favorite doll in the casket. We cried and held each other for what seemed like an hour and then closed the lid.

It was the last time that we would see her on this earth. I truly believe that the only way any of us could have gotten through these final minutes with her was because of our faith in God and our belief that someday we will all be reunited. I do not know of any other way we could have done all that needed to be done that week.

Jeri

The last time I saw the body of my precious daughter was that evening- Thursday, December 10, 2009. After everyone left, our immediate family said our final goodbyes and then Monroe and I spent a few moments alone with her before we closed the lid of her casket. While that moment broke my heart completely in two perhaps that was the moment the healing began as well. No more was she hurting. She was dancing in heaven. She was healed completely, cured, just as I had asked the Lord to heal her on that dreary day in January 2008. She was always with me through those dark days, just a thought away. All I had to do was close my eyes and there she was smiling at me- happy dark brown eyes, full head of dark curly hair, and happy, so happy. I would see her often in those days and sometimes I still do. Her presence is strongest as I'm drifting off to sleep. I believe Jesus allows me to glimpse her as she is- beautiful and spending her days praising Him. She knows her Grande who is in heaven with her now and has since welcomed many other saints into the eternal halls of worshiping Jesus. She knows her great grandparents and saves a little place for all of us not yet there.

But I digress!

Monroe

On December 11th, we got up and prepared to go to the cemetery to lay McKenzie to rest and then to the church for a celebration of her life. It would be a long day. Jeri and I had carefully orchestrated all the events and knew how we wanted the day to go. Honestly, I do not remember much other than the fact that everything went well and the day was a celebration.

Jeri

We met the next morning at the cemetery- just the five of us, my parents, Monroe's mother, and Robert and Julie Emmitt. It was raining and cold- fitting for all of our moods. I'm not sure how I got through that short graveside service. I let the tears flow. It hurt so bad that words cannot describe the pain. Were it not for my other three children, I might not have been able to bring myself to leave there. I knew they needed me and I needed them. I still do. So many days, even now, it is the children and my husband who are my reason for getting out of bed in the morning. I understand how easy it would be to sink into depression and stay in bed with the covers pulled over my head. But I don't have that luxury. My children and my husband need me and Jesus yet has work for me to do.

When we first discovered that McKenzie's cancer had recurred and decided not to treat, we began slowly making plans for the inevitable day when she would leave us. One of the details we had to discuss was where her body would be laid to rest. I hate the word "buried" because it makes me claustrophobic to think of her underground. Anyway, one place we discussed placing her is in the May family plot in Sunset Memorial Park. While there is not enough space to lay an adult there, there was just enough space for a small child like McKenzie. We needed permission from the family to do this. Monroe made a call to his uncle Jim. Within days, Jim showed up at our house. He had the deed to the plot and gave it graciously to us. As we stood discussing it, Monroe looked at the paperwork. He asked Jim how he gotten all the necessary signatures. Jim humbly admitted that he had, over a few day's time, traveled all over Texas to get the signatures of every oldest living May heir who had ties to the family plot. We were so grateful. He was such a dear man. Jim has since joined McKenzie in the throne room of heaven after losing his own fight with cancer in September 2010. Because of his kindness, McKenzie lies next to her great grandmother, Esther Lee Masden May, another lover of pink and the same woman after whom I originally wanted to name McKenzie. We will be forever grateful for Jim's hard work to help us. I think of him whenever I go to visit McKenzie's resting place.

We went directly from the cemetery to the church for McKenzie's memorial service. We had lunch at the church. My sweet friends, Muffin Camp and Mary Ellen Archer, had it all arranged for us. All we had to do was show up and eat. What a blessing.

Monroe

Jeri and I had both decided that we would speak at the memorial service. That morning, we shared with each other what we would say. It was amazing to me how similar our comments were to each other's. We had disagreed, argued and fallen apart in each other's arms many times and, at the end of this journey, our thoughts had reflected very similar to the events. Below is what I had prepared:

Life is Change

Thank you all for being here with us this week, especially those who have traveled from around Texas and my Merit Medical Friends, who have traveled from around the United States. My Merit Family has been a great support to me over the last two years and especially the last 6 months. Thank you.

Let me also clear the air about who I am. I am McKenzie's dad; I am also Rick May, Richard May, and Monroe May. Many of you may hear me called one of these today. So I did not want to confuse anyone.

I would like to take a few minutes to share McKenzie's story with you from a father's perspective.

Our journey really begin in 2004 when we found out we were expecting our fourth child. We already had three healthy children: Courtney, Caroline and Monroe. So, when we found out number four was on the way, we were surprised, but thankful. We thought we would have to make some **changes** however, at the time we had no idea how many **changes** that would be. From the moment we found out we were expecting McKenzie Jo May, our lives would **change** forever!

God used this little girl to stretch our family, our finances, our living space, our time, our hearts and our faith. After she was born, we quickly realized we needed to **change** houses. So we moved from a home we loved in Hidden Forrest to a new house in Bulverde Village. There we found the room we needed and were sure we would be there for many, many years. Shortly after the move, I had the opportunity to make a switch from sales into management. Because we now had four children, we made the decision for me to change jobs. From her birth, McKenzie helped push me to do more in order to provide for her and her brother and sisters. We were being forced to **change!**

The next couple of years were typical: family, school, soccer, volleyball, tee ball, flag football, and music lessons. We ran from event to event. We were a normal family.

Then, as most of you know, on January 1st of 2008 we started noticing a **change** in McKenzie. She was sleeping more and more, by the January 3rd we checked into the hospital, and by January 6th, a day after Jeri and my seventeenth wedding anniversary, McKenzie was diagnosed with neuroblastoma and we began on yet another **change** which would be a journey of a lifetime.

She was a month shy of her third birthday at the time. And for the next twenty-three months, our lives would be filled with more **change.** Here are a few that McKenzie and our family would be faced with:

- The diagnosis of advanced neuroblastoma.
- McKenzie would go through nine rounds of chemo, each round four to five days long, with I.V.'s at home around the clock.
- We had ten trips to the hospital, almost four and a half months total in hospital stays.
- One surgery for port placement and bone biopsy.
- One major surgery lasting ten and a half hours for the removal of the tumor.
- Two weeks in the PICU for complications and recovery, near death twice.
- Mega-dose chemo for four days around the clock.
- Bone Marrow Harvest/Bone Marrow Transplant.
- Countless CT scans and bone scans.
- Countless blood draws.
- Countless antibiotics.
- Over 117,000 hits on her website.
- Prayers from around the world.
- A Make-A-Wish Trip to Disney World Florida.
- Remission of the cancer.
- One more Christmas, one more birthday.
- All of this for just one more day and one more day after that.
- One more day with her and her family- like the MasterCard commercial says- it was priceless.

Our lives were constantly **changing**! Courtney, Caroline, and Monroe were constantly called on to adapt and **change** with each new treatment. And yet, through it all, we had hope and faith that God was leading to a final cure.

In January of 2009, yet another **change** came about and I was offered a position at our home office in Salt Lake City.

Once again, wanting to make sure that I could provide for college, cars, medical bills and all of the other needs that a growing family has, we agreed to make a **change**, and that is what is leading us to Utah. Life is **change**.

Then, July 11th of this year, the cancer returned and we began McKenzie's final chapter and that would bring us to today. Once again, she defied the odds. Originally given four to six weeks to live, she survived nineteen weeks. Each week required more **changes** in our lives.

However, today is not the end of the story...as I look back to what God has accomplished through this journey, it is almost unimaginable. He used this little girl to **change** our little corner of the world.

God used her to bring our family and friends closer together and closer to Him. He has used her to bring me closer to many people I had lost touch with over the years. He used her to teach me to love deeper and develop patience and understanding I never had before. He has used this illness to test our family in ways we could never imagine, and strengthened our love for each other for eternity. He used this illness to bring Jeri and me closer together! He has c**hanged** us all and the good news is we will never be the same! And He has **changed** many of you.

Along the way, we have been blessed by countless random acts of kindness and for that I want to thank you ALL. You painted rooms, brought meals, sent gift cards for meals, donated money, car rides, dedicated a Cross Country Season to McKenzie (thank you Coach Dykes), prayed countless prayers, and stood by our family. You all loved and reached out to each of our children. You helped take care of our family.

McKenzie's grandparents, Jane, Jerry, and Thelma all spent hours upon hours with McKenzie and our other children to make sure they were each well taken care of. They drove the wheels off their cars to provide rides and spend time at the hospital and give support. They listened and supported through countless phone conversations. They each constantly changed their schedules. And for all of this I say, thank you!

McKenzie's aunts and uncles, Kate, Russell, Shane, Gaye, Ken, Deb, and her cousins were special as well. And you each stood by our side and McKenzie's as we went through the changes of her illness. She loved you ALL!! Thank you.

I also want to thank Dr. Patel and his group. No one could have provided better care or compassion to our family over the last two years. Dr. Patel listened to our desires for our child and gave us honest and open answers. He walked beside us through this journey.

In four years, this little girl never ran for office, never fought for world peace and never wrote a book. However, she did manage to go the top of Waimea Canyon in Kauai, ride the rail to the top of Pike's Peak, journey to the bottom of the Royal Gorge in Colorado, and get every fairy princess's autograph in Disney World with the aid of her mother and two sisters. She fought her illness and many times she fought with Courtney, Caroline, and Monroe. She managed to bring a small group of people together and helped them to put their differences aside and show unconditional love to each other. She was a catalyst for changing lives. She, no doubt, will forever shape the way people who knew her view people without hair a little differently.

Her story will continue and so will all of ours.

McKenzie, you will be missed. Today, I hope that you are dancing on the streets of gold in Heaven. Your smile and Little

Mermaid voice will, no doubt, add to the joy of all around you as it did for us. You may even change Heaven.

Thank you, God, for allowing us to have her for this brief time on earth and I look forward to the day when we will all be reunited as a family.

In closing, I would like to share a poem written by Sandy Eakle entitled: "Death of a Child".

It is written from the child's point of view.

Death of a Child

Sorry I didn't get to stay.
To laugh and run and play.
To be there by your side.
I'm sorry that I had to die.
God sent me down to be with you,
to make your loving heart anew.
To help you look up and see
Both God and little me.
Mommy and Daddy, I wish I could stay.
Just like I heard you pray.
But, all the angels did cry
when they told little me goodbye.
God didn't take me cause He's mad.
He didn't send me to make you sad.
But to give us all a chance to be
a love so precious don't you see?
Up here no trouble do I see
and the pretty angels sing to me.

The streets of gold is where I play
you'll come here too, mommy and daddy, someday.
Until the day you join me here,
I'll love you both so, dear.
Each breeze you feel and see,
brings love and a kiss from me.

Thank you all for coming today and being here with us to remember McKenzie May. Your thoughts prayers and kindness mean so much to our family. Today, I will pray for each of you that you all may know the peace that surpasses all understanding in your life through Jesus Christ the Lord. One final thought as you leave today, ask yourself, "How will you let this little girl and today's experience change your life?"

Don't miss the opportunity to make a CHANGE in your life because change is life.

Isaiah 49:15-16 "I will not forget you!

See, I have engraved you on the palm of my hands." McKenzie, we will not forget you. -Thank you.

Jeri

So much of what I said that day was the backbone of this book that I won't include it here. But, I shared the gospel of Jesus Christ along with many humorous anecdotes about McKenzie.

The church was packed. I was shocked at the number of people who showed up for the memorial service of our four-year-old baby! Monroe and I had planned the service to keep it simple. We had Ray Jones and some other members of the worship team sing. At the conclusion of the worship music, Ray's son, Christopher, sang "Jesus Loves Me" and I know there was not a dry eye in the room already. Then we played the video presentation of McKenzie's pictures that the CBC staff had put together. It was beautiful. Next, Monroe spoke and then I did. We had both poured our hearts into our words. Monroe focused on how much change God had made in our lives through our precious baby girl. The Lord had shown me early in her recurrence what He had for me to say. I was to present the gospel message. I was to discuss her salvation and my own. I was excited about speaking the words that described how Jesus had come and died so that both McKenzie and I could live eternally with Him, but I doubted that I could get through the words of a prayer to lead nonbelievers into a saving belief without dissolving into a puddle of tears. So I asked Robert Emmitt, our pastor, if he would do that part and of course he said yes. He led people in that prayer in church services several times each week. He also spoke a few minutes after I did and then led the prayer. We wrapped up with a balloon release of pink balloons in the parking lot. We wanted McKenzie to see from heaven all the pink balloons being sent to her. It was sweet.

I don't know how long I talked to people after that, both out in the parking lot and then back in the church foyer. It seemed like forever. There were so many wonderful friends and family members that I wanted to greet.

It almost felt like a happy celebration (and it was supposed to be), but then I would think that I needed to find all the children and Monroe and that would lead me to remember that I would never find **all** the children after a service at CBC again. I would never pick McKenzie up from her classroom again. These kinds of thoughts still occur. My mind forgets that she is gone and I work, subconsciously, on how to get her back. I'll wonder when my mom is bringing her home from playing at her house or if we could do just one more round of chemo. Maybe then she would be healed. Maybe then I could get to her.

So we left the church and went home. We somehow managed to get through Caroline's birthday and Christmas. Those days are a blur. I know we opened presents Christmas morning and I'm sure we attended services at CBC. I know we attended the May Family Christmas party. Caroline had a major asthma attack that night and I drove a forty-minute stretch of road in about ten minutes because we had no albuterol with us. Christmas Eve, we usually get together with Monroe's mother and sister and her family. That night her boys were sick, so we postponed. Instead, the five of us went to the movies and saw Avatar. Now that was the weirdest Christmas Eve we've ever had. But we just kept telling ourselves this was our new normal- without McKenzie. It felt like nothing would ever be normal again. Some days, it still feels that way.

Monday, December 14, 2009 5:26 PM, CST

Hello everyone. It's Monday afternoon about 5:30pm. I can honestly say I don't know how we have gotten through the last week. I know all the prayers of God's people are holding us up. That is about it. On our own, we could not stand or I know, I could not survive- not without God. I was just reading all the guestbook messages from the last week. Wow, I am overwhelmed and humbled and grateful. I am still in shock. It's taking every ounce of will power to put one foot in front of the other today. I'm still expecting Meemaw to pull up in front of the house with McKenzie in the car or to need to go pick her up from a friend's house. Boy, did she know how to play.

I loved seeing so many of you at the visitation and the service on Thursday and Friday. So many faces, so little time. But it was encouraging to me to see you all. Thank you for being there. I have seen a few signatures on the guestbook of friends I missed seeing and that makes me sad. I would have loved a hug from each one there.

All right, time to make dinner...Love to you all, Jeri

Jeri

Next, we had to get ready to move to Salt Lake City. We had already closed on the new house- we joked that we bought Caroline a house for her birthday. But before we could move, we had to pack. We had to pack McKenzie's things. We had packers coming to take care of the rest of the house, but I would not let them pack her things. Monroe and I still wish we had her room set up so that we could just go and sit and feel her and hear her and smell her. But, I guess God did not want us to have that crutch. I guess He wanted us to use our memories to remember her. I spent a long time packing her room. So many things brought back so many memories that made me sit and cry. I still have all her things. They are packed away with a few exceptions. I can't bear to get rid of anything. It feels so selfish to have all these boxes of unused clothes and toys, but for now that's what I need to survive. The pain is still too fresh to take action. Maybe someday...

The packers came and packed up all the rest of our things. The movers came and put it all on the truck. We had our suitcases and we were physically ready to leave. But emotionally we were far from ready. How could we walk out the door and leave our McKenzie behind? I know she wasn't there, but it still felt like she was. Moving day came. We got in the cars. We had two cars, seven people, a cat, a dog, and fourteen hundred miles to drive. We took two days to get to Salt Lake City and arrived on New Year's Eve at 9pm.

Tuesday, December 29, 2009 1:34 PM, CST

Hello Everyone,

It is Tuesday afternoon on a raining, ugly afternoon in San Antonio. Today is moving day for the May Family and the truck is being loaded.

Tomorrow morning we will begin the drive to Utah. This has been the plan that has been on going for almost a year. It is bittersweet for us all as we are anxious to get to Salt Lake to begin yet another chapter in our lives, and sad for us as well, in the fact that we are leaving behind many family members as well as our youngest child, McKenzie.

Jeri and I have agreed to only do one or two more entries on this website and then we will be closing it down. We will let you all know when we reach Utah and that we have made it safely.

This holiday season has been a challenge to just get through at the May household. We were happy to see Christmas come and go and really glad to have it behind us. As we near New Years, we are anxious about what is ahead. We enter 2010 much different than we began 2009. Last year we celebrated New Years in Disney World Florida on McKenzie's Make-

A-Wish trip. This year we will be on the road. Life is change, and we will continue to move ahead.

Thank you all for your prayers, cards, donations and support. May God bless each of you in 2010!

Don't forget to hug your kids and be safe on New Year's Eve. -Monroe

Jeri

It was the dawn of a new year- 2010. It was a new beginning for our family. I had tried to convince Monroe right after her diagnosis of recurrence that a new adventure would be good for our family and in many ways it has. We are forced daily to adjust to our new normal once again. We are forced to rely on only each other and God to deal with our pain. In some ways, our new home in Utah has become a sanctuary for us. In so many ways it is more difficult to deal with the grief in unfamiliar surroundings, but in some ways it is good that we are not stuck in a rut of constantly being reminded that we're in the same place while McKenzie is not. If we still lived on Manhattan Way or Winding View, would we be stuck forever in the memories of the past? Maybe so. We keep pictures of her everywhere in our new home. We watch video of her regularly and talk about her all the time.

Wednesday, January 6, 2010 9:03 PM, CST

I wanted to let everyone know that we arrived safely in Utah last Thursday night about 9:00 PM. After two very long days and 1400+ miles we arrived at our house with a warm welcome from the neighborhood.

We have been moving fast ever since we arrived trying to get the house in order and the kids ready for school. They are all back in school and things are going OK. The adjustment will be a challenge but we will keep trying.

Today is the two-year anniversary of when McKenzie was first diagnosed. It is amazing how much changed in 24 months and we all miss her very, very much. We will post one or two more times, however, I wanted to let everyone know that we are safe. -Monroe

Monday, February 1, 2010 8:52 AM, MST

Hello everyone! I have missed you all! I wanted to do one more post here on McKenzie's website before I have it printed and begin work on what Monroe and I call "the book". We really do feel the Lord moving us to write eventually McKenzie's story and possibly a guide of "what not to say in a hospital room"! Don't anyone take that personally now. But be on guard that when you visit a sick friend or family member, that what they most need is your presence- not a cliché. Don't offer to "do whatever they need". What they need is for you to just choose something and do it! Just love them through actions and presence. You know, that is not what I planned on writing about today!

We have had many challenges here in Utah. Not only have we been painfully trying to adjust to life without McKenzie, but have the added challenge of adjusting to new schools, new BSF groups (that's not really painful), and new work schedules. The pets are having difficulty adjusting to the cold. Also, Courtney badly sprained her left ankle ten days ago putting her on crutches and tossing her out of basketball for the season. On the flip side, she did get her drivers' license in Texas on January 20th and is driving a little here. Her brother and sister love her new freedom especially when they get to go along. Caroline has joined a basketball team and made her first two points at her game this last Saturday. Little Monroe is very challenged by his teacher here who has expectations of him reading one hour daily! I think it's a little too much, but I am trying to be supportive of her expectations!

Now that February is here, we are finally free of our six month commitment to our rent house in San Antonio! We couldn't be happier that is behind us. We are so happy to be homeowners once again. The things I will miss are all the WONDERFUL friends we met in Summerglen. Thank you for making us feel so loved and cared for while we were there. I miss you especially: NB, LG, KG, JB, and JE. You know who you are.

During the move, I lost something very important to me. I lost a bag of jewelry. It was all my favorite pieces. I had packed these to carry in the car with us and have when we got here before the movers brought our boxes and furniture. I have no idea where that little bag went. I have looked everywhere. I will hold out hope that I will find it until the last box is unpacked. I would appreciate your prayers for recovered jewelry. It's such a stupid little thing compared to all that is going on in the world, but it is important to me.

Well, this is it. I love you guys and will always remember you in my prayers. I pray that you will be lifted up and loved by the Lord as I have been through this time in my life. We know that McKenzie dances through the streets of Heaven today. I believe that she sees us and remembers us. I believe she no longer hurts or cries. She only celebrates Jesus and I look forward to celebrating forever with her.

THANK YOU WITH LOVE, Jeri

Jeri

The milestones are hard. McKenzie died on December 8th and her fifth birthday would have been on February 8th. That was a very hard day. The first anniversary of her death the following December 8th was also a challenge. The whole family was together that day- we did another pink balloon release. We'll probably do one for many years to come. So if you happen to be flying over Salt Lake City on any given December 8th, make sure to look out the windows of the plane for pink balloons!

Grieving

Monroe

Monroe's Personal Journal Entry:

March 17th, 2010

It has been just over fourteen weeks since we said goodbye and yet a day does not pass when I do not think of you, my sweet little girl. We made it through Christmas, New Years and a move to Salt Lake and yet I still wait for you to show up. A part of me still thinks you will bust through the door at any minute and yell, "Hello? I'm back! I have just been at Meemaw's". And yet I know that is not going to happen. Your mother says she sees you everywhere and that she is certain that you have made the move with us to Utah. I am not sure, I do not dream about you and I do not hear your voice anymore. I watch old recordings of you and look at pictures daily, and long to hear your voice. I wish you would jump up in my lap one more time; I wish you would tell me you are hungry one more time and ask, "what do we have?" I miss you so much. I, at times just want to lie down and not get back up. I have said to many people that the time ahead is almost as difficult as the illness itself. And at times it is worse. I hope you are dancing on the streets of heaven and I hope that you are holding Grandee's hand, and singing loudly. Life is not the same without you. Why have you been taken away from us? We all miss you so much!

Looking back on this time in our lives, it is by far the most difficult couple of years in my forty-two year existence. However, I would not change a thing, except for the ending. I would love to have my precious daughter back and watch her grow.

This fall she would have started kindergarten. It is amazing to me how many people we meet and know that have five-year-old children beginning school. Every time I meet someone or talk to someone who has a child beginning school it touches my heart and makes me think of McKenzie. I know there will be many circumstances like this for the rest of our lives.

Jeri and I often talk about what we have learned and what we want to give back because of this experience. God brought us through and carried us every step of the way. He used the people around us to help and provide for us and constantly take care of our family. We will be forever looking for opportunities to help others because of this horrible disease called cancer.

This book was written in the hopes that it might help other families, parents and siblings going through a similar illness. We are not experts and we are not authorities on cancer or cancer treatments. We have, however, lived through the life and death of a child. In the English language, if you lose a spouse to death you are a "widow". If a child looses his or her parents you become an "orphan". If a parent loses a child there is no defining word to describe the loss.

As a parent that has lost a child, there are not enough words to describe how I feel. But as a Christian, I know that one day I will be reunited with my daughter.

My hope and prayer is that anyone who reads this book and has experienced the loss of a loved one will also know this guarantee.

Passage John 3:16-18:

16 "For God loved the world so much that he gave his one
and only Son, so that everyone who believes in him will not
perish but have eternal life. 17 God sent his Son into the world
not to judge the world, but to save the world through him.
18 "There is no judgment against anyone who believes in
him. But anyone who does not believe in him has already been
judged for not believing in God's one and only Son.

New Living Translation

Jeri

Just as Monroe's journal entry reflects, we miss McKenzie every day. We grieve deeply for her. We experienced the depression that naturally follows the loss of a loved one. Sometimes we knew what and why we were feeling things and sometimes we just felt them. One thing that really helped us was to talk about our feelings with each other. We both struggled with guilt when we felt happy. But then, slowly, I began to crave happiness, feelings of joy. I wanted everyone in our family to be happy. I am beginning to understand that everyone grieves at different rates and in different ways. It's a process, that learning. Grief is such a strange thing. It has so many different aspects to it. It has so many different stages. It helped me to talk to others, while Monroe preferred to only talk to me. We continue to turn to each other in our healing. If one of us is having a day or moment of missing her, we try to communicate it with the other. It cannot become the focus of our marriage. Our marriage, our relationship with each other and our relationship with God, should always remain our focus. We are far from perfect, but we love each other. I could not have faced such a loss on my own.

Monroe and I have done our best to allow the children to grieve in their own ways. The older girls have had a much more difficult time. It shows up in their hearts and faces when you least expect it. Sometimes I think they are doing well, but then find out they are not. Little Monroe reads me like a book and is always ready with a hug when he realizes I'm sad about missing our little angel baby. His grief comes out in very different ways. It's a thoughtful look, misbehavior, or a mention of McKenzie when I least expect it. Little Monroe missed two full years of discipline from his parents while McKenzie was going through treatment. He is one of our biggest challenges today. He is a sweet, sweet boy. But he missed the shaping we gave to the girls at that age while we were busy dealing with McKenzie. God will return to us those locust eaten years, I truly believe, if we continue trusting Him in our parenting of our children.

Back on December 6, 2009, I asked for friends to pray for our children- that God would not allow them to be stretched beyond their coping abilities. He continues to answer that prayer. Many days I worry that they have been permanently damaged. I am never quite sure if it's the loss of McKenzie or the move so soon after, but both girls have struggled to grieve appropriately. They want little to do with grief counseling.

Every time I begin to worry about them, I realize I must **trust** their Heavenly Father to carry them. We often watch videos of McKenzie with the children, we look at pictures, and we talk about funny family moments for two reasons. First, we never want them to forget. They must remember their baby sister. Also, I want them, especially the girls, to replace the memories of her death. When they remember her (not if), they need to think of her smiling, laughing, or even yelling at them. The shell that remained on December 8, 2009 and after no longer housed our vibrant daughter.

It's been a challenge explaining our situation to people who don't know us. So often when you meet someone new, you go through the gambit of questions: Where are you from? What brought you to Utah? And, of course, how many children do you have? That is obviously the hardest one to answer. If it's someone I expect to know for a while, I tell them. Sometimes, I'll just say "four" and then wait to see if they ask the ages of the children. I'll admit it's tempting to go for the shock value occasionally. I'll say, "We have four children: our oldest is Courtney (17), then Caroline (14), then Monroe (10), and McKenzie who we lost to cancer in December 2009." People's mouths drop open and then you get the head tilt and an "I'm sorry." It was hard to put into words the first few times, but it does get easier. I guess that, in itself, is a form of healing.

2 Corinthians 1:3-6 talks about praising God because He has comforted us through our trials so that we might therefore comfort others. We do suffer in this life just as Christ did. But we have the promise of God's comfort if we are His children. Sometimes He comforts us through His word and sometimes He comforts us through the hand or voice of another person. That person becomes the hand or voice of Christ comforting us.

I believe that part of the reason God allowed me to experience all that I did through McKenzie's illness and death is to be able to comfort others. I can comfort others who are going through something similar, but I can also comfort people going through any kind of challenge in their life. We all carry a bag of rocks in our lives. Is the bag of rocks I've been given to carry any heavier than yours? Maybe so, maybe not- yours may be even heavier than mine. But either way, I guarantee you that if we all put our bag of rocks in a circle in the middle of the room, none of us would want to pick up someone else's bag. We all are given circumstances unique to us because we are designed by God to carry our own bag. So, yes, my trial has been great. Yet my comfort has also been great. And I want to pay it forward. I want you to understand that no matter what you are going through, my God is a big God and He alone can carry you through. He wants to because He loves you just like He loves me.

The dictionary defines "unshakeable" as "strongly felt and unable to be changed." You know, growing up, I felt like I had a boring witness. I knew what I believed, but I had no experience in my life to which I could point that proved God's faithfulness. That is no longer the case. Now, I know, without a shadow of a doubt, that God has and can and will carry me through any circumstance in my life. My faith in God's ability to carry me in the palm of His almighty hand is unshakeable. My faith is strongly felt and unable to be changed. You, too, can have this same kind of faith in God's ability to carry you through your trials. Trust in the Lord with all your heart and lean not on your own understanding. In all your ways acknowledge Him and He will make your paths straight. (Proverbs 3:5-6) That is unshakeable faith.

I believe that once you call on the name of the Lord Jesus Christ as your Savior, believe in His death as your salvation you are saved for eternal life. There is nothing you can do to add to that salvation. No other work needs to be done. Also, nothing can then separate you from your eternal life salvation. When Jesus died on the cross to take your penalty of death and you believe in His sacrifice as your means to eternal life, it is finished. Once saved, always saved. Your faith cannot be erased. However, I know that people do choose to walk away from that faith. Jesus will not renounce us, but sometimes people do renounce Jesus. I personally believe that that does not negate their salvation; it only negates the joy of living daily walking hand in hand with Jesus. I know that a life-shaking event such as the illness and death of a child could easily be the reason for a person to walk away from their faith. However, I choose the joy of walking daily with Jesus over the anger of believing that He somehow caused this tragedy in my life. I refuse to let my faith be shaken. I refuse to walk away from Jesus. He walked with me through the valley of the shadow of death. He carried me many days. He carries me still. That is unshakeable faith.

Many times during McKenzie's illness, I cried out to God and asked Him to heal her. I truly believed then and still do believe that He is able to heal her. I have faith in His ability to heal. Initially, during her first diagnosis, my only thought was for Jesus to heal her on this earth so that she could live a long, full life. I wanted her to grow up, get married, have children of her own (even if she had to adopt), and outlive me. That was my definition of healing. But, then at her second diagnosis, I began to see healing a little differently. I no longer demanded of God that He heal her here on earth as a requirement for my faith in

Him. Even if He did not heal her here, I would yet praise Him. I saw that her death would result in ultimate healing. She would live in heaven in a body so wonderful that it would never be sick again. Again, I still believed at second diagnosis that God was able to heal her with or without man's intervention. But it was my faith that was strengthened instead of her little body. It made me reexamine all that I believed. It solidified my faith like nothing else could have. My faith today remains unshaken. My faith today is in Jesus Christ alone. He has provided a life for McKenzie much better than any healing on this earth could have. That is unshakeable faith.

Make your life count. Make McKenzie's life count. I know it counts for me.

A Single Candle or a Blazing Fire?

By Courtney May
Age 17

Five hundred rose tinted balloons bobbed above the crowd, tugging at the clutched hands of their holders, straining to follow the wind's upward lead. People clothed in black gathered just outside the church's oak doors, some dabbing at their puffy eyes or embracing. The solemn black hearse had left earlier, leaving behind car exhaust and memories. Though there was plenty of room for the group to move about under those foreboding charcoal clouds, we huddled in a compact group, together. We had gained a unity through our common loss. I observed the group of familiar faces, recognizing that I was not as alone as I had often thought. And though the clouds, clothes, and tear-smeared mascara were of a damper color, each face glimmered with the same hope and peace. I had concluded two years earlier that life wasn't all about me; but in this moment I realized that life, as much as it hurt to say, wasn't about my sister either. A single life is insignificant until it touches the lives of others. A flickering candle in the night is insignificant until it lights a blazing fire.

I am certainly no saint and have not always held this pearl of wisdom. I did not grow up in Japan or China where the community is glorified and working together is celebrated. I grew up in America, a part of the western world where the individual is all-important. My childhood was no exception. From a young age I learned that I was to fight for what I wanted, giving no care to whom I trampled in the process. Though it aimed to teach multiplication and reading, I took away a lot about individualism from my formal schooling. Ironically, at one time teaching Darwin in schools was forbidden, but his survival of the fittest theory is now reinforced by the most basic elements of the American learning system. Sure, teachers taught us to share toys in the sandbox. But then they would turn right around and forbid us to share ideas in the classroom, labeling this "cheating". Smart individual work was rewarded with yellow smiley stickers and golden grades and students were further championed with admission to advanced courses, expected to continue on to even greater future accomplishment. Cheaters paid for their so-called crimes and slow learners were punished with ignorance. Considering myself a quick learner, I figured I understood the life lesson that kindergarten was using this system of reward and punishment to teach us: sharing is good in play but in the real world true success is a result of individual excellence.

As my body grew up, my mind grew out. Bit by bit my curiosity was fed by experiences, media, and friends. I liked the subjects they taught in school but the world was, and remains, my textbook.

School was easy, as the lessons I had learned in elementary school helped me to excel there. Life was a little harder.

When I was fourteen years old my dad uttered to me the life-changing word that too many people have been confronted with: cancer. My two-year-old sister McKenzie had it. Weeks became a series of doctor visits, lethal chemo drugs, and intermittent hospital stays, tired parents, serious discussions, and questions that had no right answer. My parents made every effort to pay attention to my other two siblings and me, but McKenzie was certainly the priority. It was often lonely, but that was alright. We understood. Within days of the diagnosis, life had gone from being all about me to all about her. I even found myself begging God to take me instead.

Mahatma Gandhi once remarked that "whatever you do in life will be insignificant but is very important that you do it." On a global scale and from a historical standpoint perhaps this is true. But on a more personal level, Gandhi severely underestimated the impact that one life can have on countless others. McKenzie certainly taught me that. Though it is tough to explain to a child that they are dying, McKenzie seemed to understand that her time, like her height, was short. She made every second count. Two years later she would pass away. That was more than enough time for her to change my life and so many others. Her personality and love touched those she met and her story touched those that she could not.

It is wrong to worship the individual but it is ignorant not to acknowledge the repercussions of our actions. One is all it takes to revolutionize a community, like McKenzie did, or the world. In the Bible's book of Romans, Paul observes that it took only one man to bring sin into the world and only one to take it out. In eating the forbidden fruit, Adam would change the life of every human being to ever walk the planet. By dying on the cross, Jesus saved humanity. It is important that one does what one can in life as its effect on others will be significant.

On December 8th, 2009 McKenzie went to live with that one man who died on a cross to save her. By this point I had abandoned everything that kindergarten had taught me, besides maybe a bit of math and those oh so incredible concepts of nap and snack time. I had determined to live my life in a way that would honor McKenzie, to reach out to everyone I can in the time I have. Some may call cancer a curse but it was a blessing for all of us who were transformed through McKenzie. A greater number than had originally suspected had been touched by this short burning light, as over five hundred people showed up to celebrate McKenzie's life at her funeral. After the service, the crowd congregated outside the church, waiting for the balloon release. My dad climbed up on a short garden wall, uttering the words "3, 2, 1, release!" Soft pink, helium-filled sparks of color soon painted the heavens, hiding the sooty clouds. A pink ceiling and a band of color-coordinated witnesses were all the proof I needed to conclude that a single life is not significant; but it is important that each life be lived, as its effects on others will make all the difference.

CPSIA information can be obtained at www.ICGtesting.com
Printed in the USA
BVOW041558060213

312568BV00001B/1/P

9 781449 778781